INTRODUCTION TO LEADERSHIP

Fourth Edition

To Madison and Isla

INTRODUCTION TO LEADERSHIP

Concepts and Practice

Fourth Edition

Peter G. Northouse
Western Michigan University

Los Angeles | London | New Delhi
Singapore | Washington DC | Melbourne

FOR INFORMATION:

SAGE Publications, Inc.
2455 Teller Road
Thousand Oaks, California 91320
E-mail: order@sagepub.com

SAGE Publications Ltd.
1 Oliver's Yard
55 City Road
London EC1Y 1SP
United Kingdom

SAGE Publications India Pvt. Ltd.
B 1/I 1 Mohan Cooperative Industrial Area
Mathura Road, New Delhi 110 044
India

SAGE Publications Asia-Pacific Pte. Ltd.
3 Church Street
#10-04 Samsung Hub
Singapore 049483

Acquisitions Editor: Maggie Stanley
Development Editor: Lauren Holmes
Editorial Assistant: Neda Dallal
eLearning Editor: Katie Ancheta
Production Editor: Libby Larson
Copy Editor: Melinda Masson
Typesetter: C&M Digitals (P) Ltd.
Proofreader: Theresa Kay
Indexer: Wendy Allex
Cover Designer: Gail Buschman
Marketing Manager: Ashlee Blunk

Printed in the United States of America

ISBN: 978-1-5063-3008-2

This book is printed on acid-free paper.

17 18 19 20 21 10 9 8 7 6 5 4 3 2 1

Brief Contents

Detailed Contents

Preface

Leadership is a salient topic today. Given the volatility of global events and our national political climate, it is even more important now than it was when the third edition of this book was published. The public remains fascinated by who leaders are and what leaders do. People want to know what accounts for good leadership and how to become good leaders. Despite this strong interest in leadership, there are very few books that clearly describe the complexities of practicing leadership. I have written *Introduction to Leadership: Concepts and Practice* to fill this void.

Each chapter describes a fundamental principle of leadership and how it relates in practice to becoming an effective leader. These fundamentals are illustrated through examples, profiles of effective leaders, and case studies. The text comprises 13 chapters: **Chapter 1, "Understanding Leadership,"** analyzes how different definitions of leadership have an impact on the practice of leadership. **Chapter 2, "Recognizing Your Traits,"** examines leadership traits found to be important in social science research and explores the leadership traits of a select group of historical and contemporary leaders. **Chapter 3, "Engaging Strengths,"** discusses the emerging field of strengths-based leadership, looking at how several assessment tools can help one to recognize his or her own strengths and those of others and then put those strengths to work as an effective leader. **Chapter 4, "Understanding Philosophy and Styles,"** explores how a person's view of people, work, and human nature forms a personal philosophy of leadership and how this relates to three commonly observed styles of leadership: authoritarian, democratic, and laissez-faire. **Chapter 5, "Attending to Tasks and Relationships,"** describes how leaders can integrate and optimize task and relationship behaviors in their leadership role. **Chapter 6, "Developing Leadership Skills,"** considers three types of leadership skills: administrative, interpersonal, and conceptual. **Chapter 7, "Creating a Vision,"** explores the characteristics of a vision and how a vision is expressed and implemented. **Chapter 8, "Establishing a Constructive Climate,"** focuses on how important it is for leaders who are running groups or organizations to provide structure, clarify norms, build cohesiveness, and promote standards of excellence. **Chapter 9, "Embracing Diversity and Inclusion,"** discusses the importance of inclusive leadership and the barriers that can be encountered when trying to embrace diversity and inclusion. **Chapter 10, "Listening to Out-Group Members,"** explores the nature of out-groups, their impact, and ways leaders should respond to out-group members. **Chapter 11, "Managing Conflict,"** addresses the question of how we can manage conflict and produce positive change. **Chapter 12, "Addressing Ethics in Leadership,"** explores six factors that are related directly to ethical leadership: character, actions, goals, honesty, power, and values. Finally, **Chapter 13, "Overcoming Obstacles,"** addresses seven obstacles that subordinates may face and how a leader can help to overcome these.

NEW TO THIS EDITION

This edition retains the chapters of the previous edition but has been expanded and enhanced in several ways:

- First and foremost, it includes a new chapter on **diversity and inclusion** that examines the nature of diversity and inclusion, provides a model of inclusive behavior, describes communication practices to improve inclusion, and identifies barriers to effective inclusive leadership.
- Second, this edition **premieres the Ethical Leadership Style Questionnaire**, a self-assessment instrument that allows readers to learn what their ethical leadership behaviors tend to be. The questionnaire in this book is an abridged edition of a longer, more comprehensive assessment available to readers online.
- Third, several chapters include a look at the **dark side of leadership** in terms of the approaches explored in the book.
- Fourth, **new case studies, examples, and research** are integrated throughout the book.
- Fifth, this edition includes new **"Ask the Author" videos** that show Peter Northouse answering student questions.

SPECIAL FEATURES

Introduction to Leadership: Concepts and Practice is designed to help the reader understand how to become a better leader. While the book is grounded in leadership theory, it describes the basics of leadership in an understandable and user-friendly way. Each chapter focuses on a fundamental aspect of leadership, discusses how it can be applied in real leadership situations, and provides a relevant profile of a leader.

Perhaps the most notable features of this book are the four applied activities included in every chapter, which allow the reader to explore leadership concepts and real-world applications:

- **Case studies** illustrate the leadership concepts discussed in the chapter. At the end of each case, thought-provoking questions help the reader analyze the case using ideas presented in the chapter.
- **Self-assessment questionnaires** help the reader determine his or her own leadership style and preferences. Students may want to complete this questionnaire before reading the chapter's content. By completing the questionnaire first, the reader will be more aware of how the chapter's content specifically applies to his or her leadership tendencies.
- **Observational exercises** guide the reader in examining behaviors of leaders from his or her life experiences.
- **Reflection and action worksheets** stimulate the reader to reflect on his or her leadership style and identify actions to take to become more effective.

AUDIENCE

A practice-oriented book, *Introduction to Leadership: Concepts and Practice* is written in a user-friendly style appropriate for introductory leadership courses across disciplines. Specifically, it is well suited for programs in leadership studies and leadership courses in schools of agriculture, allied health, business, management, communication, education, engineering, military science, public administration, nursing, political science, social work, and religion. In addition, this book is appropriate for programs in continuing education, corporate training, executive development, in-service training, and government training. It is also useful for student extracurricular activities.

DIGITAL RESOURCES

SAGE coursepacks allow instructors to import high-quality online resources directly into Blackboard, Canvas, Moodle, or Brightspace by Desire2Learn

(D2L) in an intuitive, simple format. Instructors who do not use an LMS platform can still access many of the online resources by visiting **edge .sagepub.com/northouseintro4e.**

SAGE coursepacks include, for each chapter:

- A diverse range of test items with **pretests, posttests,** and **test banks** built on Bloom's Taxonomy and AACSB standards, available with **ExamView** test generation
- **Assignable SAGE Premium Video** (available via the interactive eBook version, linked through SAGE coursepacks) that includes insights from Peter G. Northouse and other leadership experts, with corresponding **multimedia assessment options** that automatically feed to a gradebook
- A comprehensive *Media Guide* for the **video resources**
- **Discussion questions** to help launch classroom interaction
- **SAGE journal articles** to show how scholarship relates to chapter concepts
- Editable, chapter-specific **PowerPoint˚ slides** that offer flexibility when creating multimedia lectures
- **Sample course syllabi** with suggested models for structuring a leadership course
- **Lecture notes** that summarize key concepts for each chapter
- Ideas for **class activities** that can be used in class to reinforce active learning
- **Web exercises** that direct students to useful websites to complete creative activities and reinforce learning
- **Suggested films** to facilitate showing examples of leadership in action
- **Case notes** that include case summaries, analyses, and sample answers to case questions
- **The Reflection and Action Worksheets** and **Observational Exercises** from the text in downloadable Word document format for more flexibility in using these resources
- **Tables and figures** from the textbook

SAGE edge for students at **edge.sagepub.com/northouseintro4e** enhances learning in an easy-to-use environment that offers, for each chapter, learning objectives, action plans to track progress, mobile-friendly flashcards and practice quizzes, SAGE Premium Video featuring author Peter G. Northouse, additional multimedia resources, and selected SAGE journal articles to strengthen learning.

Interactive eBook

An interactive eBook version of the text is available for students to provide a contemporary, multimedia-integrated presentation for learning. In addition to a fully electronic textbook, students can link directly to "Ask the Author" video, audio, additional enrichment readings from SAGE journals titles, and other relevant resources, bringing the subject matter to life in a way a traditional print text cannot.

The interactive eBook features exclusive **Interactive Leadership Assessments** to help students strengthen their leadership abilities by providing them with individualized feedback based on their responses to each questionnaire. After completing each questionnaire, a student using the interactive eBook will receive an in-depth analysis of her or his scores as well as personalized, pragmatic suggestions for further developing her or his leadership.

You can find the eBook icons in the print and electronic versions of the text. Below is a guide to the icons:

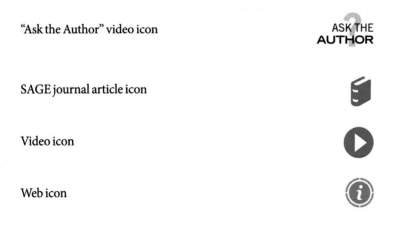

"Ask the Author" video icon

SAGE journal article icon

Video icon

Web icon

ACKNOWLEDGMENTS

I would like to express my appreciation to many individuals who directly or indirectly played a role in the development of this book. First, I would like to thank the many people at SAGE Publications, in particular my editor, Maggie Stanley, who along with her leadership team (Liz Thornton, Lauren Holmes, Neda Dallal, Katie Ancheta, Ashlee Blunk, Georgia Mclaughlin, and Gail Buschman) has competently guided this revision from the beginning review phase through the production phase. In addition, I would like to thank copy editor Melinda Masson and production editor Libby Larson. In their own unique ways, each of these people made valuable contributions that enhanced the overall quality of the book. Collectively, they are an extraordinary team that demonstrates the very highest standards of excellence in all that they do.

For their thoughtful and constructive feedback on this latest edition, I would like to thank the following reviewers:

Jens Beyer, *Hochschule Anhalt Standort Bernburg*

Carl Blencke, *University of Central Florida*

Roger Clark, *NWN Corporation*

Dan Cunningham, *McDaniel College*

D. Keith Gurley, *University of Alabama at Birmingham*

Sat Ananda Hayden, *University of Southern Mississippi*

Sharon Kabes, *Southwest Minnesota State University*

Lorin Leone, *Independence University*

Douglas Micklich, *Illinois State University*

Bryan Patterson, *Johnson C. Smith University, Northeastern University*

Robert W. Robertson, *Independence University*

Lou L. Sabina, *Stetson University*

Stephanie Schnurr, *University of Warwick*

Douglas Threet, *Foothill College*

Simone Wesner, *Birkbeck, University of London*

Paula White, *Independence University*

Cecilia Williams, *Independence University*

For comprehensive reviews of past editions, I would like to thank the following reviewers:

Maureen Baldwin, *Saint Ambrose University*

Barry L. Boyd, *Texas A&M University*

Susan Bramlett Epps, *East Tennessee State University*

Linda L. Brennan, *Mercer University*

Shannon Brown, *Benedictine University*

Lisa Burgoon, *University of Illinois at Urbana-Champaign*

Tom Butkiewicz, *University of Redlands*

Patricia Cane, *Klamath Community College*

Stephen C. Carlson, *Piedmont College*

Melissa K. Carsten, *Winthrop University*

James R. "Chip" Coldren Jr., *Governors State University*

Barbara Collins, *Cabrini College*

Stacey A. Cook, *College of Marin*

Ronald J. Cugno, *Nova Southeastern University*

Greg Czyszczon, *James Madison University*

Douglas Davenport, *Truman State University*

Edward Desmarais, *Salem State College*

Marco Dowell, *California State University, Dominguez Hills*

Tiffany Erk, *Ivy Tech Community College of Indiana*

Leon Fraser, *Rutgers Business School*

Jim Fullerton, *Idaho State University*

Jennifer Garcia, *Saint Leo University*

Don Green, *Lincoln Christian University*

Francesca Grippa, *Northeastern University*

Yael Hellman, *Woodbury University*

Vanessa Hill, *University of Louisiana at Lafayette*

Martha A. Hunt, *NHTI—Concord's Community College*

Jean Gabriel Jolivet, *Southwestern College*

Ruth Klein, *Le Moyne College*

Renee Kosiarek, *North Central College*

Robert Larison, *Eastern Oregon University*

Karen A. Longman, *Azusa Pacific University*

Maureen Majury, *Bellevue Community College*

James L. Morrison, *University of Delaware*

Terry W. Mullins, *University of North Carolina at Greensboro*

Jane Murtaugh, *College of DuPage*

Joanne E. Nottingham, *University of North Carolina, Wilmington*

Ramona Ortega-Liston, *University of Akron*

Ron Parlett, *Nova Southeastern University*

Bruce Peterson, *Sonoma State University*

Joseph W. T. Pugh, *Immaculata University*

Deana Raffo, *Middle Tennessee State University*

Melody Rawlings, *Northern Kentucky University*

Bronte H. Reynolds, *California State University, Northridge*

Louis Rubino, *California State University, Northridge*

Laurie A. Schreiner, *Azusa Pacific University*

Thomas Shields, *University of Richmond*

Pearl Sims, *Peabody College of Vanderbilt University*

Bruce Tucker, *Santa Fe Community College*

Mary Tucker, *Ohio University*

John Tummons, *University of Missouri*

Sameer Vaidya, *Texas Wesleyan University*

Natalie N. Walker, *Seminole State College*

Amy Wilson, *University at Buffalo*

Laurie Woodward, *University of South Florida*

Critiques by these reviewers were invaluable in helping to focus my thinking and writing during the revision process.

I would like to thank Dr. Bernardo Ferdman for his helpful comments and suggestions on the "Embracing Diversity and Inclusion" chapter, and Terry

Hammink for his assistance in the construction and scoring of the Ethical Leadership Style Questionnaire and James Ludema for his support.

For their outstanding work in developing creative resources for this edition, I am grateful to Isolde Anderson of Hope College, Matthew Creasy of the University of Delaware, Jeff Paul of the University of Tulsa, Lou Sabina of Stetson University, Andrea Smith-Hunter of Siena College, and Douglas Threet of Foothill College.

Finally, I wish to thank Marie Lee for her thorough editing and commitment and Laurel Northouse for her editorial insights and extraordinary support. It takes a lot of dedicated people to write a book, and I feel fortunate to have those people in my life.

About the Author

 **Peter G. Northouse,** PhD, is Professor Emeritus of Communication in the School of Communication at Western Michigan University. In addition to publications in professional journals, he is the author of *Leadership: Theory and Practice* (now in its seventh edition) and coauthor of *Health Communication: Strategies for Health Professionals* (now in its third edition) and *Leadership Case Studies in Education.* His scholarly and curricular interests include models of leadership, leadership assessment, ethical leadership, and leadership and group dynamics. For more than 30 years, he has taught undergraduate and graduate courses in leadership, interpersonal communication, and organizational communication on both the undergraduate and graduate levels. Currently, he is a consultant and lecturer on trends in leadership research, leadership development, and leadership education. He holds a doctorate in speech communication from the University of Denver, and master's and bachelor's degrees in communication education from Michigan State University.

Understanding Leadership

INTRODUCTION

This book is about *what it takes to be a leader.* Everyone, at some time in life, is asked to be a leader, whether to lead a classroom discussion, coach a children's soccer team, or direct a fund-raising campaign. Many situations require leadership. A leader may have a high profile (e.g., an elected public official) or a low profile (e.g., a volunteer leader in Big Brothers Big Sisters), but in every situation there are leadership demands placed on the individual who is the leader. Being a leader is challenging, exciting, and rewarding, and carries with it many responsibilities. This chapter discusses different ways of looking at leadership and their impacts on what it means to be a leader.

ASK THE AUTHOR

What is Leadership?

LEADERSHIP EXPLAINED

At the outset, it is important to address a basic question: *What is leadership?* Scholars who study leadership have struggled with this question for many decades and have written a great deal about the nature of leadership (Antonakis, Cianciolo, & Sternberg, 2004; Bass, 1990; Conger & Riggio, 2007). (See Box 1.1.)

▶

Leadership Basics

In leadership literature, more than 100 different definitions of leadership have been identified (Rost, 1991). Despite these many definitions, a number of concepts are recognized by most people as accurately reflecting what it is to be a leader.

"Leadership Is a Trait"

First, leadership is thought of as a *trait*. A **trait** is a distinguishing quality of an individual, which is often inherited. Defining leadership as a trait means that each individual brings to the table certain qualities that influence the way he or she leads. Some leaders are confident, some are decisive, and still others are outgoing and sociable. Saying that leadership is a trait places a great deal of emphasis on the leader and on the leader's special gifts. It follows the often-expressed belief "leaders are born, not made." Some argue that focusing on traits makes leadership an elitist enterprise because it implies that only a few people with special talents will lead. Although there may be some truth to this argument, it can also be argued that all of us are born with a wide array of unique traits and that many of these traits can have a positive impact on our leadership. It also may be possible to modify or change some traits.

Through the years, researchers have identified a multitude of traits that are associated with leadership. In Chapter 2 we will discuss some key leadership traits, and in Chapter 3 we will explain how strength-based leadership is a variation of trait leadership. Although there are many important leadership traits, what is most important for leaders is having the required traits that a particular situation demands. For example, a chaotic emergency room at a hospital requires a leader who is insightful and decisive and can bring calm to the situation. Conversely, a high school classroom in which students are bored demands a teacher who is inspiring and creative. Effective leadership results when the leader engages the right traits in the right place at the right time.

"Leadership Is an Ability"

In addition to being thought of as a trait, leadership is conceptualized as an ability. A person who has leadership **ability** is *able* to be a leader—that is, has the capacity to lead. While the term *ability* frequently refers to a natural capacity, ability can be acquired. For example, some people are naturally good at public speaking, while others rehearse to become comfortable speaking in public. Similarly, some people have the natural physical ability to excel in a sport, while others develop their athletic capacity through

BOX 1.1   The Evolution of Leadership

Leadership has long intrigued humankind and has been the topic of extensive literature for centuries. The earliest writings include philosophies of leadership such as Machiavelli's *The Prince* (1531/2005) and biographies of great leaders. With the development of the social sciences during the 20th century, inquiry into leadership became prolific. Studies on leadership have emerged from every discipline "that has had some interest in the subject of leadership: anthropology, business administration, educational administration, history, military science, nursing administration, organizational behavior, philosophy, political science, public administration, psychology, sociology, and theology" (Rost, 1991, p. 45).

As a result, there are many different leadership approaches and theories. While the words are often used interchangeably, approaches and theories are different conceptually. An **approach** is a general way of thinking about a phenomenon, not necessarily based on empirical research. A **theory** usually includes a set of hypotheses, principles, or laws that explain a given phenomenon. Theories are more refined and can provide a predictive framework in analyzing the phenomenon. For example, the spiritual leadership approach is a conceptualization of leadership that does not yet have a body of empirical research to validate it, while contingency leadership theory has a refined set of propositions based on the results of multiple research studies.

Not unlike fashion, approaches to leadership have evolved, changed focus and direction, and built upon one another during the past century.

To understand this evolution, a brief historical view can be helpful:

Trait Approach

The early **trait approach** theories were called **"Great Man" theories** because they focused on identifying the innate qualities and characteristics possessed by great social, political, and military leaders such as Catherine the Great, Mohandas Gandhi, Abraham Lincoln, Moses, and Joan of Arc. Studies of leadership traits were especially strong from 1900 to the early 1940s and enjoyed a renewed emphasis beginning in the 1970s as researchers began to examine visionary and charismatic leadership. In the 1980s, researchers linked leadership to the **"Big Five" personality factors** while interest in **emotional intelligence** as a trait gained favor in the 1990s. (For a discussion of *emotional intelligence* as a leadership skill, see Chapter 6, pages 126–127.)

Behavior Approach

In the late 1930s, leadership research began to focus on behavior—what leaders do and how they act. Groundbreaking studies by researchers at The Ohio State University and the University of Michigan in the 1940s and 1950s analyzed how leaders acted in small group situations. **Behavior approach** theories hit their heyday in the early 1960s with Blake and Moulton's (1964) work exploring how managers use **task** and **relationship behaviors** in the organizational setting.

Situational Approach

The premise of this approach is that different situations demand different kinds of leadership.

(Continued)

(Continued)

Serious examination of **situational approach** theories began in the late 1960s by Hersey and Blanchard (1969) and Reddin (1967). Situational approaches continued to be refined and revised from the 1970s through the 1990s (Vecchio, 1987). One of these, **path–goal theory**, examines how leaders use employee motivation to enhance performance and satisfaction. Another approach, **contingency theory**, focuses on the match between the leader's style and specific situational variables.

Relational Approach

In the 1990s, researchers began examining the nature of relations between leaders and followers. This research ultimately evolved into the **leader–member exchange (LMX) theory**. LMX theory predicts that high-quality relations generate more positive leader outcomes than low-quality relations. Research in the **relational approach** to leadership continues to generate moderate interest today.

"New Leadership" Approach

When these approaches began appearing in the mid-1980s—three decades ago—they were, and continue to be, called "new leadership" approaches (Bryman, 1992). Beginning with the work of Bass (1985, 1990), leadership studies generated visionary or charismatic leadership theories. From these approaches developed **transformational leadership theory**, which describes leadership as a process that changes people and organizations.

Emerging Leadership Approaches

A diverse range of approaches to leadership is emerging during the 21st century:

- **Adaptive leadership** examines how leaders help people address problems, face challenges, and adapt to change. Adaptive leadership stresses that the leaders don't solve the problems, but rather encourage others to do the problem solving and adapt to change.
- **Authentic leadership** is an approach that looks at the authenticity of leaders and their leadership and is currently enjoying strong interest.
- **Spiritual leadership** considers how leaders use values, a sense of "calling," and membership to motivate followers.
- **Servant leadership** emphasizes the "caring principle" with leaders as "servants" who focus on their followers' needs in order to help these followers become more autonomous, knowledgeable, and like servants themselves.
- **Gender-based studies**, which have gained much momentum as women continue to become more dominant in the workforce, especially on a global level, view how one's gender affects and differentiates one's leadership.

The historical timeline in Figure 1.1 is not intended to represent these approaches as separate and distinct eras, only to disappear from the picture when a new theory appears. Instead, many of these theories occur concurrently, building upon one another. Even when a certain approach's period of popularity has waned, the theory continues to influence further study and the development of new leadership approaches.

FIGURE 1.1   Development of Leadership Theories Through History

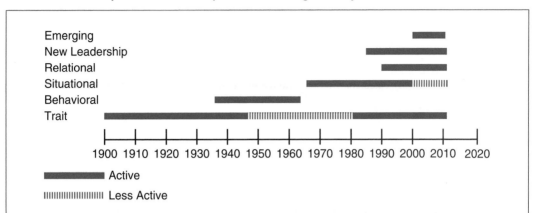

Source: Adapted from Antonakis, J., Cianciolo, A. T., & Sternberg, R. J. (Eds.). (2004). *The nature of leadership.* Thousand Oaks, CA: Sage, p. 7.

exercise and practice. In leadership, some people have the natural ability to lead, while others develop their leadership abilities through hard work and practice.

An example of leadership as ability is the legendary University of California at Los Angeles basketball coach John Wooden, whose teams won seven consecutive National Collegiate Athletic Association titles. Described first as a teacher and then as a coach, Wooden implemented four laws of learning into his coaching: explanation, demonstration, imitation, and repetition. His goal was to teach players how to do the right thing instinctively under great pressure. Less visible or well known, but also an example of leadership as ability, is the unheralded but highly effective restaurant manager who, through years of experience and learning, is able to create a successful, award-winning restaurant. In both of these examples, it is the individuals' abilities that create outstanding leadership.

Key Theories

"Leadership Is a Skill"

Third, leadership is a *skill.* Conceptualized as a **skill**, leadership is a *competency* developed to accomplish a task effectively. Skilled leaders are competent people who know the means and methods for carrying out their responsibilities. For example, a skilled leader in a fund-raising campaign knows every step and procedure in the fund-raising process and is able to use this knowledge to run an effective campaign. In short, skilled leaders are competent—they know what they need to do, and they know how to do it.

Describing leadership as a skill makes leadership available to everyone because skills are competencies that people can learn or develop. Even without natural leadership ability, people can improve their leadership with practice, instruction, and feedback from others. Viewed as a skill, leadership can be studied and learned. If you are capable of learning from experience, you can acquire leadership.

"Leadership Is a Behavior"

Leadership Behaviors

Leadership is also a *behavior*. It is *what leaders do* when they are in a leadership role. The behavioral dimension is concerned with how leaders act toward others in various situations. Unlike traits, abilities, and skills, leadership behaviors are observable. When someone leads, we see that person's leadership behavior.

Research on leadership has shown that leaders engage primarily in two kinds of general behaviors: task behaviors and process behaviors. **Task behaviors** are used by leaders to get the job done (e.g., a leader prepares an agenda for a meeting). **Process behaviors** are used by leaders to help people feel comfortable with other group members and at ease in the situations in which they find themselves (e.g., a leader helps individuals in a group to feel included). Since leadership requires both task and process behaviors, the challenge for leaders is to know the best way to combine them in their efforts to reach a goal.

"Leadership Is a Relationship"

Leadership and Change

Another, and a somewhat unusual, way to think about leadership is as a *relationship*. From this perspective, leadership is centered on the communication between leaders and followers rather than on the unique qualities of the leader. Thought of as a relationship, leadership becomes a process of collaboration that occurs between leaders and followers (Rost, 1991). A leader affects and is affected by followers, and both leader and followers are affected in turn by the situation that surrounds them. This approach emphasizes that leadership is not a linear one-way event, but rather an interactive event. In traditional leadership, authority is often top down; in the interactive type of leadership, authority and influence are shared. When leadership is defined in this manner, it becomes available to everyone. It is not restricted to the formally designated leader in a group.

Thinking of leadership as a relationship suggests that leaders must include followers and their interests in the process of leadership. A leader needs to be fully aware of the followers and the followers' interests, ideas, positions, attitudes, and motivations. In addition, this approach has an ethical overtone because it stresses the need for leaders to work with followers to achieve their mutual purposes. Stressing mutuality lessens the possibility that leaders might act toward followers in ways that are forced or unethical. It also increases the possibility that leaders and followers will work together toward a common good (Rost, 1991).

"Leadership Is an Influence Process"

A final way of thinking about leadership is as an influence process. This is the perspective that will be emphasized in this book.

> **Leadership** *is a process whereby an individual influences a group of individuals to achieve a common goal.*

Defining leadership as an influence process means that it is not a trait or an ability that resides in the leader, but rather an interactive event that occurs between the leader and the followers. Influence is central to the process of leadership because leaders affect followers. Leaders direct their energies toward influencing individuals to achieve something together. Stressing common goals gives leadership an ethical dimension because it lessens the possibility that leaders might act toward followers in ways that use coercion or are unethical.

Finally, in explaining what leadership is, it is important to make a distinction between leadership and management. In discussing what leadership is and can be, the concepts of leadership and management sometimes overlap. Both leadership and management involve influence, but leadership is about seeking constructive change, and management is about establishing order. For example, it is often said that "managers are people who do things right, and leaders are people who do the right thing." Since both leaders and managers are engaged in influencing people toward goal accomplishment, our discussion in this book will treat the roles of managers and leaders similarly and not emphasize the differences between them.

Leadership
Development

GLOBAL LEADERSHIP ATTRIBUTES

Universal Leadership Attributes

We probably all wonder at the differences in leadership around the world. Why do some countries gravitate toward the distributed leadership of a democracy, while others seem content with the hierarchical leadership of a monarchy or dictatorship? The definition and concepts of leadership outlined in this chapter are from an American perspective. If you were to travel to nations across the world, you would no doubt encounter different views of leadership specific to those ethnic and political cultures.

In 2004, Robert House led a group of 160 researchers in an ambitious study to increase our understanding of the impact culture has on leadership effectiveness. The GLOBE (Global Leadership and Organizational Behavior Effectiveness) studies drew on the input of 17,000 people in 62 countries in determining how leadership varies across the world. Among the many findings generated by the GLOBE studies was the identification of positive and negative leadership characteristics that are universally accepted worldwide (see Table 1.1).

TABLE 1.1   Universal Leadership Attributes

Positive Leader Attributes		
Trustworthy	Just	Honest
Foresighted	Plans ahead	Encouraging
Positive	Dynamic	Motivator
Builds confidence	Motivational	Dependable
Intelligent	Decisive	Effective bargainer
Win-win problem solver	Communicative	Informed
Administratively skilled	Coordinator	Team builder
Excellence oriented		
Negative Leader Attributes		
Loner	Asocial	Noncooperative
Irritable	Nonexplicit	Egocentric
Ruthless	Dictatorial	

Source: Adapted from House, R. J., Hanges, P. J., Javidan, M., Dorfman, P. W., & Gupta, V. (Eds.). (2004). *Culture, leadership, and organizations: The GLOBE study of 62 societies.* Thousand Oaks, CA: Sage, pp. 677–678. Reprinted with permission.

THE DARK SIDE OF LEADERSHIP

Those same characteristics and behaviors that distinguish leadership can also be used by leaders in nonpositive ways (Conger, 1990). The

dark side of leadership is the destructive side of leadership where a leader uses his or her influence or power for personal ends. Lipman-Blumen (2005) suggests that such leaders are "toxic," where their leadership leaves their followers worse off than they found them, often violating the basic human rights of others and playing to their followers' basest fears. Dark leadership is able to thrive when three conditions exist, according to Padilla, Hogan, and Kaiser (2007): a destructive leader, susceptible followers, and a conducive environment. Destructive leaders will prevail when the checks and balances of an organization are weak and the rules of the institution are ineffective. While many cite Adolf Hitler as the prime example of the dark side of leadership, there are many current examples in the world today from the regime of Bashar al-Assad in Syria, whose leadership has led to violent civil war that has left hundreds of thousands dead, to religious extremist groups, such as ISIS and al-Qaeda, who use their followers to engage in mass murder of innocents.

The meaning of leadership is complex and includes many dimensions. For some people, leadership is a *trait* or an *ability*, for others it is a *skill* or a *behavior*, and for still others it is a *relationship* or a *process*. In reality, leadership probably includes components of all of these dimensions. Each dimension explains a facet of leadership.

In considering these various definitions of leadership and based on the results of your Conceptualizing Leadership Questionnaire (page 14), which dimension seems closest to how you think of leadership? How would you define leadership? Answers to these questions are important because *how you think* about leadership will strongly influence *how you practice* leadership.

There is a strong demand for effective leadership in society today. This demand exists at the local and community levels, as well as at the national level, in this country and abroad. People feel the need for leadership in all aspects of their lives. They want leaders in their personal lives, at school, in the work setting, and even in their spiritual lives. Everywhere you turn, people are expressing a need for strong leadership.

When people ask for leadership in a particular situation, it is not always clear exactly what they want. For the most part, however, they want effective leadership. Effective leadership is intended influence that creates change for the greater good. Leadership uses positive means to achieve positive outcomes. Furthermore, people want leaders who listen to and understand their needs and who can relate to their circumstances. The challenge for each of us is to be prepared to lead when we are asked to be the leader.

**The Dark Side
of Leadership**

**Destructive
Leadership**

LEADERSHIP SNAPSHOT

Indra Nooyi, CEO, PepsiCo

Mark Wilson/Staff/Getty
Images News/Getty Images

The daughter of a conservative, middle-class family in southern India, Indra Nooyi didn't seem destined to one day run one of the world's largest snack food and beverage companies. But Nooyi does just that as the CEO and president of PepsiCo, making her one of the top female executives in the United States and probably the highest-ranking woman of Indian heritage in corporate America.

Nooyi, who grew up in Madras (now Chennai), India, admits she always pushed social conventions. She played on an all-girls cricket team and was a guitarist in a rock band at a time when it was deemed inappropriate for Indian girls to do such things. Despite graduating from college with bachelor's degrees in chemistry, math, and physics from Madras Christian College in 1974 and a master of business administration from the Indian Institute of Management Calcutta, Nooyi was reportedly remembered for being only a "mediocre student" (Pandey, 2006).

Nooyi's first job after college was for Tootal, a British textile company in India, but she was hired away as a brand manager for Johnson & Johnson to oversee the company's Stayfree account in India. It was a job that would have challenged the most seasoned marketing executive because, at the time, advertising women's feminine products was not allowed in her country (Murray, 2004).

By 1978, Nooyi felt she needed more preparation for the business world and applied to and was accepted to the Yale School of Management in the United States. To her surprise, her parents agreed to let her go, although it would essentially make her an unmarriageable commodity in her culture. She received financial aid from Yale, but still struggled to make ends meet, working as an overnight receptionist. She didn't have the money to buy a business suit, so she wore her traditional sari to work and later in job interviews, choosing to be herself rather than adhere to expected cultural norms.

Nooyi did not earn an MBA from Yale, choosing instead to get a master's degree in public and private management. Her first jobs after graduation were for the prestigious Boston Consulting Group and Motorola. In 1990, she joined ASEA Brown Boveri (ABB), a Swiss-Swedish industrial conglomerate. Her success in directing ABB's North American operations caught the attention of PepsiCo CEO Wayne Calloway who wooed her away to become his company's chief strategist.

Nooyi quickly left her mark at PepsiCo. She was the chief deal maker for two of PepsiCo's most important acquisitions: the Tropicana orange juice brand in 1998 and Quaker Oats in 2001. The Quaker Oats deal added a huge range of cereals and snack foods to the PepsiCo empire. Nooyi also helped the company acquire beverage maker SoBe, beating out a competing offer from Coca-Cola. Her deal-making talents elevated her to the job of PepsiCo's chief financial officer in 2000, and a year later she was given the title of president.

Nooyi's vision for PepsiCo—that "for any part of the day, we will have a little snack for you" (Byrnes, 2001)—has been implemented through development of new products and acquisitions. The company now sells a wide range of foods and beverages from Cap'n Crunch and Doritos to Mountain Dew and Gatorade. The company's 18 brands are sold in 200 countries, and it employs 198,000 people worldwide.

But the strategist in Nooyi has also foreseen the effect that growing lifestyle diseases such as obesity could have on her company. Again, she has chosen to follow an unconventional path, looking to create healthier products in an industry dominated by salt, fat, and sugar. She invested heavily in the creation of a research and development lab that took five years to complete, drawing criticism from stockholders and industry analysts. So far, the investment has had some success: PepsiCo introduced a "mid-calorie" cola, Pepsi True, which has 30% less sugar and uses stevia extract instead of artificial sweeteners, and has created potato chips that taste just as salty as the original but have less sodium. The company has also introduced a new line of craft sodas called Stubborn Soda, which contain natural flavors and sugarcane instead of high-fructose corn syrup.

SUMMARY

All of us at some time in our lives will be asked to show leadership. When you are asked to be the leader, it will be both demanding and rewarding. How you approach leadership is strongly influenced by your definitions of and beliefs about leadership. Through the years, writers have defined leadership in a multitude of ways. It is a complex, multidimensional process that is often conceptualized in a variety of ways by different people. Some of the most common ways of looking at leadership are as a trait, as an ability, as a skill, as a behavior, as a relationship, and as a process. The way you think about leadership will influence the way you practice leadership.

GLOSSARY TERMS

ability   2

adaptive leadership   4

approach   3

authentic leadership   4

behavior approach   3

"Big Five" personality factors   3

contingency theory   4

dark side of leadership   9

emotional intelligence   3

gender-based studies   4

"Great Man" theories   3

leader–member exchange (LMX)
   theory   4

leadership   7

path–goal theory   4

process behaviors   6

relational approach   4

relationship behaviors   3

servant leadership   4

situational approach   4

skill   5

spiritual leadership   4

task behaviors   3, 6

theory   3

trait   2

trait approach   3

transformational leadership
   theory   4

Sharpen your skills with SAGE edge at **edge.sagepub.com/northouseintro4e**

SAGE edge for students provides a personalized approach to help you accomplish your coursework goals in an easy-to-use learning environment.

1.1 CASE STUDY

King of the Hill

Denny Hill's career as a high school swimming coach didn't start out well. The seniors on his team quit in the first season because he required them to come to all the workouts. The team only won three meets the whole season. That was 40 years ago. Since that time, the high school chemistry teacher's success as a swimming coach has been extraordinary; his winnings include more than 900 boys' and girls' dual meets and a phenomenal 31 state titles.

Denny is noted for creating a team effort out of what is usually considered an individual sport. He begins every season with a team sleepover, followed by "Hell Week," a two-week grueling regimen in which team members swim at least 5 miles a workout and 10 miles a day. He acknowledges this is a bonding experience for the swimmers, regardless of their skill, because they are "all in the same boat."

Denny passes the mantle of leadership onto his team members. Seniors are expected to be mature leaders who inform the freshmen of the team goals and expectations. Juniors are to be role models, while sophomores serve as quiet leaders who are still learning but have a foundation in the team culture. Even the freshmen members have a job: They are required to pay attention to the coaches and other team members as they learn the team's culture and what's expected.

Denny holds a 20-minute team meeting each Monday where every member has the opportunity to present a rose or a complaint to anyone on the team including the coaches. He is tough on swimmers and makes them work, but when they need support he is always there to put an arm around them. Denny also uses humor, often making jokes that help take the edge off long, hard workouts.

And despite his teams' successes, Denny isn't about winning; he's more about preparing to win—telling his swimmers that by preparing to win, everything takes care of itself. When you do win, he says, you've done it the right way.

QUESTIONS

1. What leadership *traits* account for Denny Hill's success?

2. How would you describe Denny Hill's leadership *abilities*?

3. Leadership includes administrative skills, interpersonal skills, and conceptual skills. How does Denny Hill stack up on these *skills*?

4. How does Denny Hill integrate task and relationship *behaviors* in his leadership?

5. From a relational perspective, how would you describe Denny Hill's leadership?

6. In what way does Denny Hill's coaching exemplify leadership as an influence process?

1.4 REFLECTION AND ACTION WORKSHEET

Understanding Leadership

APPLICATION

Reflection

1. Each of us has our own unique way of thinking about leadership. What leaders or people have influenced you in your thinking about leadership? Discuss what leadership means to you and give your definition of leadership.

2. What do the scores you received on the Conceptualizing Leadership Questionnaire suggest about your perspective on leadership? Of the six dimensions on the questionnaire (trait, ability, skill, behavior, relationship, and process), which one is the most similar to your own perspective? Which one is least like your own perspective?

3. Do you think leadership is something everyone can learn to do, or do you think it is a natural ability reserved for a few? Explain your answer.

Action

1. Based on the interviews you conducted with others about leadership, how could you incorporate others' ideas about leadership into your own leadership?

2. Treating leadership as a relationship has ethical implications. How could adding the *relationship* approach to your leadership make you a better leader? Discuss.

3. Think about your own leadership. Identify one trait, ability, skill, or behavior that you could develop more fully to become a better leader.

 Visit **edge.sagepub.com/northouseintro4e** for a downloadable version of this worksheet.

REFERENCES

Antonakis, J., Cianciolo, A. T., & Sternberg, R. J. (Eds.). (2004). *The nature of leadership.* Thousand Oaks, CA: Sage.

Bass, B. M. (1985). *Leadership and performance beyond expectations.* New York, NY: Free Press.

Bass, B. M. (1990). *Bass and Stogdill's handbook of leadership: A survey of theory and research.* New York, NY: Free Press.

Blake, R. R., & Moulton, J. S. (1964). *The managerial grid.* Houston, TX: Gulf.

Bryman, A. (1992). *Charisma and leadership in organizations.* London, U K: Sage.

Byrnes, N. (2001, January 29). The power of two at Pepsi. *Businessweek.* Retrieved from http://www.bloomberg.com/news/articles/2001-01-28/the-power-of-two-at-pepsi

Conger, J. (1990). The dark side of leadership. *Organizational Dynamics, 19*(2), 44–55.

Conger, J. A., & Riggio, R. E. (Eds.). (2007). *The practice of leadership: Developing the next generation of leaders.* San Francisco, CA: Jossey-Bass.

Hersey, P., & Blanchard, K. H. (1969). Life-cycle theory of leadership. *Training and Development Journal, 23*(5), 26–34.

House, R. J., Hanges, P. J., Javidan, M., Dorfman, P. W., & Gupta, V. (2004). *Culture, leadership, and organizations:*

The GLOBE study of 62 societies. Thousand Oaks, CA: Sage.

Lipman-Blumen, J. (2005). *The allure of toxic leaders.* New York, NY: Oxford University Press.

Machiavelli, N. (2005). *The prince* (W. J. Connell, trans.). Boston, MA: Bedford/St. Martin's. (Original work published in 1531)

Murray, S. (2004, January 26). From poor Indian student to powerful U.S. business-woman. *Financial Times,* p. 3.

Padilla, A., Hogan, R., & Kaiser, R. B. (2007). The toxic triangle: Destructive leaders, susceptible followers, and conducive environments. *The Leadership Quarterly, 18*(3), 176–194.

Pandey, J. M. (2006, August 18). Nooyi: IIM-C's "average" student turns role model. *The Times of India.* Retrieved from http://timesofindia.indiatimes.com/india/Nooyi-IIM-Cs-average-student-turns-role-model/articleshow/1902571.cms

Reddin, W. J. (1967, April). The 3-D management style theory. *Training and Development Journal,* pp. 8–17.

Rost, J. C. (1991). *Leadership for the twenty-first century.* Westport, CO: Praeger.

Vecchio, R. P. (1987). Situational leadership theory: An examination of a prescriptive theory. *Journal of Applied Psychology, 72*(3), 444–451.

Recognizing Your Traits

INTRODUCTION

Why are some people leaders while others are not? What makes people become leaders? Do leaders have certain traits? These questions have been of interest for many years. It seems that all of us want to know what characteristics account for effective leadership. This chapter will address the traits that are important to leadership.

ASK THE
AUTHOR

Is Leadership a Trait?

Since the early 20th century, hundreds of research studies have been conducted on the traits of leaders. These studies have produced an extensive list of ideal leadership traits (see Antonakis, Cianciolo, & Sternberg, 2004; Bass, 1990). The list of important leadership traits is long and includes such traits as diligence, trustworthiness, dependability, articulateness, sociability, open-mindedness, intelligence, confidence, self-assurance, and conscientiousness. Because the list is so extensive, it is difficult to identify specifically which traits are essential for leaders. In fact, nearly all of the traits are probably related to effective leadership.

What traits are important when you are asked to be a leader? To answer this question, two areas will be addressed in this chapter. First, a set of selected traits that appear by all accounts to be strongly related to effective leadership in everyday life will be discussed. Second, the lives of several historical and contemporary leaders will be examined with a discussion of the traits that play a role in their leadership. Throughout this discussion, the unique ways that certain traits affect the leadership process in one way or another will be emphasized.

LEADERSHIP TRAITS EXPLAINED

Leadership Traits

From the beginning of the 20th century to the present day, researchers have focused a great deal of attention on the unique characteristics of successful leaders. Thousands of studies have been conducted to identify the traits of effective leaders. The results of these studies have produced a very long list of important leadership traits; each of these traits contributes to the leadership process.

For example, research studies by several investigators found the following traits to be important: achievement, persistence, insight, initiative, self-confidence, responsibility, cooperativeness, tolerance, influence, sociability, drive, motivation, integrity, confidence, cognitive ability, task knowledge, extroversion, conscientiousness, and openness (Judge, Bono, Ilies, & Gerhardt, 2002; Kirkpatrick & Locke, 1991; Stogdill, 1974). On the international level, House, Hanges, Javidan, Dorfman, and Gupta (2004), in a study of 17,000 managers in 62 different cultures, identified a list of 22 valued traits that were universally endorsed as characteristics of outstanding leadership in these countries. The list, which was outlined in Table 1.1 in Chapter 1, "Understanding Leadership," includes such attributes as being trustworthy, just, honest, encouraging, positive, dynamic, dependable, intelligent, decisive, communicative, informed, and a team builder. As these findings indicate, research studies on leadership traits have identified a wide array of important characteristics of leaders.

ASK THE
AUTHOR

Are There Certain Traits a Leader Needs?

However, these research findings raise an important question: If there are so many important leadership traits, which *specific traits* do people need to be successful leaders? While the answer to this question is not crystal clear, the research points to *six key traits: intelligence, confidence, charisma, determination, sociability,* and *integrity.* In the following section, we will discuss each of these traits in turn.

Intelligence

Intelligence is an important trait related to effective leadership. Intelligence includes having good language skills, perceptual skills, and reasoning ability. This combination of assets makes people good thinkers, and makes them better leaders.

While it is hard for a person to alter his or her IQ (intelligence quotient), there are certain ways for a person to improve intelligence in general. Intelligent leaders are well informed. They are aware of what is going on around them and understand the job that needs to be done. It is important for leaders to obtain information about what their leadership role entails and learn as much as possible about their work environment. This information will help leaders be more knowledgeable and insightful.

For example, a few years ago a friend, Chris, was asked to be the coach of his daughter's middle school soccer team even though he had never played soccer and knew next to nothing about how the game is played. Chris took the job and eventually was a great success, but not without a lot of effort. He spent many hours learning about soccer. He read how-to books, instructors' manuals, and coaching books. In addition, Chris subscribed to several soccer magazines. He talked to other coaches and learned everything he could about playing the game. By the time he had finished the first season, others considered Chris to be a very competent coach. He was smart and learned how to be a successful coach.

Regarding intelligence, few if any of us can expect to be another Albert Einstein. Most of us have average intelligence and know that there are limits to what we can do. Nevertheless, becoming more knowledgeable about our leadership positions gives us the information we need to become better leaders.

Confidence

Being confident is another important trait of an effective leader. Confident people feel self-assured and believe they can accomplish their goals. Rather than feeling uncertain, they feel strong and secure about their positions. They do not second-guess themselves, but rather move forward on projects with a clear vision. Confident leaders feel a sense of certainty and believe that they are doing the right thing. Clearly, **confidence** is a trait that has to do with feeling positive about oneself and one's ability to succeed.

Confidence

If confidence is a central trait of successful leaders, how can you build your own confidence? First, confidence comes from *understanding* what is required of you. For example, when first learning to drive a car, a student's confidence is low because he or she does not know *what* to do. If an instructor explains the driving process and demonstrates how to drive, the student can gain confidence because he or she now has an understanding of how to drive. Awareness and understanding build confidence. Confidence can also come from having a mentor to show the way and provide constructive feedback. This mentor may be a boss, an experienced coworker, or a significant other from outside the organization. Because mentors act as role models and sounding boards, they provide essential help to learn the dynamics of leadership.

Confidence also comes from *practice.* This is important to point out, because practice is something everyone can do. Consider Michael Phelps, one of the most well-known athletes in the world today. Phelps is a very gifted swimmer, with 23 Olympic gold medals and the record for winning the most medals, 28, of any Olympic athlete in history. But Phelps also spends an enormous amount of time practicing. His workout regimen includes swimming six hours a day, six days a week. His excellent performance and confidence are a result of his practice, as well as his gifts.

In leadership, practice builds confidence because it provides assurance that an aspiring leader can do what needs to be done. Taking on leadership roles, even minor ones on committees or through volunteer activities, provides practice for being a leader. Building one leadership activity on another can increase confidence for more demanding leadership roles. Those who accept opportunities to practice their leadership will experience increased confidence in their leadership abilities.

Charisma

Charismatic
Leadership

Of all the traits related to effective leadership, charisma gets the most attention. **Charisma** refers to a leader's special magnetic charm and appeal, and can have a huge effect on the leadership process. Charisma is a special personality characteristic that gives a leader the capacity to do extraordinary things. In particular, it gives the leader exceptional powers of influence. A good example of a charismatic leader is former president John F. Kennedy, who motivated the American people with his eloquent oratorical style (visit edge.sagepub .com/northouseintro4e to read one of his speeches). President Kennedy was a gifted, charismatic leader who had an enormous impact on others.

It is not unusual for many of us to feel challenged with regard to charisma because it is not a common personality trait. There are a few select people who are very charismatic, but most of us are not. Since charisma appears in short supply, the question arises: What do leaders do if they are not naturally charismatic?

Based on the writings of leadership scholars, several behaviors characterize charismatic leadership (Conger, 1999; House, 1976; Shamir, House, & Arthur, 1993). First, charismatic leaders serve as a *strong role model* for the values that they desire others to adopt. Mohandas Gandhi advocated nonviolence and was an exemplary role model of civil disobedience; his charisma enabled him to influence others. Second, charismatic leaders *show competence* in every aspect of leadership, so others trust their decisions. Third, charismatic leaders *articulate clear goals* and *strong values.* Martin Luther King Jr.'s "I Have a Dream" speech is an example of this type of charismatic leadership. By articulating his dream, he was able to influence multitudes of people to follow his nonviolent practices. Fourth, charismatic leaders communicate *high expectations* for followers and *show confidence* in their abilities to meet these expectations. Finally, charismatic leaders are an *inspiration* to others. They can excite and motivate others to become involved in real change, as demonstrated by John F. Kennedy and Martin Luther King Jr.

Determination

Determination is another trait that characterizes effective leaders. Determined leaders are very focused and attentive to tasks. They know *where* they are going and *how* they intend to get there. Determination is the decision to get the job done; it includes characteristics such as initiative, persistence, and drive. People with determination are willing to assert themselves, they are proactive, and they have the capacity to persevere in the face of obstacles. Being determined includes showing dominance at times, especially in situations where others need direction.

Determination

We have all heard of determined people who have accomplished spectacular things—the person with cancer who runs a standard 26.2-mile marathon, the blind person who climbs Mount Everest, or the single mom with four kids who graduates from college. A good example of determined leadership is Nelson Mandela, who is featured in the Leadership Snapshot in this chapter. Mandela's single goal was to end apartheid in South Africa. Even though he was imprisoned for many years, he steadfastly held to his principles. He was committed to reaching his goal, and he never wavered from his vision. Mandela was focused and disciplined—a determined leader.

What distinguishes all of these leaders from other people is their determination to get the job done. Of all the traits discussed in this chapter, determination is probably the one trait that is easily acquired by those who lead. All it demands is perseverance. Staying focused on the task, clarifying the goals, articulating the vision, and encouraging others to stay the course are characteristics of determined leaders. Being determined takes discipline and the ability to endure, but having this trait will almost certainly enhance a person's leadership.

Sociability

Another important trait for leaders is **sociability**. Sociability refers to a leader's capacity to establish pleasant social relationships. People want sociable leaders—leaders with whom they can get along. Leaders who show sociability are friendly, outgoing, courteous, tactful, and diplomatic. They are sensitive to others' needs and show concern for their well-being. Sociable leaders have good interpersonal skills and help to create cooperative relationships within their work environments.

Being sociable comes easier for some than for others. For example, it is easy for extroverted leaders to talk to others and be outgoing, but it is harder for introverted leaders to do so. Similarly, some individuals are naturally "people persons," while others prefer to be alone. Although people vary in the degree to which they are outgoing, it is possible to increase sociability. A sociable leader gets along with coworkers and other people in the work setting. Being friendly, kind, and thoughtful, as well as talking freely with others and giving them support, goes a long way to establish a leader's sociability. Sociable leaders bring positive energy to a group and make the work environment a more enjoyable place.

To illustrate, consider the following example. This scenario occurred in one of the best leadership classes I have had in 40 years of teaching. In this class, there was a student named Anne Fox who was a very sociable leader. Anne was an unusual student who dressed like a student from the 1960s, although it was more than two decades later. Even though she dressed differently than the others, Anne was very caring and was liked by everyone in the class. After the first week of the semester, Anne could name everyone in class; when attendance was taken, she knew instantly who was there and who was not. In class discussions, Anne always contributed good ideas, and her remarks were sensitive of others' points of view. Anne was positive about life, and her attitude was contagious. By her presence, Anne created an atmosphere in which everyone felt unique but also included. She was the glue that held us all together. Anne was not assigned to be the leader in the class, but by the semester's end she emerged as a leader. Her sociable nature enabled her to develop strong relationships and become a leader in the class. By the end of the class, all of us were the beneficiaries of her leadership.

Integrity

Integrity

Finally, and perhaps most important, effective leaders have **integrity**. Integrity characterizes leaders who possess the qualities of honesty and trustworthiness. People who adhere to a strong set of principles and take responsibility for their actions are exhibiting integrity. Leaders with integrity inspire confidence in others because they can be trusted to do what they say they are going to do. They are loyal, dependable, and transparent. Basically, integrity makes a leader believable and worthy of our trust.

Grown-ups often tell children, "Never tell a lie." For children, the lesson is "Good children are truthful." For leaders, the lesson is the same:

LEADERSHIP SNAPSHOT

Nelson Mandela, First Black President of South Africa

South Africa The Good News / www.sagoodnews
.co.za CC BY 2.0 https://creativecommons.org/
licenses/by/2.0/deed.en

In 1990, when Nelson Mandela was released from prison after serving 27 long years, he was determined not to be angry or vindictive, but instead to work to unite his country of South Africa, which had been fractured by generations of apartheid.

The descendent of a tribal king, Mandela was born in 1918 in a small African village and grew up in a country where Whites ruled through subjugation and tyranny over Blacks and other races. Mandela attended Methodist missionary schools and put himself through law school, eventually opening the first Black law partnership in 1942. His firm represented the African National Congress (ANC), which was engaged in resisting South Africa's apartheid policies, and during the 1950s, he became a leader of the ANC. Influenced by Mohandas Gandhi, Mandela was initially committed to

nonviolent resistance but shifted to supporting violent tactics when the government refused to change its apartheid policies. In 1964, Mandela received a life sentence for plotting to overthrow the government by violence.

During the nearly three decades Mandela spent in prison, he became a symbolic figure for the anti-apartheid movement. But during those years, Mandela spent time examining himself, coming to see himself as others did: as an aggressive and militant revolutionary. He learned to control his temper and strong will, instead using persuasion and emphasis to convince others. He listened to others' life stories, including those of the White guards, seeking to understand their perspectives. He was steadfast in maintaining his dignity, carefully refusing to be subservient while being respectful to the guards and others. As a result, he became a natural leader inside the prison, while outside, his fame framed him as a symbolic martyr not only to Black Africans but also to people across the globe. Free Mandela campaigns were building around the world, with other countries and international corporations being pressured by stockholders and citizens to "divest" in South Africa.

In 1990, South African president F. W. de Klerk, fearing civil war and economic collapse, released Mandela, at the time 71, from prison. Mandela emerged as a moral leader who stood by the principles of liberty and equal rights for all. He began speaking around the world, raising

(Continued)

(Continued)

financial support for the ANC while seeking to bring peace to his fractured country. In 1992, the South African government instituted a new constitution and held a popular election with all parties represented including the ANC. The result? In 1994, Mandela was elected as the first Black president of South Africa, effectively ending apartheid. For his role in negotiations to abolish apartheid, Mandela received the Nobel Peace Prize, sharing it with de Klerk.

As president of South Africa from 1994 to 1999, Mandela's mission was to transform a nation from minority rule and apartheid to a multiracial democracy. On the first day of his presidency, he set the tone with the predominantly White staff of the former president, telling them that those who wanted to keep their jobs were welcome to stay, stating "Reconciliation starts here." He developed a multiracial staff and cabinet, using his friendly smiling style and tactic of listening to all viewpoints carefully before making decisions to keep the staff focused on problems and issues rather than on partisanship.

Mandela served his five-year term as president but, at 76 years old, chose not to seek another term. In retirement, he continued to advocate for social causes, serving as a mediator in disputes outside of South Africa, and to bring a message of peace and justice throughout the world. Mandela died in 2013. While it is difficult to summarize all that he accomplished, Mandela's legacy is best described by former U.S. president Bill Clinton who in 2003 wrote, "Under a burden of oppression he saw through difference, discrimination and destruction to embrace our common humanity."

"Good leaders are honest." Dishonesty creates mistrust in others, and dishonest leaders are seen as undependable and unreliable. Honesty helps people to have trust and faith in what leaders have to say and what they stand for. Honesty also enhances a leader's ability to influence others because they have confidence in and believe in their leader.

Integrity demands being open with others and representing reality as fully and completely as possible. However, this is not an easy task: There are times when telling the complete truth can be destructive or counterproductive. The challenge for leaders is to strike a balance between being open and candid and monitoring what is appropriate to disclose in a particular situation. While it is important for leaders to be authentic, it is also essential for them to have integrity in their relationships with others.

Integrity undergirds all aspects of leadership. It is at the core of being a leader. Integrity is a central aspect of a leader's ability to influence. If people do not trust a leader, the leader's influence potential is weakened. In essence, integrity is the bedrock of who a leader is. When a leader's integrity comes into question, his or her potential to lead is lost.

Former president Bill Clinton (1993–2001) is a good example of how integrity is related to leadership. In the late 1990s, he was brought before the U.S. Congress for misrepresenting under oath an affair he had engaged in with a

White House intern. For his actions, he was impeached by the U.S. House of Representatives, but then was acquitted by the U.S. Senate. At one point during the long ordeal, the president appeared on national television and, in what is now a famous speech, declared his innocence. Because subsequent hearings provided information suggesting he might have lied during his television speech, many Americans felt Clinton had violated his duty and responsibility as a person, leader, and president. As a result, Clinton's integrity was clearly challenged and the impact of his leadership substantially weakened.

In conclusion, there are many traits related to effective leadership. The six traits discussed here appear to be particularly important in the leadership process. As will be revealed in subsequent chapters, leadership is a very complex process. The traits discussed in this chapter are important but are only one dimension of a multidimensional process.

Effective Traits

LEADERSHIP TRAITS IN PRACTICE

Throughout history, there have been many great leaders. Each of them has led with unique talents and in different circumstances. The following section analyzes the accomplishments and the traits of five famous leaders. Although there are hundreds of equally distinguished leaders, these five are highlighted because they represent different kinds of leadership at different points in history. All of these leaders are recognized as being notable leaders: Each has had an impact on many people's lives and accomplished great things.

The leaders discussed below are George Washington, Winston Churchill, Mother Teresa, Bill Gates, and Oprah Winfrey. As you read about each of them, think about their leadership traits.

**Traits of
Great Leaders**

George Washington (1732–1799)

George Washington is considered to be the founding father of the United States of America. His leadership was pivotal in the development of this country's government. He was truly respected by everyone, from low-ranking soldiers to feisty public officials. He was a man of great integrity who was a good listener. After the Revolutionary War, Washington was *the* reason that various factions did not splinter into small groups or nations. He became the United States' first president because his leadership was so well suited for the times.

Gilbert Stuart /National Gallery of Art/Getty Images

Today, there are more than 1 million workers affiliated with the Missionaries of Charity in more than 40 countries. The charity provides help to people who have been hurt by floods, epidemics, famines, and war. The Missionaries of Charity also operate hospitals, schools, orphanages, youth centers, shelters for the sick, and hospices. For her humanitarian work and efforts for peace, Mother Teresa has been recognized with many awards, including the Pope John XXIII Peace Prize (1971), the Nehru Award (1972), the U.S. Presidential Medal of Freedom (1985), and the Congressional Gold Medal (1994). Although she struggled with deteriorating health in her later years, Mother Teresa remained actively involved in her work to the very end. She died at the age of 87 in 1997. In September 2016, Pope Francis declared Mother Teresa a saint, with the official name of Saint Teresa of Kolkata. In a statement announcing the canonization, the Vatican called her a "metaphor for selfless devotion and holiness" (Lyman, 2016).

Traits and Characteristics

Mother Teresa was a simple woman of small stature who dressed in a plain blue and white sari, and who never owned more than the people she served. Mirroring her appearance, her mission was simple—to care for the poor. From her first year on the streets of Kolkata where she tended to one dying person to her last years when thousands of people were cared for by the Missionaries of Charity, Mother Teresa stayed focused on her goal. She was a true civil servant who was simultaneously determined and fearless, and humble and spiritual. She often listened to the will of God. When criticized for her stand on abortion and women's role in the family, or her approaches to eliminating poverty, Mother Teresa responded with a strong will; she never wavered in her deep-seated human values. Teaching by example with few words, she was a role model for others. Clearly, Mother Teresa was a leader who practiced what she preached (Gonzalez-Balado, 1997; Sebba, 1997; Spink, 1997; Vardey, 1995).

Yamaguchi Haruyoshi/Contributor/
Corbis Historical/Getty Images

Bill Gates (1955–)

For many years, William (Bill) H. Gates III, cofounder and chair of Microsoft Corporation, the world's largest developer of software for personal computers, was the wealthiest person in the world with assets estimated at more than $70 billion. A self-made man, Gates began his interest in computers at the age of 13 when he and a friend developed their first computer software program. He later attended Harvard

University but left, without graduating, to focus on software development. He cofounded Microsoft in 1975. Under Gates's leadership, Microsoft developed the well-known Microsoft Disk Operating System (MS-DOS), Windows operating system, and Internet Explorer browser. Microsoft is one of the fastest-growing and most profitable companies ever established. From the success of Microsoft, Gates and his wife established the Bill & Melinda Gates Foundation in 2000 to reduce inequities and improve lives around the world. This foundation promotes education, addresses global health issues (such as malaria, HIV/AIDS, and tuberculosis), sponsors libraries, and supports housing and community initiatives in the Pacific Northwest. Beginning in 2006, Gates transitioned away from his day-to-day operating role at Microsoft to spend more time working with his foundation, but he remained the corporation's chair. But in February 2014, Gates stepped down as the company's board chairman in order to increase his involvement in the company's operations, serving in a new role of technology adviser and mentor to the company's new CEO Satya Nadella. Gates continues to tackle global challenges as co-chair of the Bill & Melinda Gates Foundation, which has become the world's largest private charitable foundation.

Traits and Characteristics

Bill Gates is both intelligent and visionary. When he cofounded Microsoft, he had a vision about how to meet the technological needs of people in the future, and he hired friends to help him accomplish that vision. Gates is also task oriented and diligent, often working 12 or more hours a day to promote his interest in software product development. Furthermore, Gates is focused and aggressive. When Microsoft was accused by the U.S. government of antitrust violations, Gates appeared before congressional hearings and strongly defended his company. When asked about whether he has a "win at all cost" mentality, he answered that you bring people together to work on products and make products better, but there is never a finish line—there are always challenges ahead (Jager & Ortiz, 1997, pp. 151–152). In his personal style, Gates is simple, straightforward, unpretentious, and altruistic: He has demonstrated a strong concern for the poor and underserved.

Intelligence in Leadership

Oprah Winfrey (1954–)

An award-winning television talk show host, Oprah Winfrey is one of the most powerful and influential women in the world. Born in rural Mississippi into a

Frederick M. Brown/Stringer/Getty Images Entertainment/Getty Images

dysfunctional family, she was raised by her grandmother until she was 6. Winfrey learned to read at a very early age and skipped two grades in school. Her adolescent years were difficult: While living in inner-city Milwaukee with her mother who worked two jobs, Winfrey was molested by a family member. Despite these experiences, she was an honors student in high school and received national accolades for her oratory ability. She received a full scholarship to Tennessee State University, where she studied communication and worked at a local radio station. Winfrey's work in the media eventually led her to Chicago where she became host of the highly acclaimed *Oprah Winfrey Show*. In 2007, Winfrey was the highest-paid entertainer in television, earning an annual salary estimated at $260 million. She also is an actor, a producer, a book critic, and a magazine publisher, and, in 2011, left her successful television show to concentrate on her television network, OWN. For years, Winfrey had publicly battled her weight, using her struggles as inspiration for her millions of fans to lead healthier lives. In 2015, Winfrey become a 10% stockholder and board member of the diet empire Weight Watchers. Winfrey, who has long shown an interest in health issues and dieting programs, serves as an adviser to the company, using her undeniable clout to further encourage others to engage in healthier lifestyles.

Her total wealth is estimated at more than $3.1 billion. Winfrey is also a highly regarded philanthropist: Her giving has focused on making a difference in the lives of the underprivileged and poor. Winfrey has paid special attention to the needs of people in Africa, raising millions of dollars to help AIDS-affected children there and creating a leadership academy for girls in a small town near Johannesburg, South Africa.

Traits and Characteristics

Oprah Winfrey's remarkable journey from rural poverty to influential world leader can be explained by several of her strengths (Harris & Watson, 2007; Illouz, 2003; McDonald, 2007). Foremost, Winfrey is an excellent communicator. Since she was a little girl reciting Bible passages in church, she has been comfortable in front of an audience. On television, she is able to talk to millions of people and have each person feel as if she is talking directly to him or her. Winfrey is also intelligent and well read, with a strong business sense. She is sincere, determined, and inspirational. Winfrey has a charismatic style of leadership that enables her to connect with people. She is spontaneous and expressive, and has a fearless ability to self-disclose. Because she has "been in the struggle" and survived, she is seen as a role model. Winfrey has overcome many obstacles in her life and encourages others to overcome their struggles as well. Her message is a message of hope.

All of these individuals have exhibited exceptional leadership. While each of these leaders is unique, together they share many common characteristics. All are visionary, strong willed, diligent, and inspirational. As purpose-driven leaders, they are role models and symbols of hope. Reflecting on the characteristics of these extraordinary leaders will provide you with a better understanding of the traits that are important for effective leadership. Although you may not aspire to be another Bill Gates or Mother Teresa, you can learn a great deal from these leaders in understanding how your own traits affect your leadership.

SUMMARY

This chapter describes the traits required of a leader. Social science research has provided insight into leadership traits. Thousands of leadership studies have been performed to identify the traits of effective leaders; the results of these studies point to a very long list of important leadership traits. From this list, the traits that appear to be especially important for effective leadership are *intelligence, confidence, charisma, determination, sociability,* and *integrity*.

Traits and Leadership Styles

From an examination of a select group of well-known historical and contemporary leaders including George Washington, Winston Churchill, Mother Teresa, Bill Gates, and Oprah Winfrey, it is clear that exemplary leaders exhibit many similar traits. In the main, these leaders were or are visionary, strong willed, diligent, inspirational, purpose driven, and hopeful. These leadership figures provide useful models for understanding the traits that are important and desirable for achieving effective leadership.

Because leadership is a complex process, there are no simple paths or guarantees to becoming a successful leader. Each individual is unique, and each of us has our own distinct talents for leadership. Those who are naturally strong in the six traits discussed in this chapter will be well equipped for leadership. If you are not strong on all of these traits but are willing to work on them, you can still become an effective leader.

Remember that there are many traits related to effective leadership. By becoming aware of your own traits and how to nourish them, you will be well on your way to becoming a successful leader.

APPLICATION

(Continued)

face of this earth and not help somebody. My persuasion has to have a purpose."

After finishing college, Tim went on to get a master's degree in communication and, at the age of 28, became the executive director of the Douglass Community Association, a 90-year-old private, nonprofit, inner-city agency that provides opportunities for youth development, education, healthy living, and leadership. Tim managed the center's $1.2 million budget and 24 people. He spent much of his time out in the larger community raising money and resources and putting out fires. Although Tim enjoyed his role as executive director, he admits he had difficulty handling the day-to-day personnel issues at the agency.

"I spent a lot of time managing external human resources, but not paying attention to the needs of internal human resources at the center. When my staff did an assessment of me, they consistently said, 'He does a great job as a leader, but he is our boss and we need him here.'"

To enhance his skills, he took advanced leadership training at the Center for Creative Leadership in North Carolina and Harvard University in Cambridge, Massachusetts. Tim left the community center after four years to become an associate vice president at Southwest Michigan First, a regional agency focused on catalyzing job creation and economic growth in an area that has been hard hit by job losses. For Tim, it's an opportunity that makes the most of his double set of DNA.

"This is the place where my talent and my passions meet. I can help people. I can sift through problems and take big issues and break them down in ways people understand. I can persuade and motivate people and organizations to grow," he says. "And I am still helping others in ways that people can't take away."

But Tim still wants to find more ways to help others by creating an independent foundation to help people and kids in need. "My experience has been that it is hard to help hurting people because there is so much bureaucracy and BS tied up in how we do it. I want to help people without strings. If you give people money to help them, don't give it to them if you need it back. If you're gonna do something for someone, just do it."

QUESTIONS

1. What is your reaction to Tim's story?

2. Nature and nurture play a significant role in Tim's leadership journey. From your perspective, which has the greatest impact on Tim? Discuss your answer.

3. Of the six major traits described in the chapter (i.e., intelligence, confidence, charisma, determination, sociability, and integrity), which traits are Tim's strongest, and which traits are his weakest?

4. What characteristics of Tim's leadership would you like to incorporate into your own style of leadership?

2.2 LEADERSHIP TRAITS QUESTIONNAIRE

Purpose

1. To gain an understanding of how traits are used in leadership assessment
2. To obtain an assessment of your own leadership traits

Directions

1. Make five copies of this questionnaire. It should be completed by you and five people you know (e.g., roommates, coworkers, relatives, friends).
2. Using the following scale, have each individual indicate the degree to which he or she agrees or disagrees with each of the 14 statements below regarding your leadership traits. Do not forget to complete this exercise for yourself.
3. _____ (your name) is

Statements	Strongly disagree	Disagree	Neutral	Agree	Strongly agree
1. Articulate: Communicates effectively with others	1	2	3	4	5
2. Perceptive: Is discerning and insightful	1	2	3	4	5
3. Self-confident: Believes in oneself and one's ability	1	2	3	4	5
4. Self-assured: Is secure with self, free of doubts	1	2	3	4	5
5. Persistent: Stays fixed on the goals, despite interference	1	2	3	4	5
6. Determined: Takes a firm stand, acts with certainty	1	2	3	4	5
7. Trustworthy: Is authentic, inspires confidence	1	2	3	4	5
8. Dependable: Is consistent and reliable	1	2	3	4	5
9. Friendly: Shows kindness and warmth	1	2	3	4	5
10. Outgoing: Talks freely, gets along well with others	1	2	3	4	5
11. Conscientious: Is thorough, organized, and careful	1	2	3	4	5
12. Diligent: Is industrious, hardworking	1	2	3	4	5
13. Sensitive: Shows tolerance, is tactful and sympathetic	1	2	3	4	5
14. Empathic: Understands others, identifies with others	1	2	3	4	5

(Continued)

Visit **edge.sagepub.com/northouseintro4e** for a downloadable version of this questionnaire.

APPLICATION

2.2 LEADERSHIP TRAITS QUESTIONNAIRE

(Continued)

Scoring

1. Enter the responses for Raters 1, 2, 3, 4, and 5 in the appropriate columns on the scoring sheet on this page. An example of a completed chart is provided on page 41.

2. For each of the 14 items, compute the average for the five raters and place that number in the "average rating" column.

3. Place your own scores in the "self-rating" column.

Leadership Traits Questionnaire Chart

	Rater 1	Rater 2	Rater 3	Rater 4	Rater 5	Average rating	Self-rating
1. Articulate							
2. Perceptive							
3. Self-confident							
4. Self-assured							
5. Persistent							
6. Determined							
7. Trustworthy							
8. Dependable							
9. Friendly							
10. Outgoing							
11. Conscientious							
12. Diligent							
13. Sensitive							
14. Empathic							

Summary and interpretation:

Scoring Interpretation

The scores you received on this questionnaire provide information about how you see yourself and how others see you as a leader. The chart allows you to see where your perceptions are the same as those of others and where they differ. There are no "perfect" scores for this questionnaire. The purpose of the instrument is to provide a way to assess your strengths and weaknesses and to evaluate areas where your perceptions are similar to or different from those of others. While it is confirming when others see you in the same way as you see yourself, it is also beneficial to know when they see you differently. This assessment can help you understand your assets as well as areas in which you may seek to improve.

2.2 LEADERSHIP TRAITS QUESTIONNAIRE

(Continued)

Example 2.1 Leadership Traits Questionnaire Ratings

		Rater 1	Rater 2	Rater 3	Rater 4	Rater 5	Average rating	Self-rating
1.	Articulate	4	4	3	2	4	3.4	4
2.	Perceptive	2	5	3	4	4	3.6	5
3.	Self-confident	4	4	5	5	4	4.4	4
4.	Self-assured	5	5	5	5	5	5	5
5.	Persistent	4	4	3	3	3	3.4	3
6.	Determined	4	4	4	4	4	4	4
7.	Trustworthy	5	5	5	5	5	5	5
8.	Dependable	4	5	4	5	4	4.4	4
9.	Friendly	5	5	5	5	5	5	5
10.	Outgoing	5	4	5	4	5	4.6	4
11.	Conscientious	2	3	2	3	3	2.6	4
12.	Diligent	3	3	3	3	3	3	4
13.	Sensitive	4	4	5	5	5	4.6	3
14.	Empathic	5	5	4	5	4	4.6	3

Summary and interpretation: The scorer's self-ratings are higher than the average ratings of others on articulate, perceptive, conscientious, and diligent. The scorer's self-ratings are lower than the average ratings of others on self-confident, persistent, dependable, outgoing, sensitive, and empathic. The scorer's self-ratings on self-assured, determined, trustworthy, and friendly are the same as the average ratings of others.

Improve Your Leadership Skills

If you have the interactive eBook version of this text, log in to access the interactive leadership assessment. After completing this chapter's questionnaire, you will receive individualized feedback and practical suggestions for further strengthening your leadership based on your responses in this questionnaire.

APPLICATION

APPLICATION

2.3 OBSERVATIONAL EXERCISE

Leadership Traits

Purpose

1. To gain an understanding of the role of traits in the leadership process

2. To examine the traits of selected historical and everyday leaders

Directions

1. Based on the descriptions of the historical leaders provided in the chapter, identify the three major leadership traits for each of the leaders listed below.

2. Select and briefly describe two leaders in your own life (e.g., work supervisor, teacher, coach, music director, business owner, community leader). Identify the three major leadership traits of each of these leaders.

Historical leaders   The leader's three major traits

George Washington   1. _____   2. _____   3. _____

Winston Churchill   1. _____   2. _____   3. _____

Mother Teresa   1. _____   2. _____   3. _____

Bill Gates   1. _____   2. _____   3. _____

Oprah Winfrey   1. _____   2. _____   3. _____

 Visit **edge.sagepub.com/northouseintro4e** for a downloadable version of this exercise.

2.3 OBSERVATIONAL EXERCISE

(Continued)

Everyday leaders

Leader #1 _____

Brief description _____

_____

_____

_____

Traits   1. _____ 2. _____ 3. _____

Leader #2 _____

Brief description _____

_____

_____

_____

Traits   1. _____ 2. _____ 3. _____

Questions

1.   Based on the leaders you observed, which leadership traits appear to be most important?

2.   What differences, if any, did you observe between the historical and everyday leaders' traits?

3.   Based on your observations, what one trait would you identify as the definitive leadership trait?

4.   Overall, what traits do you think should be used in selecting our society's leaders?

2.4 REFLECTION AND ACTION WORKSHEET

Leadership Traits

Reflection

1. Based on the scores you received on the Leadership Traits Questionnaire, what are your strongest leadership traits? What are your weakest traits? Discuss.

2. In this chapter, we discussed five leadership figures. As you read about these leaders, which leaders did you find most appealing? What was it about their leadership that you found remarkable? Discuss.

3. As you reflect on your own leadership traits, do you think some of them are more "you" and authentic than others? Have you always been the kind of leader you are today, or have your traits changed over time? Are you a stronger leader today than you were five years ago? Discuss.

Action

1. If you could model yourself after one or more of the historical leaders we discussed in this chapter, whom would you model yourself after? Identify two of their traits that you could and should incorporate into your own style of leadership.

2. Based on the case study of Tim T., which of his traits could you incorporate into your own leadership? Discuss.

3. Although changing leadership traits is not easy, which of your leadership traits would you like to change? Specifically, what actions do you need to take to change your traits?

4. All of us have problematic traits that inhibit our leadership but are difficult to change. Which single trait distracts from your leadership? Since you cannot easily change this trait, what actions can you take to "work around" this trait? Discuss.

Visit **edge.sagepub.com/northouseintro4e** for a downloadable version of this worksheet.

REFERENCES

Antonakis, J., Cianciolo, A. T., & Sternberg, R. J. (Eds.). (2004). *The nature of leadership.* Thousand Oaks, CA: Sage.

Asmal, K., Chidester, D., & Wilmot, J. (2003). *Nelson Mandela: In his own words.* New York, NY: Little, Brown.

Bass, B. M. (1990). *Bass and Stogdill's handbook of leadership: A survey of theory and research.* New York, NY: Free Press.

Brookhiser, R. (1996). *Founding father: Rediscovering George Washington.* New York, NY: Free Press.

Burns, J. M., & Dunn, S. (2004). *George Washington.* New York, NY: Times Books.

Clinton, W. J. (2003). Foreword. In K. Asmal, D. Chidester, & J. Wilmot (Eds.), *Nelson Mandela: In his own words* (pp. xv–xvi). New York, NY: Little, Brown.

Conger, J. A. (1999). Charismatic and transformational leadership in organizations: An insider's perspective on these developing streams of research. *Leadership Quarterly, 10*(2), 145–170.

Fishman, E. (2001). Washington's leadership: Prudence and the American presidency. In E. Fishman, W. D. Pederson, & R. J. Rozell (Eds.), *George Washington: Foundation of presidential leadership and character* (pp. 125–142). Westport, CT: Praeger.

Gonzalez-Balado, J. L. (1997). *Mother Teresa: Her life, her work, her message.* Liguori, MO: Liguori.

Hadland, A. (2003). Nelson Mandela: A life. In K. Asmal, D. Chidester, & J. Wilmot (Eds.), *Nelson Mandela: In his own words* (pp. xxix–xxxvii). New York, NY: Little, Brown.

Harris, J., & Watson, E. (Eds.). (2007). *The Oprah phenomenon.* Lexington: The University Press of Kentucky.

Hayward, S. F. (1997). *Churchill on leadership: Executive success in the face of adversity.* Rocklin, CA: Prima.

Higginbotham, R. D. (2002). *George Washington: Uniting a nation.* Lanham, MD: Rowman & Littlefield.

House, R. J. (1976). A 1976 theory of charismatic leadership. In J. G. Hunt & L. L. Larson (Eds.), *Leadership: The cutting edge* (pp. 189–207). Carbondale: Southern Illinois University Press.

House, R. J., Hanges, P. J., Javidan, M., Dorfman, P. W., & Gupta, V. (2004). Leadership, culture, and organizations: The GLOBE study of 62 societies. Thousand Oaks, CA: Sage.

Illouz, E. (2003). *Oprah Winfrey and the glamour of misery.* New York, NY: Columbia University Press.

Jager, R. D., & Ortiz, R. (1997). *In the company of giants: Candid conversations with the visionaries of the digital world.* New York, NY: McGraw-Hill.

Joseph, J. A. (2003). Promoting peace and practicing diplomacy. In K. Asmal, D. Chidester, & J. Wilmot (Eds.), *Nelson Mandela: In his own words* (pp. 499–506). New York, NY: Little, Brown.

Judge, T. A., Bono, J. E., Ilies, R., & Gerhardt, M. W. (2002). Personality and leadership: A qualitative and quantitative review. *Journal of Applied Psychology, 87*(4), 765–780.

Keegan, J. (2002). *Winston Churchill.* New York, NY: Viking.

Kirkpatrick, S. A., & Locke, E. A. (1991). Leadership: Do traits matter? *The Executive, 5*(2), 48–60.

Lyman, E. J. (2016). Mother Teresa declared a saint by Pope Francis. *USA Today.* Retrieved from http://www.usatoday.com

McDonald, K. B. (2007). *Embracing sisterhood: Class, identity, and contemporary black women.* Lanham, MD: Rowman & Littlefield.

Sandys, C., & Littman, J. (2003). *We shall not fail: The inspiring leadership of Winston Churchill.* New York, NY: Penguin.

Schwartz, B. (1987). *George Washington: The making of an American symbol.* New York, NY: Free Press.

Sebba, A. (1997). *Mother Teresa: Beyond the image.* New York, NY: Doubleday.

Shamir, B., House, R. J., & Arthur, M. B. (1993). The motivational effects of charismatic leadership: A self-concept based theory. *Organization Science, 4*(4), 577–594.

Spink, K. (1997). *Mother Teresa: A complete authorized bibliography.* New York, NY: HarperCollins.

Stogdill, R. M. (1974). *Handbook of leadership: A survey of theory and research.* New York, NY: Free Press.

Turn 2 Foundation. (2010). *Proud to Be Me.* Retrieved from http://derekjeter.mlb.com/players/jeter_derek/turn2/proud_douglass.jsp

Vardey, L. (1995). Introduction. In L. Vardey (Ed.), *Mother Teresa: A simple path* (pp. xv–xxxviii). New York, NY: Ballantine.

Wills, G. (1994). *Certain trumpets: The call of leaders.* New York, NY: Simon & Schuster.

Engaging Strengths

INTRODUCTION

Think of a time or circumstance when you were at the top of your game. Now, step back and try to explain why you were so effective in that situation. What was it about *you* or the *way you presented yourself* that made you feel good? What did you *do* that worked so well? Why did others respond to you the way they did? The answers to each of these questions are related to your strengths—the central theme of this chapter.

Every one of us has identifiable leadership strengths, areas in which we excel or thrive. But we often fail to recognize these strengths. As a result, many times our strengths are used ineffectively or not at all. The same is true for the strengths of our coworkers and followers; sometimes their strengths are known, but often they go untapped. The challenge we face as leaders is to identify our own strengths as well as the strengths of others and then use these to make our organizations and followers more efficient, productive, and satisfied.

Identifying individual strengths is a unique challenge because people often feel hesitant and inhibited about acknowledging positive aspects of

ASK THE
AUTHOR

**What Do You Mean
By Strengths?**

themselves. In the American culture, expressing positive self-attributes is often seen as boastful or self-serving. In fact, focusing on self is disdained in many cultures, while showing humility and being self-deprecating is seen as virtuous. In this chapter, you will be asked to set aside your inhibitions about identifying your own strengths in an effort to better understand the inextricable role these strengths play in leading and working with others.

Our goal in this chapter is to explore how understanding strengths can make one a better leader. First, we will explain the concept by defining *strengths* and describing the *historical background* of strengths-based leadership. We will examine *how to identify strengths*, followed by a description of different *measures* that can be used to assess your strengths. The final section of the chapter will look at the concept of strengths-based leadership in *practice*, including specific strategies that leaders can employ to use strengths to become more effective leaders.

STRENGTHS-BASED LEADERSHIP EXPLAINED

ASK THE
AUTHOR

What is Strengths-Based Leadership?

Before discussing the development and principles of strength leadership, we first need to clarify what is meant by strengths. A **strength** is *an attribute or quality of an individual that accounts for successful performance.* It is the characteristic, or series of characteristics, we demonstrate when our performance is at its best. Strength researchers (Buckingham & Clifton, 2001; Rath, 2007) suggest that strengths are the ability to consistently demonstrate exceptional work. Similarly, Linley (2008) defines strength as a preexisting capacity that is authentic and energizing and enables peak performance. Simply put, strengths are positive features of ourselves that make us effective and help us flourish. For example, Antonio was born with a talent for drawing and design. He worked as a construction laborer for years while he attended a university to study architecture. As a result, when Antonio became an architect, his experiences in building made his design skills stronger because he more fully understood the concepts of actual construction. His clients often comment that one of his strengths is his "construction-friendly" designs.

Historical Background

Studying leadership from the perspective of strengths is a new area of study, which came to the forefront in the late 1990s as a result of two overlapping research developments. First, researchers at the Gallup Organization initiated a massive study that included interviews of over 2 million people to describe what's right with people—that is, their talents and what they are good at—rather than what's wrong with people (Rath, 2007).

Second, academic research scholars began to question the exclusive focus in psychology on the disease model of human problems and started to study mentally and physically healthy people and what accounted for their well-being. From this work, a new field called *positive psychology* emerged (Peterson & Seligman, 2003). Each of these two developments helped to explain the rising popularity of strengths-based leadership.

Gallup Organization

Best known as a public opinion research organization that conducts political polling, the **Gallup Organization** also conducts research in other areas of the social sciences. For nearly 40 years, the study of people's strengths has been a major research focus at Gallup. This work was spearheaded by the late Donald O. Clifton, under whose leadership millions of people were interviewed regarding their performance and human strengths. Based on these interview data, Gallup researchers designed and published the StrengthsFinder profile, an online assessment of people's talents and potential strengths. This profile was subsequently titled the Clifton StrengthsFinder in honor of its chief designer and since 2007 has been called StrengthsFinder 2.0. Later in the chapter, we will discuss more extensively StrengthsFinder and the specific talent-based strengths it measures.

The Strengths Finder

StrengthsFinder is one of the most widely used self-assessment questionnaires in the world and has been completed by more than 10 million people to date. This assessment has been adopted by many universities and organizations to help individuals identify their strengths, become more engaged, and improve their performance. While Gallup has not published a theory about strengths, the widely accepted use of StrengthsFinder has elevated strengths as a key variable in discussions of factors that account for effective leadership development and performance.

Positive Psychology

At the same time Gallup's StrengthsFinder profile was growing in popularity, a major change was occurring in the discipline of psychology. Researchers were challenging the discipline to expand its focus on not only what is wrong with people and their weaknesses, but also what is right with people and their positive attributes. This expanded focus, which was initiated by Martin Seligman in an address to the American Psychological Association in 1998 (see Fowler, Seligman, & Kocher, 1999), soon became the field of *positive psychology*. Since its inception a decade ago, positive psychology has grown exponentially and developed into a credible and important area of psychological research.

Positive
Psychology

**Positive Psychology
in Action**

Specifically, **positive psychology** can be defined as "the 'scientific' study of what makes life most worth living" (Peterson, 2009, p. xxiii). Rather than study the frailties and flaws of individuals (the disease model), positive psychology focuses on individuals' strengths and the factors that allow them to thrive (Fredrickson, 2001; Seligman, 2002; Seligman & Csikszentmihalyi, 2000). It addresses people's positive experiences, such as their happiness and joy; people's positive traits, such as their characteristics and talents; and people's positive institutions, such as families, schools, and businesses that influence them (Cameron, Dutton, & Quinn, 2003).

Most prominently, positive psychology is devoted to the study of people's positive characteristics—their *strengths*. This makes it invaluable for understanding strengths-based leadership. Positive psychology launched the analysis of people's strengths into the mainstream of scientific research (Linley, 2008). Concepts and theories from the field of positive psychology directly relate to learning how strengths-based leadership works.

Identifying and Measuring Strengths

As indicated in the historical background, most of the research on strengths has been done by scholars connected with Gallup and scholars studying positive psychology. This body of research has produced multiple ways of identifying strengths and a wide-ranging list of individual strengths. This section explores the way strengths have been identified by three major groups: (1) Gallup Organization, (2) Values in Action Institute, and (3) Centre of Applied Positive Psychology in Great Britain. Although there is much overlap in their work, each research group provides a unique perspective on identifying and measuring individual strengths. Collectively, this research provides an extensive list of specific strengths, a clear picture of how strengths can be measured, and an expansive view of how strengths can be used to understand human behavior.

Gallup and the StrengthsFinder Profile

Gallup researchers interviewed an enormous number of executives, salespeople, teachers, doctors, nurses, and other professionals about their strengths and what made them good at what they did. The goal of the interviews was to identify the qualities of high-performing individuals. From interviews, Gallup researchers extracted 34 patterns or themes that they thought did the best job at explaining excellent performance (see Table 3.1). These 34 items are "the most common themes that emerged from the study of human talent" (Buckingham & Clifton, 2001, p. 12). For the last decade, these themes have been the benchmark for discussing strengths in the workplace.

It is important to point out that Gallup researchers identified **themes of human talent**, not strengths. Talents are similar to personality traits—they are relatively stable, fixed characteristics that are not easily changed. From talents, strengths emerge. The equation for developing a strength is talent times investment (see Figure 3.1). Strengths are derived from having certain talents and then further developing those talents by gaining additional knowledge, skills, and practice (Rath, 2007). For example, you may have the talent for being able to communicate easily with others. If you were to invest time in learning more about the intricacies of effective communication and practicing it with the help of Toastmasters International, a club that helps individuals develop public speaking skills, you could enhance your communication strength. Similarly, if you were born with talent as an initiator, you could develop it further into one of your strengths by studying how to "think outside of the box" and then practicing this thought process in your organization. To summarize, talents are not strengths, but they provide the basis for developing strengths when they are coupled with knowledge, skills, and practice.

How are strengths measured from the Gallup perspective? Gallup's StrengthsFinder is a 177-item questionnaire that identifies "the areas *where you have the greatest potential to develop strengths*" (Rath, 2007, p. 31). After taking this questionnaire, you receive a list of your five strongest talents. You can build on these talents, furthering your personal growth and development. The questionnaire, which takes about 30 minutes to complete, is available through an access code that appears in the back of strengths books published by Gallup. It is also available on the organization's website at www .strengthsfinder.com.

Becoming Influential

TABLE 3.1 34 Talent Themes

Executing	Influencing	Relationship Building	Strategic Thinking
Achiever	Activator	Adaptability	Analytical
Arranger	Command	Developer	Context
Belief	Communication	Connectedness	Futuristic
Consistency	Competition	Empathy	Ideation
Deliberative	Maximizer	Harmony	Input
Discipline	Self-Assurance	Includer	Intellection
Focus	Significance	Individualization	Learner
Responsibility	Woo	Positivity	Strategic
Restorative		Relator	

FIGURE 3.1   Strength Equation

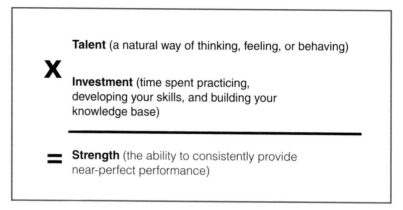

Talent (a natural way of thinking, feeling, or behaving)

X

Investment (time spent practicing, developing your skills, and building your knowledge base)

=   **Strength** (the ability to consistently provide near-perfect performance)

How can leaders use strengths in their leadership? In the book *Strengths Based Leadership*, Rath and Conchie (2008) explain how a leader's scores on the StrengthsFinder profile can be interpreted. To facilitate understanding, they developed a configuration that depicts four domains of leadership strengths (see Table 3.2). The four domains are executing, influencing, relationship building, and strategic thinking. These domains were derived from information obtained during interviews with thousands of executive teams and from a factor analysis of the Gallup talent data set. Taken together, the four domains represent the four kinds of strengths that help create successful teams.

Effective teams possess broad groupings of strengths and work best when all four domains of leadership strengths are represented on their teams (Rath & Conchie, 2008). Effective teams are generally well rounded, and they have different group members who fulfill different needs of the group. Leaders bring unique strengths to teams, but leaders do not have to demonstrate strengths in all four domains. Strong and cohesive teams bring into play everyone's strengths to make the team effective.

For example, Maria Lopez, who has owned a successful bridal shop for 10 years, took the StrengthsFinder profile and found her dominant strengths were in the *strategic thinking* domain. Maria is known for her futuristic thinking and deliberate planning. She is outstanding at forecasting trends in bridal wear and helping her team navigate the constantly changing bridal market. Maria hired Claudia, whose dominant strengths are in *relationship building*. Claudia is the most positive person on the staff and connects with everyone. It is Claudia who treats customers in the store like they are part of "the

TABLE 3.2 Four Domains of Leadership Strength

Executing
Influencing
Relationship Building
Strategic Thinking

family." To run the store on a day-to-day basis, Maria brought on Kristen who is a hard worker and uses her strengths in *executing* to get the job done. She is highly disciplined and motivated to make the bridal shop the best in the city. Lastly, Maria hired Brianna because of her strengths in the domain of *influencing*. Brianna is always out in the community promoting the shop. She is seen as a credible professional by other shop owners because she is self-assured and knowledgeable. In the store, people like Brianna because she is not afraid to be in charge and give directions to others. In summary, Maria, the store's owner, is a leader with strengths in one domain, but has the wisdom to hire personnel who have strengths in other domains. Collectively, the combined strengths of Maria and her team allow them to have a very successful bridal shop.

Values in Action Institute and Inventory of Strengths

At the same time the StrengthsFinder profile was gaining prominence, researchers at the Values in Action (VIA) Institute, led by Martin Seligman and Christopher Peterson, were engaged in a project to develop a framework for the field of positive psychology that defined and conceptualized character strengths. This classification focused on what is best in people rather than their weaknesses and problems. To develop the classification, they reviewed philosophical and spiritual literature in Confucianism, Buddhism, Hinduism, Judeo-Christianity, Ancient Greece, and Islam to determine whether there were commonalities that consistently emerged across cultures regarding virtues (Peterson & Park, 2009; Peterson & Seligman, 2004). From the review, they identified six universal core virtues: *courage, justice, humanity, temperance, transcendence,* and *wisdom.* These six virtues represent the basic structure around which Seligman and Peterson developed the Values in Action Classification of Character Strengths (see Table 3.3). The VIA Classification includes 24 strengths organized under these six basic virtues.

As illustrated in Table 3.3, the 24 character strengths identified in the VIA Classification are somewhat different from the strengths identified in

TABLE 3.3   VIA Classification of Character Strengths

Classification	Strengths
WISDOM & KNOWLEDGE *Cognitive Strengths*	1. Creativity 2. Curiosity 3. Open-mindedness 4. Love of learning 5. Perspective
COURAGE *Emotional Strengths*	6. Authenticity 7. Bravery 8. Perseverance 9. Zest
HUMANITY *Interpersonal Strengths*	10. Kindness 11. Love 12. Social intelligence
JUSTICE *Civic Strengths*	13. Fairness 14. Leadership 15. Teamwork
TEMPERANCE *Strengths Over Excess*	16. Forgiveness 17. Modesty 18. Prudence 19. Self-regulation
TRANSCENDENCE *Strengths About Meaning*	20. Appreciation of beauty and excellence 21. Gratitude 22. Hope 23. Humor 24. Religiousness

Source: Adapted from *A Primer in Positive Psychology,* by Christopher Peterson, 2006, pp. 142–146.

Gallup's StrengthsFinder profile (see Table 3.1). For example, "justice" and "love," which are strengths in the VIA Classification, seem more encompassing and virtue oriented than "connectedness" and "ideation," which are strengths identified in the Gallup list. Furthermore, the strengths outlined by the StrengthsFinder are more closely tied to the workplace and helping individuals perform better, while VIA strengths are focused more directly on a person's character and how one can become more virtuous.

From the VIA perspective, character strengths are measured with the Values in Action Inventory of Strengths (VIA-IS), a questionnaire designed to create a profile of your character strengths. It takes about 30 minutes to complete and is available free at www.viacharacter.org. After completing the questionnaire, you will receive reports and feedback identifying your top five

Values in Action

character strengths as well as a rank order of your scores on all 24 character strengths.

Centre of Applied Positive Psychology and the R2 Strengths Profiler Assessment

Based on the principles of positive psychology, researchers at the Centre of Applied Positive Psychology (CAPP) in the United Kingdom developed an approach to strengths that differs from the approaches used in Gallup's StrengthsFinder and the Values in Action perspectives. Rather than focusing exclusively on the identification of a specific number of strengths, CAPP researchers created a more dynamic model of strengths that emphasizes the changing nature of strengths (see Figure 3.2). They also examined different kinds of strengths and weaknesses. CAPP argued that strengths are more fluid than personality traits and can emerge over a lifetime through the different situations we experience.

From CAPP's perspective, strengths were conceptualized as "the things that we are good at and that give us energy when we are using them" (Linley & Dovey, 2012, p. 4). The three central elements of this definition became the criteria in CAPP's questionnaire (R2 Strengths Profiler) for assessing strengths: (1) performance—how good we are at doing something; (2) energy—how much vitality we get out of it; and (3) use—how often we are able to do it. Therefore, the R2 Strengths Profiler assesses 60 strengths in relation to three dimensions of energy, performance, and use. Based on an individual's combined scores across these dimensions, CAPP provides feedback that specifies the individual's realized strengths, unrealized strengths, learned behaviors, and weaknesses. It takes about 20 minutes to complete the R2 Strengths Profiler, which is available for a fee at www.cappeu.com.

The CAPP strengths perspective is represented in the R2 Strengths Profiler Quadrant Model (see Figure 3.2). It is divided into quadrants labeled *realized strengths*, *unrealized strengths*, *learned behaviors*, and *weaknesses*. As you can see in Figure 3.2, each quadrant lists attributes based on the dimensions of performance, energy generation, and use. Each quadrant characterizes different individual attributes and how they can be put into use.

Realized Strengths. **Realized strengths** are personal attributes that represent our strongest assets. We are energized when we use them because they help us perform well. For example, one of Rachel's strengths is *narrator*. She is a wonderful storyteller and uses these stories to convey her message and express her values. The model suggests that people should make every effort to *maximize* the use of these realized strengths, when it is appropriate to do so.

Unrealized Strengths. **Unrealized strengths** are personal attributes that are less visible. We feel good when we tap into unrealized strengths because they

FIGURE 3.2   R2 Strengths Profiler 4M Model

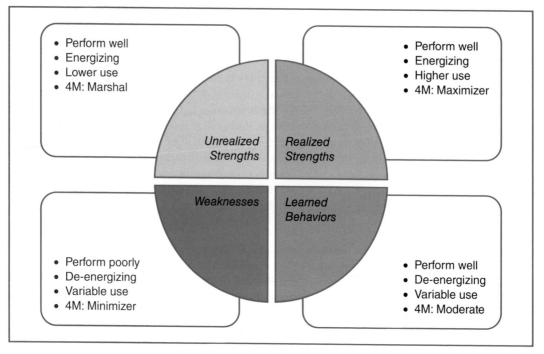

- Perform well
- Energizing
- Lower use
- 4M: Marshal

- Perform well
- Energizing
- Higher use
- 4M: Maximizer

Unrealized Strengths

Realized Strengths

Weaknesses

Learned Behaviors

- Perform poorly
- De-energizing
- Variable use
- 4M: Minimizer

- Perform well
- De-energizing
- Variable use
- 4M: Moderate

Source: Centre of Applied Positive Psychology (CAPP), Coventry, UK: CAPP Press.

support our efforts and help us achieve our goals. One of Jason's unrealized strengths is *creativity*. He is good at coming up with new ideas and concepts, but more often than not he just goes with the flow and does not express his creativity. The model challenges individuals to become more aware of these strengths and to use them more frequently—thus to *marshal* them as a resource.

Learned Behaviors. Learned behaviors represent those ingrained things we have learned throughout our life experience. Although valuable, they do not excite or inspire us. For example, one of Sunil's learned behaviors is *driver*. As the eldest of five, he was driven to graduate from college. Highly self-motivated, Sunil constantly pushes himself to succeed in everything he does, often to the detriment of his own health. Many times Sunil doesn't recognize when his goals are unrealistic, and not succeeding in these leads to feelings of self-doubt and worthlessness. The model suggests limiting, or *moderating*, the use of these behaviors because they are draining and do not energize us.

Weaknesses. Weaknesses are our limiting attributes. They often drain our energy and result in poor performance. One of Kaylee's weaknesses is *unconditionality.* She finds it hard to genuinely accept people for who they are, without being judgmental about them and expecting them to change to meet her ideals. As a leader, she is constantly frustrated by others because they don't meet her standards in a number of areas. The model suggests that effective people try to *minimize* their weaknesses so as to make them irrelevant or of less concern.

Unlike the previous approaches to strengths, the CAPP model is prescriptive and pragmatic. The R2 Strengths Profiler suggests ways people can be more effective by increasing their strengths and minimizing their weaknesses. The model recommends that individuals use their realized strengths when possible, but also intentionally look for ways to increase use of their unrealized strengths. Stated another way, we should capitalize on our strengths but also seek out ways to express our unrealized strengths. In addition, the model recommends that we try to moderate our use of learned behaviors and minimize our use of our weaknesses. We are energized by our strengths (the top two quadrants), and we lose energy when we express our weaknesses and learned behavior (the bottom two quadrants).

A good example of using the CAPP model is Tamaria, who has recently taken on the role of project manager for a team that is developing a new website for her company. Tamaria's *realized strength* is her focus on details and organization; her *weakness* is that she isn't as technically skilled as some of the members of her team. As a child, Tamaria struggled in school, and one of her coping mechanisms was to ask a lot of questions so that she thoroughly understood assignments. That has become a *learned behavior* she still employs. Finally, one of Tamaria's *unrealized strengths* is her ability to problem-solve and mediate in conflict.

In order for her team to succeed, Tamaria will need to *maximize* the use of her realized strengths of organization and attention to detail in outlining the tasks and deadlines for the project. To deal with her weakness in technical skills, she will need to *minimize* her involvement in the technical development of the website, relying on other team members' technical skills. By employing her learned behavior of asking her team members a lot of questions about what they are doing and why, Tamaria will slow down the team's progress and frustrate team members who may feel she's micromanaging them. In this case, she will need to *moderate* her inquisitiveness, identifying the questions that she really needs answered or finding a way to research the questions on her own. Finally, working within a team can result in disparate opinions and ideas, and Tamaria will need to *marshal* her unrealized strength in the mediation and problem solving so the team works smoothly together and meets deadlines while creating a dynamic website.

To summarize, researchers have developed three unique assessment tools to identify strengths: (1) StrengthsFinder, (2) Values in Action Inventory of

Strengths, and (3) R2 Strengths Profiler (see Table 3.4). Each of these assessments provides a unique approach to strengths, and together they help to define and clarify the meaning of strengths. All of the questionnaires are accessible online, and they are worthwhile self-assessment tools for identifying and exploring your personal strengths.

STRENGTHS-BASED LEADERSHIP IN PRACTICE

Using Strengths in a Pharmacy

How are strengths used in leadership? Although there are no established leadership theories on how to practice leadership from a strengths perspective, many useful applications can be made from strengths research in everyday leadership situations. In this section, we discuss several specific ways to incorporate strengths in your personal and work settings. The steps include (1) discovering your strengths, (2) developing your strengths, (3) recognizing and engaging the strengths of others, and (4) fostering a positive strengths-based environment around you. Following these steps will not be a panacea for becoming a perfect strengths-based leader, but they will most certainly help you, as a leader, to maximize the use of your strengths as well as those of others.

Discovering Your Strengths

As we discussed earlier in this chapter, strengths emerge from our basic personality traits. We all have unique personality traits, and therefore we all have unique strengths. No one is without strengths. As suggested by psychologist Howard Gardner (1997), extraordinary individuals are "distinguished less by their impressive 'raw power' than by their ability to identify their strengths

TABLE 3.4   Approaches to Identifying Strengths

Approach	Purpose	Number of Strengths
Strengths of Competence **Gallup**	To identify traits/strengths of peak performers	24
Strengths of Character **Values in Action (VIA-IS)**	To identify virtuous/moral character strengths	36
Strengths Fully Realized **CAPP R2 Strengths Profiler**	To identify strengths and weaknesses to improve performance	60+

and then exploit them" (p. 15). MacKie (2016) suggests that our leadership capability is enhanced when we are able to discover our fully utilized strengths, underutilized strengths, and weaknesses. The challenge we face is identifying our strengths and then employing them effectively in our leadership and personal lives.

Discovering your strengths requires you to concentrate on your positive attributes and those times when you feel inspirited. To do so, you need to pay attention to your successes rather than focusing on your weaknesses or failures. For example, when are you at the top of your game? What is it about you or your interactions with others that contributes to that feeling? What accounts for your best performance? When things are going really well for you, what attributes are behind this success? Answering these questions will help you discover your strengths. They are the first and most important step in practicing strengths-based leadership.

There are several ways you can discover your strengths. First, you can complete one or more of the strengths questionnaires (e.g., StrengthsFinder 2.0, VIA-IS, and R2 Strengths Profiler) that are available online. Each questionnaire gives a unique snapshot of your greatest strengths. Second, you can fill out the Leadership Strengths Questionnaire that appears in this chapter. This questionnaire will provide you with specific feedback regarding your relative strengths in the areas of implementation, innovation, encouragement, analysis, and mediation. Third, you can complete the Reflected Best Self Exercise (RBSE) (Quinn, Dutton, & Spreitzer, 2003), which can be found at http://positiveorgs.bus.umich .edu/cpo-tools/reflected-best-self-exercise-2nd-edition/. The RBSE can assist you in identifying unrecognized and unexplored area of strengths (Roberts et al., 2005). Fourth, you can complete the "discovering your strengths" exercise that appears at the end of this chapter in Reflection and Action Worksheet 3.4. This exercise allows people you know to tell you what they see as your strengths when you are performing at your best. It is a powerful exercise you can use to become more aware of your strengths, and it may help you learn about some you have not recognized. Fifth, you can engage in a self-assessment of what you believe to be your strongest attributes. Intuitively, we all have a sense of what we do well, but taking the time to intentionally contemplate and consider our own strengths leads us to become more fully aware of our strengths.

Discovering Strengths

This myriad of methods for discovering strengths will allow you to painlessly develop a definitive list of your major strengths. This process is not only enlightening but is also a vital first step in developing strengths-based leadership.

Developing Your Strengths

Once you have discovered your strengths, what do you do with that knowledge? How do you make use of this information to be a stronger leader?

Developing Strengths

Developing one's strengths is a multifaceted process that involves several steps. First, you must acknowledge your strengths and be prepared to reveal them to others. As we discussed at the beginning of this chapter, it is often difficult to share our strengths with others because we may feel inhibited about openly and verbally acknowledging positive aspects of ourselves. But expressing our strengths is essential to making others aware of our leadership.

Telling others about our strengths is important because it lets them know how we can be most useful when working or collaborating together, clarifying the unique contributions we can make to others and their work. In essence, disclosing strengths declares "this is what I bring to the table, this is what I am best at, this is what I can do for you," and that allows others to know what they can expect from us. For example, when Tanya lets others know that her strongest quality is that she is an *achiever*, others learn that Tanya is not likely to allow mediocrity in their work. She is going to be demanding and push others toward excellence. Similarly, when Jason tells his staff that his strength is *listening*, his staff learns that Jason will have an open door and be willing to hear their problems or concerns. Putting our strengths out in the open makes us more transparent to others, and this helps others predict how we are going to act and how they might want to act toward us.

People use a variety of ways to reveal their strengths. Some people post their top five strengths on Facebook or LinkedIn, add them to their email signature, or list them on their résumé as a way of making their strengths more visible to others. Several unique examples of how some people share their strengths are illustrated in Figure 3.3. Disclosing our strengths to others does not need to be a daunting or embarrassing task, but can be done in a fairly simple, straightforward manner.

Expressing strengths has a cultural element to it as well. What one culture may see as a strength that should be revealed, another may see as something to be kept hidden. For example, many Western cultures encourage women to recognize and celebrate their intelligence. In some cultures, such as those in religiously conservative, patriarchal societies of the Middle East, women expressing intelligence is not seen as a strength. Many girls are prohibited from attending school.

In addition to revealing your strengths, practice working consistently with others based on your strengths. For example, if your strength is being an *innovator*, find ways to be creative in your leadership. For example, do not hesitate to engage in activities like brainstorming or creating a vision for your group or organization. Similarly, if your strength is that you are *deliberative*, place yourself in a position where your strength in providing structure and order to a project can be put to use. Add your well-thought-out perspective by being vigilant and practical when people around you are coming up with

FIGURE 3.3 **Examples of Ways to Express Strengths**

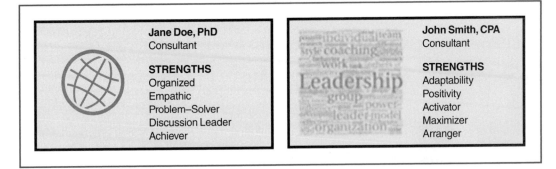

ideas that have never been tested. The point is that you should lead from your strengths; your strengths represent the best you have to offer in influencing others. As Anderson (2004) from the Gallup Organization has suggested, "The best of the best invent ways of developing and applying strengths in areas where they want to improve, achieve, and become more effective" (p. 7).

A good example of practicing strengths is Warren Buffett, one of the wealthiest people in the world. Buffett is known for his *patience, practicality,* and *trustfulness,* and he used these strengths to make Berkshire Hathaway, a multinational conglomerate, successful (Buckingham & Clifton, 2001). His patience led him to adopt the now famous "20-year perspective" on investing only in companies that he believed would be successful for the long term. His practicality explains how he selected specific companies whose services and products he understood (e.g., American Express). Finally, Buffett's trustfulness allowed him to select senior managers who were reputable and dependable to run his company. Clearly, Buffett recognized his strengths and carved out a role for himself that allowed him to practice these strengths every day (Buckingham & Clifton, 2001).

Addressing Your Weaknesses

Leaders must not only recognize and capitalize on their strengths, but also be able to identify their weaknesses and address them (MacKie, 2016). Harvard leadership professor John P. Kotter states, "Great leadership doesn't mean running away from reality . . . sharing difficulties can inspire people to take action that will make the situation better" (Blagg & Young, 2001).

While some of the models discussed here advocate minimizing your weaknesses, understanding them can allow you to work to improve them and to recognize situations where your weaknesses can be a liability to your leadership. For example, Lisa owns a small business developing e-commerce

LEADERSHIP SNAPSHOT

Steve Jobs, Founder, Apple Inc.

© Bloomberg/Contributor/
Bloomberg/Getty Images

While Steve Jobs was undoubtedly brilliant, he didn't possess the technical abilities to be a computer genius. In fact, Jobs didn't know how to write computer code or program a computer. But he succeeded—twice—in building one of the most successful and profitable computer companies in the world.

Jobs had many notable strengths, including his creativity, team building, strategic vision, and influencing. He had intuitive vision, imagining products and applications of which no one else dared to dream. When he created Apple in 1976 with partner Steve Wozniak, he sought to create an attractive, simple, inexpensive computer marketed as the first home computer. Jobs micromanaged every detail of the computer's creation from its unique operating software to the color of its casing.

Jobs was an influencer, using his indomitable will and charisma to convince himself and others of almost anything. He believed rules were meant to be broken, and in 1984, Apple did just that, introducing a truly revolutionary product, the Macintosh. It used graphics, icons, a mouse, and the point-and-click technology that is still standard. It was innovative and influential.

But Jobs wasn't perfect. He could be confrontational, and this quality eventually resulted in him being booted out of his own company by Apple's board of directors.

Jobs moved on, using his visionary skills and passion for perfection to create NeXT Computer, recognized as a great product that never caught on with consumers.

Undaunted, Jobs branched out into movie animation by acquiring Pixar Animation Studios, bringing his vision, passion, and influencing skills to a new industry. Under his leadership, Pixar revolutionized movie animation and made Jobs a multibillionaire.

His old company, Apple, hadn't done so well. A decade after Jobs exited, Apple was nearly bankrupt. It decided to buy NeXT Computer and the services of Jobs as a consultant. But he would soon take over as CEO. His first move was to employ another of his strengths—focus. He took the two-dozen products Apple was producing—printers, computers, and software—and winnowed them down to only laptop and desktop computers for the professional and home consumer.

Jobs didn't stop there. Over the next 14 years, he dreamt up the iPod, the iPad, and the iPhone. By combining creativity, technology, and feats of engineering, Apple produced new devices that consumers hadn't even thought of or knew they needed. Jobs insisted these devices be intuitive and simple to use and oversaw every detail of design from creating specialized glass for the screens to the width of their metal casings.

In the end, Jobs's vision revolutionized seven industries: personal computers, animated movies, music, telephones, tablet computing, digital publishing, and retail stores. When he returned to Apple in 1997, he personally created the company's new ad campaign—"Think Different"—which was as much a statement of his own strengths as a leader as it was a mission statement for Apple.

websites for companies that sell products online. Her strengths are her structural and process-oriented thinking and technical expertise. She is adept at anticipating and managing the many small details for creating a website that is secure and provides a good user experience. However, Lisa can't describe what she does in normal "layperson" terms for clients. In her proposals and presentations, she tends to lose clients with her use of technical language and minutiae of detail. In Lisa's case, it isn't enough that she minimize her weakness—she can't *not* talk to clients because that's how she generates new business. She must find a way to communicate better with her clients.

After losing out on several possible projects, Lisa listened to the feedback of the clients when they said that what she was proposing was "too complicated." Lisa brought in a marketing professional, Julie, to help her develop and pitch proposals to clients. Julie understands enough of the technical parts of Lisa's work to be able to put it in easier-to-understand terms for potential clients. Julie is very strong in communication and social interactions, and Lisa is finding that by observing and working with Julie, she is learning to communicate more effectively with clients.

While making the most of our strengths is important for leaders, recognizing our weaknesses is also important in effective leadership. In the case of Lisa, she had to address her communication problems; there was no way around it. Working to improve on your weaknesses or using them as opportunities for others to contribute their strengths will improve your leadership.

Recognizing and Engaging the Strengths of Others

In addition to employing their own strengths, leaders need to recognize and engage the strengths of their followers. They need to determine what followers are good at doing and help them to do it. Educators who study group dynamics and the roles individuals play in effective groups often say "people do what they do best." What they mean by this is that individuals often become engaged and contribute positively to groups when they are allowed to do what they are good at and feel comfortable doing. People feel comfortable in groups when they can contribute to the group from their strengths.

How do leaders know what people are good at? Sometimes people are very up front and freely express their strengths. Mia, for example, often says when she joins a new work project, "I'm a good note taker, so you can plan on me to be the record keeper for our meetings." Similarly, Josh often says on the first day of a roofing project, "I am pretty fast with the nail gun, so you might want me on the roof nailing shingles." Clearly, sometimes followers openly inform leaders of their strengths. When this occurs, it is important for leaders to acknowledge these individuals' strengths if possible and assign them to roles in the work setting that capitalize on these strengths.

While recognizing strengths sounds simple, it is not uncommon for leaders to overlook followers' strengths. Oftentimes, the strengths of followers are not evident to leaders or even to the followers themselves. This becomes a challenging situation, because leaders need to ascertain followers' strengths from what they observe rather than what followers explicitly express to them. Cordelia was a struggling graduate student who was just plodding along, uncertain about her direction and goals. When she received an A++ on a challenging reaction paper, she became excited and was surprised to learn that her strength was *creativity*, particularly in writing. Cordelia and her instructor both became aware of her strengths in writing by the work she did on her assignment. Juan is good with solving computer glitches in the office, suggesting his strengths lie in the area of *technology*. When he was assisting a staff member who was having a problem downloading a file from the web, he found that he liked the challenge of solving these problems. Or consider Ashley, who is a good worker, always present, and never oppositional. She is a wonderful team member whose strengths are *consistency*, *kindness*, and being *fun-loving*. She fosters the *esprit de corps* in the athletic center where she works. In each of these examples, an effective leader tries to identify the followers' strengths and then incorporate them into building a more productive team.

However, it is important to note that others' strengths may not always be directly recognizable. Followers may have strengths that are not observable because their situations don't allow for many facets of their overall abilities to emerge. Therefore, it is important to find opportunities outside followers' normal realm of duties or activities that will allow their strengths to emerge. For example, Jeff works on an assembly line at a golf cart manufacturer attaching seats to the chassis of golf carts. The position is very repetitive and structured, and Jeff, like the other assembly line employees, spends most of his workday at his station with limited interaction with other workers. However, with the blessing of his supervisor, Jeff recently organized a softball team made up of other plant workers to play in a local league. Jeff has recruited team members, arranged all the practices, communicated practice and game schedules to the team, organized the purchase of team uniforms, and promoted the team's games in the plant through flyers and the company newsletter. As a result, many individuals who work with Jeff have observed his strengths in *organization*, *inclusion*, and *communication*, which would not be observable through his day-to-day work on the assembly line.

As we discussed earlier in this chapter, high-performing teams and work groups possess strengths in four domains: executing, influencing, relationship building, and strategic thinking (see Table 3.2). When leaders become aware of their followers' strengths as well as their own, they can use this information to design work groups that have individuals with strengths representing each of the domains. Knowing followers' unique strengths allows leaders to make work assignments that maximize each individual's contribution to the collective goals of the group (Rath & Conchie, 2008). If a leader is strong on executing and knows how to make new ideas come to fruition, but is not as strong in building relationships, the leader should identify followers with strengths in that area. Or if a leader has strengths in connecting with people and taking command, the leader can identify others who are strong in executing and strategic thinking. Knowledge of followers' strengths is a valuable tool to help leaders to build effective groups.

Leadership and Followership

Fostering a Positive Strengths-Based Environment

A final way to practice strengths-based leadership is to create and promote a positive work environment in which people's strengths play an integral role. Multiple studies by researchers in positive organizational scholarship indicate that companies and organizations that create positive work environments have a positive physiological impact on employees and, in turn, this has an advantageous impact on their performance (Cameron, 2012; Dutton & Ragins, 2007). Similarly, research suggests that when employees have the opportunity to engage their strengths, they are more productive and more loyal, and their companies experience less turnover (Clifton & Harter, 2003). In short, people feel better and work better when the climate in which they work is positive.

In his book *Positive Leadership*, Cameron (2012) argues that leaders who want to create a positive work environment should attend to four areas: *climate*, *relationships*, *communication*, and *meaning*. To create a *positive climate*, leaders should foster among their employees virtues such as compassion, forgiveness, and gratitude. When these qualities are present, people feel encouraged and are more productive. Leaders can also promote celebrating people's strengths. Doing so helps people feel valued as individuals and respected for their contribution to the organization. To build *positive relationships*, leaders need to highlight individuals' positive images and strengths rather than their negative images and weaknesses. Acknowledging and building on people's strengths encourages others to do the same, and this results in the development of an environment where positive relationships flourish. To develop *positive communication*, leaders must be supportive, make more positive than negative statements, and be less negatively evaluative of others. Positive communication helps people feel connected and encourages them to capitalize on their strengths. Finally, leaders can foster *positive meaning* in their organizations by emphasizing the connection between employees' values and the long-term impact of their work. Employees who find meaning in their work and see it as valuable are more engaged and productive.

A Positive Climate

Fostering a positive strengths-based organizational environment is embraced by a multitude of organizations. For example, more than 500 colleges and universities have integrated dimensions of a strengths-based perspective into their student learning, faculty, and culture, including Baylor University, Texas A&M University, Azusa Pacific University, University of Arkansas, Texas Tech University, San Jose State University, and University of Minnesota. Among the many companies that have adopted strengths as a systematic program are Fortune 500 companies Pfizer, Hilton, Facebook, Chick-fil-A, Coca-Cola, Cisco, Microsoft, and Best Buy.

SUMMARY

Strengths-based leadership has been given much attention in recent years because researchers believe it can have a significant impact on the way leaders choose to lead and on the performance of followers. In this chapter, we explored people's strengths and how leaders can make use of these strengths to become more effective leaders. Although we all have strengths, they often go unrecognized and unused. Understanding strengths can make one a better leader.

A strength is defined as an attribute or quality of an individual that accounts for successful performance. In simple terms, a strength is what we do when we are performing at our best. Strengths often begin with our inborn talents and can be further developed through knowledge, skills, and practice. The equation for developing a strength is *talent times investment* (Rath, 2007).

Strengths-based leadership has come to the forefront in recent years as a result of two research developments. First, spearheaded by Donald O. Clifton, the Gallup Organization interviewed millions of people about their strengths and what made them good at what they did. From interviews, Gallup extracted 34 themes that best explained excellent performance. Second, academic scholars created a new field called positive psychology that focused less on the disease model and more on the study of healthy people and what accounted for their well-being. Prominent in this new field is the study of people's positive characteristics—their strengths. Taken together, research at Gallup and in positive psychology explains the rising popularity of strengths-based leadership.

People's strengths have been measured in different ways. The benchmark is Gallup's *StrengthsFinder*, which is a 177-item questionnaire that identifies an individual's five strongest talents across four domains (i.e., executing, influencing, relationship building, and strategic thinking). Strengths can also be measured using the *Values in Action Inventory of Strengths*, which provides an individual's top five character strengths as well as a rank order of his or her scores on 24 virtue-derived character strengths. A third measure, the *R2 Strengths Profiler*, assesses 60 strengths in relationship to an individual's energy, performance, and use, and provides feedback on an individual's realized strengths, unrealized strengths, learned behaviors, and weaknesses.

Although there are no established theories about the practice of strengths-based leadership, there are several straightforward ways for individuals to incorporate strengths into their leadership. First, leaders need to discover their own strengths. They can do this through completing questionnaires and other self-assessment activities. The goal is to develop a definitive list of one's strengths. Second, leaders need to be prepared to acknowledge their strengths and reveal them to others. Although we may feel inhibited about disclosing our strengths to others, it is essential for making others aware of our capabilities. We need to make ourselves transparent to others and lead from our strengths. Third, leaders must make a concerted effort to recognize and engage the strengths of others. Because "people do what they do best," leaders have an obligation to help uncover others' strengths and then integrate these strengths into building more productive teams. Finally, leaders can practice strengths-based leadership by fostering work environments in which people's strengths play an integral role. Leaders can do this by creating for their followers a positive climate, positive relationships, positive communication, and positive meaning (Cameron, 2012). Research shows that people feel better and work better when the climate in which they work is positive.

To summarize, strengths-based leadership is a new area of research that offers a unique approach to becoming a more effective leader. Not a panacea, strengths concepts provide an innovative and valuable perspective to add to our leadership toolbox.

GLOSSARY TERMS

Gallup Organization 49

learned behaviors 56

positive psychology 50

realized strengths 55

strengths 48

themes of human talent 51

unrealized strengths 55

weaknesses 56

⑤SAGE edge™

Sharpen your skills with SAGE edge at **edge.sagepub.com/northouseintro4e**

SAGE edge for students provides a personalized approach to help you accomplish your coursework goals in an easy-to-use learning environment.

3.1 Case Study

Ready to Be CEO?

Christine Jorgens was shocked when the board of Begin the Future Foundation, the nonprofit organization she worked for, asked her to apply for the position of CEO of the organization. For 40 years, Begin the Future Foundation had provided programs in a nine-county region to help children living in poverty in urban and rural areas succeed in school and life, and the CEO's job was a big one.

Christine had never aspired to be a CEO. She had grown up on a small farm in a rural area, one of seven children in a family that struggled financially. In high school, she worked at a local restaurant, first as a dishwasher and then as a waitress, continuing to work there while she attended college studying social work.

In her senior year of college, she landed an internship at Begin the Future Foundation overseeing an after-school program for middle school students. Christine ended up working for Begin the Future Foundation for 12 more years, with many of her colleagues joking that she was "the intern who never left." Friendly and approachable, she eagerly took on whatever work the organization had for her to do. She worked as a receptionist, became a grant writer, helped out in public relations and marketing, and then was given a position developing and initiating new programs and working with donors to fund those programs.

She thrived at program development, finding ways to implement community resources that

were often overlooked. Her program, Study Buddies, paired up volunteer tutors from a local college with children to meet three times a week for a half-hour of tutoring followed by a half-hour of recreation and games. Christine also initiated Girl Power, a program allowing middle school girls to spend an afternoon each week shadowing a local female professional or businesswoman who worked in a career that they were interested in pursuing.

Christine's enthusiasm was contagious, especially with donors. Her programs were all successfully funded, and potential donors often approached Christine with ideas they had for new initiatives that they were willing to fund.

But despite all her successes, Christine wasn't sure she was CEO material. She saw herself as a local girl who had lucked into some great opportunities. The board had been clear about what credentials a new CEO must have: strategic thinking, experience running a nonprofit organization, ability to work with people on all levels of society from the poorest to the richest, ability to manage people, and a commitment to the organization's mission of helping kids escape poverty. Christine didn't have direct experience overseeing a nonprofit and felt she needed more experience in the day-to-day management of the organization.

At the suggestion of the board members, she took a strengths assessment and learned her strengths were in strategic planning, relationship building, creativity, compassion, and influencing. In addition, the board members pointed out that she had a deep knowledge and commitment to the organization and the children they served. Despite Christine's hesitancy, the board was convinced Christine was the right candidate.

QUESTIONS

1. Strengths are considered inborn traits that can be enhanced with experience. What experiences in Christine's background helped her develop her strengths?

2. Of the strengths identified by the assessment, which were directly observable in Christine's work? Were there any that were not?

3. Christine admitted having some weaknesses, especially in day-to-day management of the organization. Which of her strengths could she put into use to help her deal with that, and how?

4. What strengths should Christine seek from others that would complement her own and fill some gaps?

3.2 LEADERSHIP STRENGTHS QUESTIONNAIRE

Purpose

1. To develop an understanding of your leadership strengths
2. To rank your strengths in selected areas of performance

Directions

1. Please answer the statements below in terms of whether the statement describes *what you are like.*
2. For each of the statements, circle the number that indicates the degree to which *you feel the statement is like you.*

Statements	Very Much Unlike Me	Unlike Me	Neutral	Like Me	Very Much Like Me
1. I am an energetic participant when working with others.	1	2	3	4	5
2. Brainstorming is one of my strengths.	1	2	3	4	5
3. I am good at encouraging coworkers when they feel frustrated about their work.	1	2	3	4	5
4. I want to know "why" we are doing what we are doing.	1	2	3	4	5
5. I look for common ground in opposing opinions of others.	1	2	3	4	5
6. I enjoy implementing the details of projects.	1	2	3	4	5
7. I like to explore creative approaches to problems.	1	2	3	4	5
8. I go out of my way to help others feel good about their accomplishments.	1	2	3	4	5
9. Examining complex problems or issues is one of my strengths.	1	2	3	4	5
10. I am a mediator in conflict situations.	1	2	3	4	5
11. I stick with the task until the work is completed.	1	2	3	4	5
12. I can initiate change, if it is needed, when working with others.	1	2	3	4	5
13. I show concern for the personal well-being of others.	1	2	3	4	5
14. I like to consider various options for doing things.	1	2	3	4	5

(Continued)

Visit **edge.sagepub.com/northouseintro4e** for a downloadable version of this questionnaire.

3.2 LEADERSHIP STRENGTHS QUESTIONNAIRE

(Continued)

APPLICATION

Statements	Very Much Unlike Me	Unlike Me	Neutral	Like Me	Very Much Like Me
15. I am effective communicating with people who are inflexible.	1	2	3	4	5
16. I try to follow through with ideas so that the work gets done.	1	2	3	4	5
17. I enjoy creating a vision for a work-related project.	1	2	3	4	5
18. I am the "glue" that helps hold the group together.	1	2	3	4	5
19. I like exploring the details of a problem before trying to solve it.	1	2	3	4	5
20. I can draw the best out of people with diverse opinions.	1	2	3	4	5
21. I like making to-do lists so that the work gets completed.	1	2	3	4	5
22. I can "think outside of the box."	1	2	3	4	5
23. Encouraging others comes easily for me.	1	2	3	4	5
24. I like thinking things through before engaging in work projects.	1	2	3	4	5
25. I am good at finding common ground when a conflict is present.	1	2	3	4	5
26. I enjoy scheduling and coordinating activities so the work is completed.	1	2	3	4	5
27. I am good at developing new ideas for others to consider.	1	2	3	4	5
28. I am good at encouraging others to participate on projects.	1	2	3	4	5
29. I like to explore problems from many different perspectives.	1	2	3	4	5
30. I am effective at helping coworkers reach consensus.	1	2	3	4	5

3.2 LEADERSHIP STRENGTHS QUESTIONNAIRE

(Continued)

Scoring

1. Sum the responses on items 1, 6, 11, 16, 21, and 26 (implementer score).

2. Sum the responses on items 2, 7, 12, 17, 22, and 27 (innovator score).

3. Sum the responses on items 3, 8, 13, 18, 23, and 28 (encourager score).

4. Sum the responses on items 4, 9, 14, 19, 24, and 29 (analytic score).

5. Sum the responses on items 5, 10, 15, 20, 25, and 30 (mediator score).

Total Scores:

_____ _____ _____ _____ _____

Implementer   Innovator   Encourager   Analytic   Mediator

Scoring Interpretation

The Leadership Strengths Questionnaire is designed to measure your strengths in the areas of implementation, innovation, encouragement, analysis, and mediation. By assessing the rank order of your scores, you can determine the areas in which you have the greatest strengths and the areas in which you are weaker. A high score in a certain area indicates where you are strong; a low score shows where you are weak. As discussed in this chapter, every person has multiple strengths. In addition to the strengths revealed by the Leadership Strengths Questionnaire, you may wish to complete other strengths assessments to obtain a more complete picture of all of your strengths.

If your score is 26–30, you are in the very high range.

If your score is 21–25, you are in the high range.

If your score is 16–20, you are in the moderate range.

If your score is 11–15, you are in the low range.

If your score is 6–10, you are in the very low range.

Improve Your Leadership Skills

If you have the interactive eBook version of this text, log in to access the interactive leadership assessment. After completing this chapter's questionnaire, you will receive individualized feedback and practical suggestions for further strengthening your leadership based on your responses in this questionnaire.

APPLICATION

3.3 OBSERVATIONAL EXERCISE

Strengths

Purpose

1. To learn to recognize people's strengths
2. To gain an understanding of the role of strengths in the leadership process

Directions

1. In this exercise, your task is to observe a leader *in action*. The leader can be a teacher, a supervisor, a coach, a manager, or anyone who has a position that involves leadership.
2. Based on your observations of the leader in action, identify areas in which the leader has strengths and areas in which the followers have strengths.

Questions

1. Based on the virtue-based strengths listed in Table 3.3, identify two strengths you observed the leader exhibit. How did these strengths affect his or her followers?

2. Discuss what strengths group members appeared to exhibit and how these strengths may complement or distract from the leader's leadership.

3. Do you think the followers in this situation would feel comfortable expressing their own strengths to others? Discuss.

4. If you were coaching the leader in this situation, what specific things could she or he do to create a positive environment where the expression of people's strengths was welcomed?

 Visit **edge.sagepub.com/northouseintro4e** for a downloadable version of this exercise.

3.4 REFLECTION AND ACTION WORKSHEET

Strengths

Reflection

1. For this exercise, you are being asked to interview several people you know about your strengths. Instructions:

    -   First, identify three people (e.g., friends, coworkers, colleagues, family members) from whom you feel comfortable asking for feedback about yourself.
    -   Second, ask each of these individuals to do the following:

        a. Think of a time or situation when they saw you at your best

        b. Tell a brief story about what you were doing

        c. Describe why they thought you were performing well in this situation

        d. Based on this story, describe what unique benefits you offered others in this situation

    -   Third, from the answers the individuals gave, identify two or three recurring themes. These themes represent your strengths.

2. What is your reaction to what others (in Step 1) have identified as your strengths? Are the strengths others identified about you consistent with your own perceptions of your strengths? In what way are they consistent with your scores on the Leadership Strengths Questionnaire?

3. This chapter suggests that it is important for leaders to reveal their strengths to others. As a leader, how do you feel about disclosing your strengths to others? How do you react when others express their strengths to you?

Action

1. Based on the questionnaire in this chapter and your own insights, create a business card for yourself that lists your five signature strengths.

2. Of the four domains of leadership strengths (see Table 3.2), which are your strongest? Describe how you could solicit support from followers to complement these areas of strength.

3. Imagine you are the leader of a classroom group required to do a semester-long service learning project. Identify and discuss specific things you could do to create a positive climate, positive relationships, positive communication, and positive meaning.

 Visit **edge.sagepub.com/northouseintro4e** for a downloadable version of this worksheet.

REFERENCES

Anderson, E. C. (2004). *StrengthsQuest: Curriculum outline and learning activities.* Princeton, NJ: Gallup Organization.

Biswas-Diener, R. (2010). *Practicing positive psychology coaching: Assessment, activities, and strategies for success.* Hoboken, NJ: John Wiley & Sons.

Blagg, D., & Young, S. (2001, February 1). What makes a good leader. *Harvard Business School Alumni Stories.* Retrieved from https://www.alumni.hbs.edu/stories/Pages/story-bulletin.aspx?num=3059

Buckingham, M., & Clifton, D. (2001). *Now, discover your strengths.* New York, NY: Free Press.

Cameron, K. S. (2012). *Positive leadership: Strategies for extraordinary performance* (2nd ed.). San Francisco, CA: Berrett-Koehler.

Cameron, K. S., Dutton, J. E., & Quinn, R. E. (2003). Foundations of positive organizational scholarship. In K. S. Cameron, J. E. Dutton, & R. E. Quinn (Eds.), *Positive organizational scholarship* (pp. 3–14). San Francisco, CA: Berrett-Koehler.

Clifton, D. O., & Harter, J. K. (2003). Investing in strengths. In K. S. Cameron, J. E. Dutton, & R. E. Quinn (Eds.), *Positive organizational scholarship* (pp. 111–121). San Francisco, CA: Berrett-Koehler.

Dutton, J. E., & Ragins, B. R. (2007). *Exploring positive relationships at work.* Mahwah, NJ: Erlbaum.

Fowler, R. D., Seligman, M. E. P., & Kocher, G. P. (1999). The APA 1998 annual report. *American Psychologist, 54*(8), 537–568.

Fredrickson, B. L. (2001). The role of positive emotions in positive psychology: The broaden-and-build theory of positive emotions. *American Psychologist, 56*, 218–226.

Gardner, H. (1997). *Extraordinary minds: Portraits of exceptional individuals and an examination of our extraordinariness.* New York, NY: Basic Books.

Kaplan, R. E., & Kaiser, R. B. (2010). Toward a positive psychology for leaders. In P. A. Linley, S. A. Harrington, & N. Garcea (Eds.), *Oxford handbook of positive psychology and work* (pp. 107–117). Oxford, UK: Oxford University Press.

Lewis, S. (2011). *Positive psychology at work: How positive leadership and appreciative inquiry create inspiring organizations.* Oxford, UK: Wiley-Blackwell.

Linley, A. (2008). *Average to A+: Realising strengths in yourself and others.* Coventry, UK: CAPP Press.

Linley, A., & Dovey, H. (2012). *Technical manual and statistical properties for Realise2.* Coventry, UK: CAPP Press.

Luthans, F., & Avolio, B. J. (2002). Authentic leadership development. In K. S. Cameron, J. E. Dutton, & R. E. Quinn (Eds.), *Positive organizational scholarship* (pp. 241–258). San Francisco, CA: Berrett-Koehler.

MacKie, D. (2016). *Strength-based leadership coaching in organizations: An evidence-based guide to positive leadership development.* London, UK: Kogan Page.

Peterson, C. (2006). *A primer in positive psychology.* New York, NY: Oxford University Press.

Peterson, C. (2009). Foreword. In S. J. Lopez & C. R. Snyder (Eds.), *Oxford handbook of positive psychology* (p. xxiii). New York, NY: Oxford University Press.

Peterson, C., & Park, N. (2009). Classifying and measuring strengths of character. In S. J. Lopez & C. R. Snyder (Eds.), *Oxford handbook of positive psychology* (pp. 25–34). New York, NY: Oxford University Press.

Peterson, C., & Seligman, M. E. P. (2003). Positive organizational studies: Lessons from positive psychology. In K. S. Cameron, J. E. Dutton, & R. E. Quinn (Eds.), *Positive organizational scholarship* (pp. 14–28). San Francisco, CA: Berrett-Koehler.

Peterson, C., & Seligman, M. E. P. (2004). *Character strengths and virtues: A handbook and classification.* New York, NY: Oxford University Press; Washington, DC: American Psychological Association.

Quinn, R. E., Dutton, J., & Spreitzer, G. (2003). *Reflected Best Self Exercise: Assignment and instructions to participants* (Product number 001B). Ann Arbor: University of Michigan Regents, Positive Organizational Scholarship Research Group.

Rath, T. (2007). *Strengths Finder 2.0.* New York, NY: Gallup Press.

Rath, T., & Conchie, B. (2008). *Strengths based leadership: Great leaders, teams, and why people follow.* New York, NY: Gallup Press.

Roberts, L. M., Spreitzer, G., Dutton, J., Quinn, R., Heaphy, E., & Barker, B. (2005, January). How to play to your strengths. *Harvard Business Review*, pp. 75–80.

Seligman, M. E. P. (2002). *Authentic happiness: Using the new positive psychology to realize your potential for lasting fulfillment.* New York, NY: Free Press.

Seligman, M. E. P., & Csikszentmihalyi, M. (2000). Positive psychology. *American Psychologist, 55*(1), 5–14.

Understanding Philosophy and Styles

INTRODUCTION

What is your philosophy of leadership? Are you an in-charge type of leader who closely monitors followers? Or are you a laid-back type of leader who gives followers a lot of rein? Whether you are one or the other or somewhere in between, it is important to recognize your personal philosophy of leadership. This philosophy affects how others respond to you, how they respond to their work, and, in the end, how effective you are as a leader.

In this chapter, we will discuss how a person's view of people, work, and human nature forms a personal philosophy of leadership. In addition, this chapter will examine how that philosophy is demonstrated in three of the most commonly observed styles of personal leadership: the authoritarian, democratic, and laissez-faire styles. We will discuss the nature of these styles and the implications each has for effective leadership performance.

ASK THE
AUTHOR

What Does "Philosophy of Leadership" Mean?

LEADERSHIP PHILOSOPHY EXPLAINED

Understanding Leadership Philosophy

Each of us approaches leadership with a unique set of beliefs and attitudes about the nature of people and the nature of work. This is the basis for our **philosophy of leadership**. For example, some think people are basically good and will happily work if given the chance. Others think people are prone to be a bit lazy and need to be nudged to complete their work. These beliefs about people and work have a significant impact on an individual's leadership style and probably come into play in every aspect of a person's leadership.

Do you think people like work, or do you think people find work unpleasant? This was one of the central questions addressed by Douglas McGregor in his famous book *The Human Side of Enterprise* (1960). McGregor believed that managers need to understand their core assumptions about human nature and assess how these assumptions relate to their managerial practice.

In particular, McGregor was interested in how managers view the motivations of workers and their attitudes toward work. He believed that understanding these motivations was central to knowing how to become an effective manager. To explain the ways that managers approach workers, McGregor proposed two general theories—Theory X and Theory Y. McGregor believed that by exploring the major assumptions of each of these theories people could develop a better understanding of their own viewpoints on human behavior and the relationship of these viewpoints to their leadership style. Below is a description of both theories. As you read, ask yourself if the assumptions of the theory are consistent or inconsistent with your own attitudes and philosophy of leadership.

Theory X

Theory X is made up of three assumptions about human nature and human behavior (see Table 4.1). Taken together, these assumptions represent a philosophy of leadership that many leaders exhibit to one degree or another.

Assumption #1. The average person dislikes work and will avoid it if possible.

This assumption argues that people do not like work; they view it as unpleasant, distasteful, or simply a necessary evil. According to this assumption, if given the chance, people would choose not to work. An example of this assumption is the worker who says, "I only go to work to be P-A-I-D. If I

TABLE 4.1 Assumptions of McGregor's Theory X

Theory X

McGregor's Theory X
1. People dislike work. 2. People need to be directed and controlled. 3. People want security, not responsibility.

didn't need to pay my bills, I would never work." People with this philosophy would avoid work if they could.

Assumption #2. People need to be direct and controlled.

This assumption is derived directly from the first assumption. Since people naturally do not like work, management needs to set up a system of incentives and rewards regarding work that needs to be accomplished because workers are often unwilling or unable to motivate themselves. This assumption says that without external direction and incentives people would be unmotivated to work. An example of this is the high school teacher who persuades students to hand in homework assignments by threatening them with bad grades. The teacher forces students to perform because the teacher thinks that the students are unwilling to do it or incapable of doing it without that force being applied. From the perspective of Theory X, leaders play a significant role in encouraging others to accomplish their work.

Assumption #3. People want security, not responsibility.

The picture this assumption paints is of workers who want their leaders to take care of them, protect them, and make them feel safe. Because it is too difficult to set their own goals, workers want management to do it for them. This can only happen when managers establish the guidelines for workers. An example of this assumption can be observed at a fast-food restaurant where the employees only have to focus on completing the specific tasks set before them (e.g., cleaning the shake machines or making fries) and are not required to take initiative on their own. In general, many fast-food restaurant workers are not required to accept many challenging responsibilities. Instead, they are told what to do, and how and when to do it. Consistent with this assumption, this example highlights how some workers are not ambitious but want job security above everything else.

So what does it mean if a person's personal leadership style or philosophy is similar to Theory X? It means these leaders have a tendency to view workers as lazy and uninterested in work because they do not value work. As a result, Theory X leaders tend to be directive and controlling. They supervise followers closely and are quick to both praise and criticize them as they see fit. At times, these leaders remind workers of their goal (e.g., to be P-A-I-D) or threaten them with punishment to persuade them to accomplish tasks. As the person in charge, a Theory X leader sees his or her leadership role as instrumental in getting the job done. Theory X leaders also believe it is their role to motivate followers because these workers have little self-motivation. Because of this belief, these leaders take on the responsibility for their followers' actions. From the Theory X perspective, it is clear that followers have a *need* for leadership.

Theory Y

Theory X and Theory Y

Like Theory X, **Theory Y** is based on several specific assumptions about human nature and behavior (see Table 4.2). Taken together, the assumptions of Theory Y present a distinctly different perspective from the ideas set forth in Theory X. It is a perspective that can be observed to a degree in many leaders today.

Assumption #1. The average person does not inherently dislike work. Doing work is as natural as play.

Rather than viewing work as a burden or bad, this assumption suggests people see work as satisfying and not as a punishment. It is a natural activity for them. In fact, given the chance, people are happy to work. An example of this can be seen in what former president Jimmy Carter has done in his retirement. He has devoted much of his time and energy to constructing homes throughout the United States and around the world with Habitat for Humanity. Certainly, the former president does not need to work: He does so because work is natural for him. All his life, Carter has been used to making a contribution to the well-being of others. Working with Habitat for Humanity is another opportunity for him to contribute. Some people view work as a natural part of their lives.

Assumption #2. People will show responsibility and self-control toward goals to which they are committed.

As opposed to Theory X, which suggests that people need to be supervised and controlled, Theory Y suggests that people can and will make a conscious choice to work on their own.

TABLE 4.2   Assumptions of McGregor's Theory Y

McGregor's Theory Y
1. People like work.
2. People are self-motivated.
3. People accept and seek responsibility.

People can be committed to the objectives of their work. Consider some examples from the sports world. Successful athletes are often highly committed to their goals and usually do not need to be controlled or supervised closely. Coaches design training plans for these athletes, but the athletes do the work themselves. A successful long-distance runner does not need to be pushed to run 60 training miles a week in preparation for a marathon because the runner is already motivated to run long distances. Similarly, an Olympic swimmer does not need to be forced to do daily 3-mile pool workouts at 5:00 A.M. because the swimmer chooses to do this independently of any coach's urging. These athletes are self-directed because they are committed to their goals. This is the point of Theory Y. When people can find commitment in their work, they will work without needing leaders to motivate or cajole them. Put another way, when people have a passion for their work, they will do it even without outside direction.

Assumption #3. In the proper environment, the average person learns to accept and seek responsibility.

While Theory X argues that people lack ambition, prefer to be directed, and want security, Theory Y assumes that the average person is inherently resourceful and, if given the chance, will seek to take responsibility. If given the chance, people have the capacity to engage in a wide range of goal-setting and creative problem-solving activities. Theory Y argues that, given the opportunity, people will act independently and be productive.

For example, two university students working in the main stacks section of the library were required to complete a checklist whenever they worked to be sure that they correctly carried out various sorting and shelving activities. The checklist was long, cumbersome, and repetitious, however. Frustrated by the checklist, the students took it upon themselves to design an entirely new, streamlined checklist. The new checklist for sorting and shelving was very clear and concise, and was playful in appearance. After reviewing the checklist and giving it a short trial period, management at the library adopted the new checklist and required that it be implemented throughout the entire library. In this example, library management provided an environment where students felt comfortable suggesting a rather major change in how their work was to be completed. In addition, management was willing to accept and adopt a student-initiated work change. It is not unrealistic to imagine that these students will be more confident initiating ideas or taking on new challenges in other work settings in the future.

So if a leader's philosophy of leadership is similar to Theory Y, what does it mean? It means that the leader views people as capable and interested in working. Even though Theory Y leaders may define work requirements, they do not try to control workers. To these leaders, followers are not lazy; on the contrary, they naturally want to work. In addition, these leaders do not think they need to try to motivate followers or make them work since workers are capable of motivating themselves. Using coercion or external reinforcement schemes is not a part of their leadership repertoire. Theory Y leaders are very attuned to helping followers find their passion for what they want to do. These leaders know that when followers are committed to their work, they are more motivated to do the job. Allowing followers to seek and accept responsibilities on their own comes easily for Theory Y leaders. In short, Theory Y leadership means supporting followers without the need to direct or control them.

In the late 1970s and 1980s, a new leadership theory tangentially related to Theory X and Theory Y was developed by William Ouchi (1981). Ouchi contrasted the collectivistic culture of Japanese companies—which had begun to dominate markets, especially in automobiles and electronics—with the individualism stressed in American organizations and developed an approach that was a hybrid of the two called **Theory Z**. A Theory Z organization is one that emphasizes common cultural values, beliefs, and objectives among its members with a focus on communication, collaboration, and consensual decision making. At the same time, some of the individualistic values of American organizations are also incorporated. Theory Z organizations still maintain formal authority structures and an emphasis on individual contributions and recognizing individual achievements. However, the individual decision making of the leader that is found in both Theory X and Theory Y is not a characteristic of a Theory Z organization.

In summary, all of us maintain certain basic beliefs and assumptions about human nature and work that form our leadership philosophy. The next section discusses how that philosophy impacts your behaviors as a leader, or your *leadership style*. Whether a person's philosophy is similar to Theory X or similar to Theory Y, it affects his or her style of leadership. The challenge is to understand the philosophical underpinnings of your own leadership style.

Leadership in Challenging Times

LEADERSHIP STYLES EXPLAINED

What behaviors do you exhibit as a leader? Do you like to be in control and keep up on the activities of your followers? Or do you believe in a more hands-off approach in leading others, letting them make decisions on their own?

Whatever your behaviors are as a leader, they are indicative of your leadership style. **Leadership style** is defined as the behaviors of leaders, focusing on what leaders do and how they act. This includes leaders' actions toward followers in a variety of contexts. As noted in the previous section, your leadership style is driven by your personal leadership philosophy. In the following section, we discuss the most commonly observed leadership styles associated with Theory X and Theory Y: authoritarian, democratic, and laissez-faire. While none of these styles emerges directly from Theory X or Theory Y, the authoritarian and democratic styles closely mirror the ideas set forth in these theories, respectively.

The primary work on styles of leadership was by Lewin, Lippitt, and White (1939), who analyzed the impact of various leadership styles on small group behavior. Using groups of 10-year-old boys who met after school to engage in hobby activities, the researchers analyzed what happened when their adult leaders used one of three styles: authoritarian, democratic, or laissez-faire. The groups of boys experienced each of the three styles of leadership for a six-week period.

The outcome of the study by Lewin and colleagues was a detailed description of the nature of the leadership behaviors used for each of the three styles (White & Lippitt, 1968). They also described the impact each of these three styles had on group members.

The following sections describe and elaborate on their findings and the implications of using each of these leadership styles. Be aware that these styles are not distinct entities (e.g., like personality traits). They overlap each other. That is, a leader can demonstrate more than one style in any given situation. For example, a leader may be authoritarian about some issues and democratic about others, or a leader may be authoritarian at some points during a project and democratic at others. As leaders, we may display aspects of all of these styles.

Authoritarian Leadership Style

In many ways, the **authoritarian leadership style** is very similar to Theory X. For example, authoritarian leaders perceive followers as needing direction. The authoritarian leader needs to control followers and what they do. Authoritarian leaders emphasize that they are in charge, exerting influence and control over group members. They determine tasks and procedures for group members but may remain aloof from participating in group discussions. Authoritarian leaders do not encourage communication among group members; instead, they prefer that communication be directed to them. In evaluating others, authoritarian leaders give praise and criticism freely, but it is given based on their own personal standards rather than based on objective criticism.

Styles of Leaders and Managers

▶

**The Authoritarian
Leadership Style**

Some have argued that authoritarian leadership represents a rather pessi-mistic, negative, and discouraging view of others. For example, an authori-tarian leader might say something like "Because my workers are lazy, I need to tell them what to do." Others would argue that authoritarian leadership is a much-needed form of leadership—it serves a positive purpose, particu-larly for people who seek security above responsibility. In many contexts, authoritarian leadership is used to give direction, set goals, and structure work. For example, when employees are just learning a new job, authori-tarian leadership lets them know the rules and standards for what they are supposed to do. Authoritarian leaders are very efficient and successful in motivating others to accomplish work. In these contexts, authoritarian leadership is very useful.

What are the *outcomes* of authoritarian leadership? Authoritarian leadership has both pluses and minuses. On the positive side, it is efficient and produc-tive. Authoritarian leaders give direction and clarity to people's work and accomplish more in a shorter period. Furthermore, authoritarian leadership is useful in establishing goals and work standards. On the negative side, it fos-ters dependence, submissiveness, and a loss of individuality. The creativity and personal growth of followers may be hindered. It is possible that, over time, followers will lose interest in what they are doing and become dissatis-fied with their work. If that occurs, authoritarian leadership can create dis-content, hostility, and even aggression.

In addition, authoritarian leadership can become abusive leadership, where these leaders use their influence, power, and control for their per-sonal interests or to coerce followers to engage in unethical or immoral activities. For example, a coach who withholds playing time from athletes who openly disagree with his play calls or a boss who requires salaried employees to work up to 20 hours of overtime each week or "be replaced with someone who will" are both examples of the dark side of authoritar-ian leadership.

While the negative aspects of authoritarian leadership appear to outweigh the positive, it is not difficult to imagine contexts where authoritarian lead-ership would be the preferred style of leadership. For example, in a busy hospital emergency room, it may be very appropriate for the leader in charge of triaging patients to be authoritarian with various types of emer-gencies. The same could be true in other contexts, such as the chaperone of a middle school canoe trip, or the coach of a high school team during the state finals basketball tournament. Despite the negatives of authoritar-ian leadership, this form of leadership is common and necessary in many situations.

Democratic Leadership Style

**The Democratic
Leadership Style**

The **democratic leadership style** strongly resembles the assumptions of Theory Y. Democratic leaders treat followers as fully capable of doing work on their own. Rather than controlling followers, democratic leaders *work with* followers, trying hard to treat everyone fairly, without putting themselves above followers. In essence, they see themselves as guides rather than as directors. They give suggestions to others, but never with any intention of changing them. Helping each follower reach personal goals is important to a democratic leader. Democratic leaders do not use "top-down" communication; instead, they speak on the same level as their followers. Making sure everyone is heard is a priority. They listen to followers in supportive ways and assist them in becoming self-directed. In addition, they promote communication between group members and in certain situations are careful to draw out the less-articulate members of the group. Democratic leaders provide information, guidance, and suggestions, but do so without giving orders and without applying pressure. In their evaluations of followers, democratic leaders give objective praise and criticism.

The *outcomes* of democratic leadership are mostly positive. First, democratic leadership results in greater group member satisfaction, commitment, and cohesiveness. Second, under democratic leadership there is more friendliness, mutual praise, and group mindedness. Followers tend to get along with each other and willingly participate in matters of the group, making more "we" statements and fewer "I" statements. Third, democratic leadership results in stronger worker motivation and greater creativity. People are motivated to pursue their own talents under the supportive structure of democratic leadership. Finally, under a democratic leader group members participate more and are more committed to group decisions. The downside of democratic leadership is that it takes more time and commitment from the leader. Work is accomplished, but not as efficiently as if the leader were authoritarian.

Laissez-Faire Leadership Style

**Destructive
Laissez-Faire Leadership**

The **laissez-faire leadership style** is dissimilar to both Theory X and Theory Y. Laissez-faire leaders do not try to control followers as Theory X leaders do, and they do not try to nurture and guide followers as Theory Y leaders do. Laissez-faire stands alone as a style of leadership; some have labeled it *nonleadership.* The laissez-faire leader is a nominal leader who engages in minimal influence. As the French phrase implies, *laissez-faire* leadership means the leader takes a "hands-off, let it ride" attitude toward followers. These leaders recognize followers but are very laid back and make no attempt to influence their activities. Under laissez-faire leadership, followers have freedom to do pretty much what they want to do whenever they want to do it. Laissez-faire leaders make no attempt to appraise or regulate the progress of followers.

The Laissez-Faire Leadership Style

Given that laissez-faire leadership involves nominal influence, what are the *effects* of laissez-faire leadership? Laissez-faire leadership tends to produce primarily negative outcomes. The major effect is that very little is accomplished under a laissez-faire leader. Because people are directionless and at a loss to know what to do, they tend to do nothing. Giving complete freedom results in an atmosphere that most followers find chaotic. Followers prefer some direction; left completely on their own, they become frustrated. Without a sense of purpose and direction, group members have difficulty finding meaning in their work; they become unmotivated and disheartened. As a result, productivity goes down.

However, there are situations where the laissez-faire style is successful. People who are self-starters, who excel at individualized tasks and don't require ongoing feedback, may prefer working under laissez-faire leaders.

For example, Angela is the president of a website development company who uses independent contractors from across the globe. In certain respects, you could describe her leadership style as laissez-faire. The programmers who develop the websites' code are in Poland, the designer is in India, the content writer is in the United Kingdom, and Angela is in the United States. When developing a site, Angela maps out and communicates the basic framework for the website and then relies on all of the individual contractors to determine the tasks they need to do for the site's development. Because their tasks can be dependent upon another's—for example, the designer needs the programmers to write the code to make the page display graphics and images in a certain way—they do communicate with one another, but because of time zone differences, this is mostly done by email. As their leader, Angela is kept apprised of issues and developments through an electronic project management system they share, but because all of the contractors are experts at what they do and trust the other team members to do what they do best, she lets them problem-solve issues and concerns with one another and rarely gets involved.

While there are a few situations where laissez-faire leadership is effective, in a majority of situations, it proves to be unsuccessful and unproductive.

LEADERSHIP SNAPSHOT

Victoria Ransom, Chief Executive, Wildfire

© Bloomberg/Contributor/
Bloomberg/Getty Images

"I don't believe in hierarchy or creating hierarchy. I believe in earning respect."

That comes from Victoria Ransom, cofounder of social media software company Wildfire Interactive, which grew from an idea to a company with 400 employees and 21,000 clients. The company, which Ransom cofounded with Alain Chuard in 2008, helps companies reach customers over social networks, and was acquired in 2012 by Google for $350 million.

Wildfire's success is largely due to the leadership style and philosophy of Ransom, who serves as the company's chief executive. Ransom grew up in Scotts Ferry, a rural village in New Zealand where her father was an asparagus farmer and her mother was an office manager for a farming equipment company. Ransom worked in the fields, and it was there that she learned the values of hard work, leading by example, and humility that she brings to Wildfire.

Wildfire was actually an afterthought, created to solve a problem that Ransom and Chuard had encountered in running the first company they had formed, Access Trips. Access Trips was an adventure travel company that took small groups of travelers, ages 20–45, to remote destinations, and Ransom and Chuard were looking for a way to promote Access Trips online by giving away a trip on Facebook. They discovered, however, that no software existed to do what they wanted, so they developed their own software to design sweepstakes, contests, or other promotions that could run on Facebook.

The software, and Wildfire, was profitable within a year. Clients soon ranged from two-person catering businesses to Sony and Unilever (Coster, 2012).

The company grew very quickly, which put Ransom's values-based culture to the test.

"I've learned as the company grows, you're only as good as the leaders you have underneath you," she says. "You might think that because you're projecting our values, then the rest of the company is experiencing the values. . . . [D]irect supervisors become the most important influence on people in the company. Therefore, a big part of leading becomes your ability to pick and guide the right people" (Bryant, 2013).

In order to find those right people, it was critical that Wildfire spell out its values and company

(Continued)

(Continued)

culture to employees from the outset. To do so, Ransom and Chuard identified what they valued in the people at Wildfire and then met with all the employees in small groups to get their feedback on these values. What resulted was a list of values that the company instilled and demonstrated: passion, team player, humility, and integrity. Also on the list were having the courage to speak up and curiosity.

"We really encourage people to constantly question, to stay on top of what's happening in our industry, to learn what other people in the company are doing. The hope was to break down these walls of 'them versus us,'" Ransom says (Bryant, 2013).

Ransom says a final value they identified was to "do good, and do right by each other" (Bryant, 2013).

The values a company purports to have, however, are not so readily maintained. Values and culture have to be universally embraced, or they will crumble.

"I think the best way to undermine a company's values is to put people in leadership positions who are not adhering to the values," Ransom says, noting that others begin to lose faith in the values. "Until you take action and move those people out, and then everyone gets faith in the values again" (Bryant, 2013).

Ransom says one way the company showed its values was when it would let employees go who didn't live up to the values. Making these hard decisions about people, even if they were good performers, showed employees that "yeah, this company actually puts its money where its mouth is" (Bryant, 2013).

LEADERSHIP STYLES IN PRACTICE

Leadership and Collaboration

Each leader has a unique style of leadership. Some are very demanding and assertive while others are more open and participative. Similarly, some leaders could be called micromanagers, while others could be labeled nondirective leaders. Whatever the case, it is useful and instructive to characterize your leadership regarding the degree to which you are authoritarian, democratic, or laissez-faire.

It is important to note that these styles of leadership are not distinct entities; it is best to think of them as occurring along a continuum, from high leader influence to low leader influence (see Figure 4.1). Leaders who exhibit higher amounts of influence are more authoritarian. Leaders who show a moderate amount of influence are democratic. Those who exhibit little to no influence are laissez-faire. Although we tend to exhibit primarily one style over the others, our personal leadership styles are not fixed and may vary depending on the circumstances.

FIGURE 4.1   Styles of Leadership

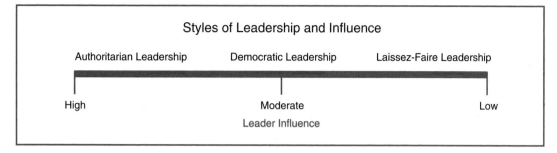

Consider what your results of the Leadership Styles Questionnaire on page 95 tell you about your leadership style. What is your main style? Are you most comfortable with authoritarian, democratic, or laissez-faire leadership? If you are the kind of leader who likes to structure work, likes to lay out the ground rules for others, likes to closely supervise your followers, thinks it is your responsibility to make sure followers do their work, wants to be "in charge" or to know what others are doing, and believes strongly that rewarding and punishing followers is necessary, then you are *authoritarian*. If you are the kind of leader who seldom gives orders or ultimatums to followers, instead trying to work with followers and help them figure out how they want to approach a task or complete their work, then you are primarily *democratic*. Helping each follower reach his or her own personal goals is important to a democratic leader.

In some rare circumstances, you may find you are showing *laissez-faire leadership*. Although not a preferred style, it is important to be aware when one is being laissez-faire. Laissez-faire leaders take a very low profile to leadership. What followers accomplish is up to them. If you believe that your followers will thrive on complete freedom, then the laissez-faire style may be the right style for you. However, in most situations, laissez-faire leadership hinders success and productivity.

SUMMARY

All of us have a philosophy of leadership that is based on our beliefs about human nature and work. Some leaders have a philosophy that resembles Theory X: They view workers as unmotivated and needing direction and control. Others have a philosophy similar to Theory Y: They approach workers as self-motivated and capable of working independently without strong direct influence from a leader.

Our philosophy of leadership is played out in our style of leadership. There are three commonly observed styles of leadership: *authoritarian, democratic,* and *laissez-faire.* Similar to Theory X, *authoritarian leaders* perceive followers as needing direction, so they exert strong influence and control. Resembling Theory Y, *democratic leaders* view followers as capable of self-direction, so they provide counsel and support. *Laissez-faire leaders* leave followers to function on their own, providing nominal influence and direction.

Effective leadership demands that we understand our philosophy of leadership and how it forms the foundations for our style of leadership. This understanding is the first step to becoming a more informed and competent leader.

GLOSSARY TERMS

authoritarian leadership style 83	philosophy of leadership 78
democratic leadership style 85	Theory X 78
laissez-faire leadership style 85	Theory Y 80
leadership style 82	Theory Z 82

$SAGE edge™

Sharpen your skills with SAGE edge at **edge.sagepub.com/northouseintro4e**

SAGE edge for students provides a personalized approach to help you accomplish your coursework goals in an easy-to-use learning environment.

4.1 CASE STUDY

Many Managers, Different Styles

Vanessa Mills was recently hired to work at a branch of Lakeshore Bank as a personal banker. The branch is very busy and has a large staff, including three on-site managers. As a new employee, Vanessa is trying to figure out how to succeed as a personal banker while meeting the expectations of her three very different managers.

Vanessa is paid a salary, but also receives a commission for activities including opening new accounts and selling new services to customers such as credit cards, lines of credit, loans, and stock accounts. Personal bankers are expected to open a certain number of accounts each month and build relationships with customers by exploring their various banking needs and offering services to meet those needs.

Marion Woods is one of the managers at Vanessa's branch. She has worked for Lakeshore Bank for 10 years and prides herself on the success of the branch. Marion openly talks about employees' progress in terms of the number of accounts opened or relationships established, and then commends or scolds people depending on their productivity. Marion stresses to Vanessa the importance of following procedures and using the scripts that Marion provides to successfully convince customers to open new accounts or accept new services with the bank.

As a new banker, Vanessa has not opened many accounts and feels very uncertain about her competence. She is intimidated by Marion, believing that this manager is continually watching and evaluating her. Several times Marion has publically criticized Vanessa, commenting on her shortcomings as a personal banker. Vanessa tries hard to get her sales numbers up so she can keep Marion off her back.

Bruce Dexter, another manager at Vanessa's branch, has been with Lakeshore Bank for 14 years. Bruce started out as a teller and worked his way up to branch manager. As a manager, Bruce is responsible for holding the bank staff's Monday morning meetings. At these staff meetings, Bruce relays the current numbers for new accounts as well as the target number for new accounts. He also lists the number of new relationships the personal bankers have established. After the meetings, Bruce retreats back into his office where he sits hidden behind his computer monitor. He rarely interacts with others. Vanessa likes when Bruce retreats into his office because she does not have to worry about having her performance scrutinized. However, sometimes when Vanessa is trying to help customers with a problem that falls outside of her banking knowledge, she is stressed because Bruce does not provide her with any managerial support.

The third manager at the branch is Heather Atwood. Heather just started at Lakeshore

(Continued)

(Continued)

Bank within the last year, but worked for nine years at another bank. Vanessa finds Heather to be very helpful. She often pops in when Vanessa is with a customer to introduce herself and make sure everything is going well. Heather also allows Vanessa to listen in when she calls disgruntled customers or customers with complicated requests, so Vanessa can learn how to manage these types of interactions. Heather trusts her staff and enjoys seeing them grow, encouraging them by organizing games to see who can open the most accounts and offering helpful feedback when customer interactions do not go as planned. Vanessa is grateful for the advice and support she receives from Heather, and looks up to her because she is competent and kind.

Vanessa is coming up on her three-month review and is very nervous that she might get fired based on her low sales record and the negative feedback she has received from Bruce and Marion regarding her performance. Vanessa decides to talk to Heather about her upcoming review and what to expect. Heather assures Vanessa that she is doing fine and shows promise even if her numbers have not reached that of a seasoned banker. Still, Vanessa is concerned about Bruce and Marion. She has hardly had more than two conversations with Bruce and feels intimidated by Marion who, she perceives, manages by running around barking numbers at people.

QUESTIONS

1. Based on the assumptions of Theory X and Theory Y, how would you describe each manager's philosophy and style of leadership? In what way do their attitudes about Vanessa affect their leadership?

2. In this type of customer service setting, which leadership style would be most effective for the bank to meet its goals? From the bank's perspective, which (if any) manager exhibits the most appropriate leadership? Discuss.

3. What advice would you give to each of the managers to enhance their leadership skills within the bank?

4. What do you think Vanessa can do to prepare herself for her three-month review?

4.2 LEADERSHIP STYLES QUESTIONNAIRE

Purpose

1. To identify your style of leadership
2. To examine how your leadership style relates to other styles of leadership

Directions

1. For each of the statements below, circle the number that indicates the degree to which you agree or disagree.
2. Give your immediate impressions. There are no right or wrong answers.

Statements	Strongly disagree	Disagree	Neutral	Agree	Strongly agree
1. Employees need to be supervised closely, or they are not likely to do their work.	1	2	3	4	5
2. Employees want to be a part of the decision-making process.	1	2	3	4	5
3. In complex situations, leaders should let followers work problems out on their own.	1	2	3	4	5
4. It is fair to say that most employees in the general population are lazy.	1	2	3	4	5
5. Providing guidance without pressure is the key to being a good leader.	1	2	3	4	5
6. Leadership requires staying out of the way of followers as they do their work.	1	2	3	4	5
7. As a rule, employees must be given rewards or punishments in order to motivate them to achieve organizational objectives.	1	2	3	4	5
8. Most workers prefer supportive communication from their leaders.	1	2	3	4	5
9. As a rule, leaders should allow followers to appraise their own work.	1	2	3	4	5
10. Most employees feel insecure about their work and need direction.	1	2	3	4	5
11. Leaders need to help followers accept responsibility for completing their work.	1	2	3	4	5
12. Leaders should give followers complete freedom to solve problems on their own.	1	2	3	4	5
13. The leader is the chief judge of the achievements of the members of the group.	1	2	3	4	5
14. It is the leader's job to help followers find their "passion."	1	2	3	4	5

(Continued)

Visit **edge.sagepub.com/northouseintro4e** for a downloadable version of this questionnaire.

APPLICATION

4.2 LEADERSHIP STYLES QUESTIONNAIRE

(Continued)

Statements	Strongly disagree	Disagree	Neutral	Agree	Strongly agree
15. In most situations, workers prefer little input from the leader.	1	2	3	4	5
16. Effective leaders give orders and clarify procedures.	1	2	3	4	5
17. People are basically competent and if given a task will do a good job.	1	2	3	4	5
18. In general, it is best to leave followers alone.	1	2	3	4	5

Scoring

1. Sum the responses on items 1, 4, 7, 10, 13, and 16 (authoritarian leadership).

2. Sum the responses on items 2, 5, 8, 11, 14, and 17 (democratic leadership).

3. Sum the responses on items 3, 6, 9, 12, 15, and 18 (laissez-faire leadership).

Total Scores

Authoritarian Leadership _____

Democratic Leadership _____

Laissez-Faire Leadership _____

Scoring Interpretation

This questionnaire is designed to measure three common styles of leadership: authoritarian, democratic, and laissez-faire. By comparing your scores, you can determine which styles are most dominant and least dominant in your own style of leadership.

If your score is 26–30, you are in the very high range.

If your score is 21–25, you are in the high range.

If your score is 16–20, you are in the moderate range.

If your score is 11–15, you are in the low range.

If your score is 6–10, you are in the very low range.

Improve Your Leadership Skills

If you have the interactive eBook version of this text, log in to access the interactive leadership assessment. After completing this chapter's questionnaire, you will receive individualized feedback and practical suggestions for further strengthening your leadership based on your responses in this questionnaire.

APPLICATION

4.3 OBSERVATIONAL EXERCISE

Leadership Styles

Purpose

1. To become aware of authoritarian, democratic, and laissez-faire styles of leadership

2. To compare and contrast these three styles

Directions

1. From all of the coaches, teachers, music directors, or managers you have had in the past 10 years, select one who was authoritarian, one who was democratic, and one who was laissez-faire.

   Authoritarian leader (name) _____

   Democratic leader (name) _____

   Laissez-faire leader (name) _____

2. On another sheet of paper, briefly describe the unique characteristics of each of these leaders.

Questions

1. What differences did you observe in how each leader tried to influence you?

2. How did the leaders differ in their use of rewards and punishment?

3. What did you observe about how others reacted to each leader?

4. Under which leader were you most productive? Why?

 Visit **edge.sagepub.com/northouseintro4e** for a downloadable version of this exercise.

4.4 REFLECTION AND ACTION WORKSHEET

Leadership Styles

APPLICATION

Reflection

1. As you reflect on the assumptions of Theory X and Theory Y, how would you describe your own philosophy of leadership?

2. Of the three styles of leadership (authoritarian, democratic, and laissez-faire), what style comes easiest for you? Describe how people respond to you when you use this style.

3. One of the aspects of democratic leadership is to help followers take responsibility for themselves. How do you assess your own ability to help others help themselves?

Action

1. If you were to try to strengthen your philosophy of leadership, what kinds of changes would you have to make in your assumptions about human nature and work?

2. As you look at your results on the Leadership Styles Questionnaire, what scores would you like to change? What would you have to do to make those changes?

3. List three specific activities you could use to improve your leadership style.

4. If you make these changes, what impact will this have on others?

 Visit **edge.sagepub.com/northouseintro4e** for a downloadable version of this worksheet.

REFERENCES

Bryant, A. (2013, January 26). If supervisors respect the values, so will everyone else. *The New York Times*. Retrieved from http://www.nytimes.com/2013/01/27/business/victoria-ransom-of-wildfire-on-instilling-a-companys-values.html?_r=0

Coster, H. (2012, October 19). Victoria Ransom's wild ride. *Fortune*. Retrieved from http://tech.fortune.cnn.com/2012/10/19/victoria-ransom-wildfire/

Lewin, K., Lippitt, R., & White, R. K. (1939). Patterns of aggressive behavior in experimentally created "social climates." *Journal of Social Psychology, 10*, 271–299.

McGregor, D. (1960). *The human side of enterprise*. New York, NY: McGraw-Hill.

Ouchi, W. G. (1981). *Theory Z: How American business can meet the Japanese challenge*. Reading, MA: Addison-Wesley.

White, R., & Lippitt, R. (1968). Leader behavior and member reaction in three "social climates." In D. Cartwright & A. Zander (Eds.), *Group dynamics* (pp. 318–335). New York, NY: Harper & Row.

Attending to Tasks and Relationships

INTRODUCTION

Most people would agree that good doctors are experts at treating disease *and*, at the same time, care about their patients. Similarly, good teachers are informed about the subject matter *and*, at the same time, are sensitive to the personal lives of their students. In leadership, the same is true. Good leaders understand the work that needs to be done *and*, at the same time, can relate to the people who help them do the job.

When we look at what leaders do—that is, at their behaviors—we see that they do two major things: (1) They attend to tasks, and (2) they attend to their relationships with people. The degree to which leaders are successful is determined by how these two behaviors are exhibited. Situations may differ, but every leadership situation needs a degree of both task and relationship behaviors.

ASK THE
AUTHOR

**Which Behaviors Are
Central to Leadership?**

**Task and Relationship
Theories**

Through the years, many articles and books have been written on how leaders behave (Blake & McCanse, 1991; Kahn, 1956; Misumi, 1985; Stogdill, 1974). A review of these writings underscores the topic of this chapter: The essence of leadership behavior has two dimensions—task behaviors and relationship behaviors. Certain circumstances may call for strong task behavior, and other situations may demand strong relationship behavior, but some degree of each is required in every situation. Because these dimensions are inextricably tied together, it is the leader's challenge to integrate and optimize the task and relationship dimensions in his or her leadership role.

One way to explore our own task and relationship perspectives on leadership is to explore our **personal styles** in these two areas. All of us have developed unique habits regarding work and play, which have been ingrained over many years, probably beginning as far back as elementary school. Rooted in the past, these habits regarding work and play form a very real part of who we are as people and of how we function. Many of these early habits stay with us over the years and influence our current styles.

**Analyzing
Leadership Styles**

In considering your personal style, it is helpful to describe in more detail your task-oriented and relationship-oriented behaviors. What is your inclination toward tasks and relationships? Are you more work oriented or people oriented in your personal life? Do you find more rewards in the process of "getting things done" or in the process of relating to people? We all have personal styles that incorporate some combination of work and play. Completing the Task and Relationship Questionnaire on page 113 can help you identify your personal style. Although these descriptions imply that individuals have either one style or the other, it is important to remember that each of us exhibits both behaviors to some degree.

TASK AND RELATIONSHIP STYLES EXPLAINED

Task Style

Task-oriented people are goal oriented. They want to achieve. Their work is meaningful, and they like things such as to-do lists, calendars, and daily planners. Accomplishing things and doing things is the raison d'être for this type of person. That is, these individuals' reason for being comes from doing. Their "in-box" is never empty. On vacations, they try to see and do as much as they possibly can. In all avenues of their lives, they find meaning in doing.

In his book titled *Work and Love: The Crucial Balance* (1980), psychiatrist Jay Rohrlich showed how work can help people organize, routinize, and structure their lives. Doing tasks gives people a sense of control and self-mastery. Achievement sharpens our self-image and helps us define ourselves. Reaching a goal, like running a race or completing a project, makes people feel good because it is a positive expression of who they are.

Some clear examples of task-oriented people include those who use color codes in their daily planners, who have sticky notes in every room of their house, or who, by 10:00 on Saturday morning, have washed the car, done the laundry, and cleaned the apartment. Task-oriented people also are likely to make a list for everything, from grocery shopping to the series of repetitions in their weight-lifting workouts. Common to all of these people is their interest in achieving the goal and accomplishing the work.

Relationship Style

Relationship-oriented people differ from task-oriented people because they are not as goal directed. The relationship-oriented person finds meaning in being rather than in doing. Instead of seeking out tasks, relationship-oriented people want to connect with people. They like to celebrate relationships and the pleasures relationships bring.

Relationship Style

Furthermore, relationship-oriented people often have a strong orientation in the present. They find meaning in the moment rather than in some future objective to be accomplished. In a group situation, sensing and feeling the company of others is appealing to these people. They have been described by some as "relationship junkies." They are the people who are the last to turn off their cell phones as the airplane takes off and the first to turn the phones back on when the airplane lands. Basically, they are into connectedness.

In a work setting, the relationship-oriented person wants to connect or attach with others. For example, the relationship-oriented person would not be afraid to interrupt someone who was working hard on a task to talk about the weather, sports, or just about anything. When working out a problem, relationship-oriented people like to talk to and be associated with others in addressing the problem. They receive satisfaction from being connected to other people. A task-oriented friend described a relationship-oriented person perfectly when he said, "He is the kind of person who stands and talks to you, coffee mug in hand, when you're trying to do something like mow the lawn or cover the boat." The meaning in "doing" is just not paramount in the relationship-oriented person's style.

LEADERSHIP SNAPSHOT

Mick Wilz, Director of Enterprise Excellence, Sur-Seal

© Terry Duffy

Innovation is key to survival in manufacturing, and Mick Wilz has the accolades to prove it. As the director of enterprise excellence at Sur-Seal in Cincinnati, Ohio, Wilz made changes to the manufacturing process that led to the company receiving the Excellence Award from the Association for Manufacturing Excellence in 2012. Working within an industry where task and routine are absolutely critical, it was actually Wilz's unique relationship-oriented approach to those tasks that made the most difference.

Wilz is dyslexic and finds reading, writing, and spelling to be very difficult. Not a lot was known about this condition when he was growing up during the late 1950s and 1960s, and Wilz says his childhood was lonely and hard. But his mother was very supportive, advocating for him with teachers and shifting him to five different grammar schools in order to find the best help.

After high school, Wilz began working in building maintenance at the family business, Sur-Seal, a manufacturer of rubber and plastic gaskets. In the 1990s he became the company's head of operations, and in 2006 he took on the position of director of enterprise excellence charged with reaching peak efficiencies in the manufacturing process. One of his efforts was to initiate a redesign of the factory's layout, moving work groups to new locations on the manufacturing floor to improve production (www.sur-seal.com).

Because of his difficulties, Wilz relies heavily on visual communication, which was one reason he decided to inform employees about the redesign by showing, rather than telling, them. He used children's Lego blocks to set up a mock version of the current factory arrangement, right down to using Lego figurines to represent each individual worker. With the employees watching, he changed the Lego layout to show the new design. As the employees stood in front of this demonstration, they were able to see for themselves the plan, make suggestions, and become involved in the redesign.

Wilz took his visual communication efforts elsewhere in the factory, making Sur-Seal a visual workplace. Large posters and signs providing safety directions, instructions on operating the equipment, and diagrams of the products are posted at every machine.

Wilz's struggles and achievements have made him a more compassionate boss. "Because I had a difficult time when I was young, I believe in treating others as I would like to have been treated. I give employees second chances because I know what it's like to struggle," Wilz says. As an example, he talks about the time when one of the company's maintenance workers was given several chances to improve his work habits and succeeded, becoming the head of his department and a leader in Sur-Seal's manufacturing initiatives.

"We hire a lot of high school graduates who aren't inclined to try college because they feel it would be too difficult," Wilz says. "You have to find a seat on the bus for everyone. I'm a perfect example" (Wilz, 2012).

TASK AND RELATIONSHIP STYLES IN PRACTICE

In the previous section, you were asked to consider your *personal* style regarding tasks and relationships. In this section, we are going to consider the task and relationship dimensions of your *leadership* style.

Figure 5.1 illustrates dimensions of leadership along a task–relationship continuum. **Task-oriented leadership**, which appears on the left end of the continuum, represents leadership that is focused predominantly on procedures, activities, and goal accomplishments. **Relationship-oriented leadership**, which appears on the right end of the continuum, represents leadership that is focused primarily on the well-being of followers, how they relate to each other, and the atmosphere in which they work. Most leadership falls midway between the two extremes of task- and relationship-oriented leadership. This style of leadership is represented by the midrange area, a blend of the two types of leadership.

As discussed at the beginning of this chapter, good leaders understand the work that needs to be done, as well as the need to understand the people who will do it. The process of "doing" leadership requires that leaders attend to both tasks and relationships. The specific challenge for the leader is to decide how much task and how much relationship is required in a given context or situation.

Focusing on Tasks and People

Task Leadership

Task leadership behaviors facilitate goal accomplishment—they are behaviors that help group members to achieve their objectives. Researchers have found that task leadership includes many behaviors. These behaviors are frequently labeled in different ways, but are always about task accomplishment. For example, some have labeled task leadership as **initiating structure**,

FIGURE 5.1   Task–Relationship Leadership Continuum

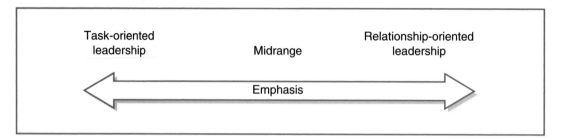

Task Leadership

which means the leader organizes work, defines role responsibilities, and schedules work activities (Stogdill, 1974). Others have labeled task leadership as **production orientation**, which means the leader stresses the production and technical aspects of the job (Bowers & Seashore, 1966). From this perspective, the leader pays attention to new product development, workload matters, and sales volume, to name a few aspects. A third label for task leadership is **concern for production** (Blake & Mouton, 1964). It includes policy decisions, new product development, workload, sales volume, or whatever the organization is seeking to accomplish.

In short, task leadership occurs anytime the leader is doing something that assists the group in reaching its goals. This can be something as simple as handing out an agenda for an upcoming meeting or as complex as describing the multiple quality control standards of a product development process. Task leadership includes many behaviors: Common to each is influencing people toward goal achievement.

As you would expect, people vary in their ability to show task-oriented leadership. There are those who are very task oriented and those who are less task oriented. This is where a person's personal style comes into play. Those who are task oriented in their personal lives are naturally more task oriented in their leadership. Conversely, those who are seldom task oriented in their personal lives will find it difficult to be task oriented as a leader.

Whether a person is very task oriented or less task oriented, the important point to remember is that, as a leader, he or she will always be required to exhibit some degree of task behavior. For certain individuals this will be easy and for others it will present a challenge, but some task-oriented behavior is essential to each person's effective leadership performance.

Relationship Leadership

Relationship leadership behaviors help followers feel comfortable with themselves, with each other, and with the situation in which they find themselves.

For example, in the classroom, when a teacher requires each student to know every other student's name, the teacher is demonstrating relationship leadership. The teacher is helping the students to feel comfortable with themselves, with other students, and with their environment.

Researchers have described relationship leadership in several ways that help to clarify its meaning. It has been labeled by some researchers as **consideration behavior** (Stogdill, 1974), which includes building camaraderie, respect, trust, and regard between leaders and followers. Other researchers describe relationship leadership as having an **employee orientation** (Bowers & Seashore, 1966), which involves taking an interest in workers as human beings, valuing their uniqueness, and giving special attention to their personal needs. Another line of research has simply defined relationship leadership as **concern for people** (Blake & Mouton, 1964). Within an organization, concern for people includes building trust, providing good working conditions, maintaining a fair salary structure, and promoting good social relations.

Essentially, relationship leadership behavior is about three things: (1) treating followers with dignity and respect, (2) building relationships and helping people get along, and (3) making the work setting a pleasant place to be. Relationship leadership behavior is an integral part of effective leadership performance.

In our fast-paced and very diverse society, the challenge for a leader is finding the time and energy to listen to all followers and do what is required to build effective relationships with each of them. For those who are highly relationship oriented in their personal lives, being relationship oriented in leadership will come easily; for those who are highly task oriented, being relationship oriented in leadership will present a greater challenge. Regardless of your personal style, every leadership situation demands a degree of relationship leadership behavior.

As discussed earlier in this chapter, task and relationship leadership behaviors are inextricably tied together, and a leader's challenge is to integrate the two in an optimal way while effectively adapting to followers' needs. For example, task leadership is critically important in a company or an organization with a large number of newly hired employees or at a charter school with a cadre of new faculty members. It is also called for in an adult fitness class when the instructor is introducing a new exercise. Or, consider the family members of a patient going home after a major heart surgery who have to learn how to change dressings and give medications; they want the health professionals to tell them exactly what to do and how to do it. In situations like these, the followers feel uncertain about their roles and responsibilities, and they want a leader who clarifies their tasks and tells them what is expected of them. In fact, in nearly every group or situation there are some individuals who want and need task direction from their leader, and in these

Relationship
Leadership

Ethical Leadership
and Relationships

BOX 5.1   Student Perspectives on Task and Relationship Styles

The following examples are personal observations written by college students. These papers illuminate the distinct differences task and relationship orientations can have in real-life experiences.

Taken to Task

I am definitely a task-oriented person. My mother has given me her love of lists, and my father has instilled in me the value of finishing things once you start them. As a result, I am highly organized in all aspects of my life. I have a color-coded planner with all of the activities I need to do, and I enjoy crossing things off my lists. Some of my friends call me a workaholic, but I don't think that is accurate. There are just a lot of things I have to do.

My roommate Steph, however, is completely different from me. She will make verbal lists for her day, but usually will not accomplish any of them [the items listed]. This drives me crazy when it involves my life. For example, there were boxes all over the place until about a month after we moved into our house. Steph would say every day that she was going to focus and get her room organized that day, but she'd fail miserably most of the time. She is easily distracted and would pass up the opportunity to get unpacked to go out with friends, get on Facebook, or look at YouTube videos.

No matter how much Steph's life stresses me out, I have learned from it. I'm all about having a good time in the right setting, but I am coming to realize that I don't need to be so planned and scheduled. No matter how carefully you do plan, something will always go awry. I don't know that Steph is the one who has taught me that or if I'm just getting older, but I'm glad I'm learning that regardless.

—*Jessica Lembke*

Being Rather Than Doing

I am an extremely relationship-oriented person. While I know that accomplishing tasks is important, I believe the quality of work people produce is directly related to how they feel about themselves and their leader.

I had the privilege of working with fifth graders in an after-school program last year. There was a range of issues we dealt with including academic, behavioral, and emotional problems, as well as kids who did not have safe homes (i.e., no running water or electricity, physical and emotional abuse, and drug addictions within the home). The "goal" of our program was to help these kids become "proficient" students in the classroom.

The task-oriented leaders in administration emphasized improving students' grades through repetition of school work, flash cards, and quizzes. It was important for our students to improve their grades because it was the only way statistically to gauge if our program was successful. Given some of the personal trials these young people were dealing with, the last thing in my "relationship-oriented" mind was working on their academics. These young people had so much potential and wisdom that was stifled when they were asked to blindly follow academic assignments. In addition, they did not know how to self-motivate, self-encourage, or get the work done with so many of life's obstacles in their way.

Instead of doing school work, which the majority of my students struggled with and hated, I focused on building relationships with and between the students. We used discussion, role play, dance parties, and leadership projects to build their self-confidence and emotional intelligence. The students put together service projects to improve their school and community including initiating a trash pickup and recycling initiative at the school and making cards for a nearby nursing home. By the end of the year almost every one of my students had improved his or her grades significantly. More important, at our daily "cheer-for-each-other" meetings, the students would beam with pride for their own and others' successes.

I guess my point in telling this story is that relationship-oriented leadership is more important to me than task. I much prefer "being" than "doing." I am not an organized, goal-oriented person. I rarely make it out of my house without going back two or three times to grab something I forgot, and my attention span is shorter than that of a fruit fly. However, I feel that my passion for relationships and human connection is what motivates me.

—*Elizabeth Mathews*

A Blend of Both

The Style Approach categorizes leaders as being either task oriented or relationship oriented. While I agree that there are these styles of leadership, I disagree that everyone can be placed concretely into one or the other. The Ohio State study says it well by stating that there are "two different continua." When it comes to determining where I stand on each continuum, I'd have to say I'm about even. Not surprisingly, my results of the Task and Relationship Questionnaire reflect these thoughts: I scored a solid 41 in both task- and relationship-oriented styles; I'm equally task and relationship oriented, with each of these styles becoming more prevalent in certain situations.

While I truly enjoy being around other people, making sure everyone is happy and that we all enjoy our time, I'm very focused and goal oriented. If I'm at the movies with my friends, I'm not worrying about a to-do list; alternatively, if I'm working on a group project for school, I'm not as concerned about making friends with the group members.

Completing tasks is very important to me. I have an agenda that I keep with me at all times, partly because without it I would never remember anything, and partly because it provides satisfaction and peace of mind. I make to-do lists for myself: groceries, household chores, homework, and goals. I thrive when I'm busy, but not if I'm disorganized. For example, this semester I'm taking 20 credits, applying to graduate schools, taking the GRE, and working at the bookstore. For me it is comforting to have so many responsibilities. If I have downtime, I usually waste it, and I hate that feeling.

I also feel, however, that I'm very relationship oriented. My task-oriented nature doesn't really affect how I interact with people. I like to make sure people are comfortable and confident in all situations. While I pressure myself to get things done and adhere to a schedule, I'd never think of pushing those pressures onto someone else. If I were the leader of a group that wasn't getting things done, I'd set an example, rather than tell someone what he or she should be doing.

For me, the idea of "two continua" really makes sense. Whether I am task or relationship focused depends on the situation. While I certainly want to have fun with people, I'm a proponent of the "time and place" attitude, in which people remember when it is appropriate to socialize and when it is appropriate to get a job done.

—*Sally Johnson*

circumstances it is paramount that the leader exhibit strong task-oriented leadership.

Team Experiences

On the other hand, it is also true that many groups or situations will have individuals who want to be affiliated with or connected to others more than they want direction. For example, in a factory, in a classroom, or even at a workplace like McDonald's, there are individuals who want the leader to befriend them and relate to them on a human level. The followers are willing to work, but they are primarily interested in being recognized and feeling related to others. An example would be individuals who attend a cancer support group. They like to receive information from the leader, but even more importantly, they want the leader to relate to them. It is similar with individuals who attend a community-sponsored reading club. They want to talk about the book, but they also want the leader to relate to them in a more familiar way. Clearly, in these situations, the leader needs to connect with these followers by utilizing relationship-oriented behaviors.

In addition to task and relationship behaviors, Yukl, Gordon, and Taber (2002) identified a third category of leader behaviors relevant to effective leadership, which they labeled *change behaviors*. Based on an analysis of a large number of earlier leadership measures, the researchers found that change behaviors included visioning, intellectual stimulation, risk taking, and external monitoring. This category of behaviors has been less prominent in the leadership literature but still is a valuable way to characterize what leaders do. Change behaviors are closely related to leadership skills and creating a vision, which we discuss in the next two chapters of the book.

In society, the most effective leaders recognize and adapt to followers' needs. Whether they are team leaders, teachers, or managers, they appropriately demonstrate the right degrees of task and relationship leadership. This is no small challenge because different followers and situations demand different amounts of task and relationship leadership. When followers are unclear, confused, or lost, the leader needs to show direction and exhibit task-oriented leadership. At the same time, a leader needs to be able to see the need for affiliation and attachment in followers and be able to meet those needs, without sacrificing task accomplishment.

Leaders' Value Systems

In the end, the best leader is the leader who helps followers achieve the goal by attending to the task and by attending to each follower as a person. We all know leaders who do this: They are the coaches who force us to do drills until we are blue in the face to improve our physical performance, but who then caringly listen to our personal problems. They are the managers who never let us slack off for even a second but who make work a fun place to be. The list goes on, but the bottom line is that the best leaders get the job done and care about others in the process.

SUMMARY

Good leaders are both task oriented and relationship oriented. Understanding your personal styles of work and play can provide a better recognition of your leadership. Task-oriented people find meaning in doing, while relationship-oriented people find meaning in being connected to others. Effective leadership requires that leaders be both task oriented and relationship oriented.

GLOSSARY TERMS

concern for people 105

concern for production 104

consideration behavior 105

employee orientation 105

initiating structure 103

personal styles 100

production orientation 104

relationship-oriented leadership 103

task-oriented leadership 103

⑤SAGE edge™

Sharpen your skills with SAGE edge at **edge.sagepub.com/northouseintro4e**

SAGE edge for students provides a personalized approach to help you accomplish your coursework goals in an easy-to-use learning environment.

5.1 Case Study

From Two to One

Mark Schmidt runs Co-Ed Cleaners, a business that employs college students to clean offices and schools during the night hours. Due to an economic downturn, Co-Ed Cleaners has lost customers, and although Mark has trimmed everywhere he can think of, he has come to the conclusion that he has to cut back further. This will require letting one of his two managers go and consolidating responsibilities under the other manager's leadership.

Dan Cali manages groups of students who clean school buildings. Dan is always on the go, visiting cleaning teams at each school while they are working. His employees describe him as an efficient taskmaster with checklists they are all required to follow and sign off on as they complete each job. Dan initiates most ideas for changing processes based on efficiency. When something goes wrong on a job, Dan insists he be alerted and brought in to solve it. "Dan is a very task-oriented guy," says one of his team members. "There is no one who works harder than he does or knows more about our jobs. This guy gets more done in an hour than most guys do in a day. In the two years I've been here, I don't think I've ever seen him stop and take a break or even have a cup of coffee." Dan's efforts have helped Co-Ed Cleaners

be recognized as "The Best Professional Cleaning Service" for three years running.

Asher Roland is the manager of groups of students who clean small offices and businesses. Asher has up to 10 teams working a night and relies on his employees to do their jobs and keep him apprised of problems. He takes turns working alongside his teams to understand the challenges they may face, getting to know each of his employees in the process. Once a month, he takes the teams to a restaurant for a "Great Job Breakfast" where they talk about sports, the weather, politics, their relationships and families, and, when they have time, work issues. One of his employees describes him this way: "Asher is a really good guy. Never had a better boss. If I am having problems, I would go to Asher first. He always advocates for us and listens when we have ideas or problems, but allows us to manage our own jobs the way we think best. He trusts us to do the right things, and we trust him to be fair and honest with us."

Mark likes both Dan and Asher, and in their own way they are both good managers. Mark worries, however, about how each manager's individual style will affect his ability to take on the responsibilities of the manager he replaces. He must let one go, but he doesn't know which one.

QUESTIONS

1. Using ideas from the chapter, describe Dan's and Asher's styles of leadership.

2. How will Asher's employees, who are used to being able to manage themselves in their own way, respond to Dan's task-oriented style?

3. How will Dan's employees, who are used to being given clear direction and procedures, respond to Asher's more relationship-oriented style?

4. If you were an employee at Co-Ed Cleaners, would you want Mark to let Dan or Asher go? Explain your choice.

5.2 Task and Relationship Questionnaire

Purpose

1. To identify how much you emphasize task and relationship behaviors in your life
2. To explore how your task behavior is related to your relationship behavior

Directions

For each item below, indicate on the scale the extent to which you engage in the described behavior. Move through the items quickly. Do not try to categorize yourself in one area or another.

Statements	Never	Rarely	Sometimes	Often	Always
1. Make a to-do list of the things that need to be done.	1	2	3	4	5
2. Try to make the work fun for others.	1	2	3	4	5
3. Urge others to concentrate on the work at hand.	1	2	3	4	5
4. Show concern for the personal well-being of others.	1	2	3	4	5
5. Set timelines for when the job needs to be done.	1	2	3	4	5
6. Help group members get along.	1	2	3	4	5
7. Keep a checklist of what has been accomplished.	1	2	3	4	5
8. Listen to the special needs of each group member.	1	2	3	4	5
9. Stress to others the rules and requirements for the project.	1	2	3	4	5
10. Spend time exploring other people's ideas for the project.	1	2	3	4	5
11. Pay close attention to project deadlines.	1	2	3	4	5
12. Act friendly toward other group members.	1	2	3	4	5
13. Clarify each group member's job responsibilities.	1	2	3	4	5
14. Express support for other group members' ideas.	1	2	3	4	5
15. Emphasize performance standards for the group.	1	2	3	4	5
16. Talk with other group members about their personal concerns.	1	2	3	4	5
17. Keep other group members focused on goals.	1	2	3	4	5
18. Emphasize everyone's unique contributions to the group.	1	2	3	4	5
19. Follow rules and regulations closely.	1	2	3	4	5
20. Express positive feelings toward others in the group.	1	2	3	4	5

(Continued)

 Visit **edge.sagepub.com/northouseintro4e** for a downloadable version of this questionnaire.

APPLICATION

5.2 TASK AND RELATIONSHIP QUESTIONNAIRE

(Continued)

Scoring

1. Sum scores for the odd-numbered statements (task score).

2. Sum scores for the even-numbered statements (relationship score).

Total Scores

Task score: _____

Relationship score: _____

Scoring Interpretation

This questionnaire is designed to measure your task-oriented and relationship-oriented leadership behavior. By comparing your scores, you can determine which style is more dominant in your own style of leadership. If your task score is higher than your relationship score, you tend to give more attention to goal accomplishment and some-what less attention to people-related matters. If your relationship score is higher than your task score, your primary concern tends to be dealing with people, and your secondary concern is directed more toward tasks. If your scores are very similar to each other, it suggests that your leadership is balanced and includes an equal amount of both behaviors.

> If your score is 45–50, you are in the very high range.
>
> If your score is 40–44, you are in the high range.
>
> If your score is 35–39, you are in the moderately high range.
>
> If your score is 30–34, you are in the moderately low range.
>
> If your score is 25–29, you are in the low range.
>
> If your score is 10–24, you are in the very low range.

Improve Your Leadership Skills

If you have the interactive eBook version of this text, log in to access the interactive leadership assessment. After completing this chapter's questionnaire, you will receive individualized feedback and practical suggestions for further strengthening your leadership based on your responses in this questionnaire.

5.3 OBSERVATIONAL EXERCISE

Task and Relationship

Purpose

1. To understand how leadership includes both task and relationship behaviors
2. To contrast different leaders' task and relationship behaviors

Directions

1. Over the next couple of days, observe the leadership styles of two different leaders (e.g., teacher, athletic coach, choir director, restaurant manager, work supervisor).
2. Record your observations of the styles of each person.

Leader #1 (name) _____

Task behaviors	Relationship behaviors
• _____	• _____
• _____	• _____
• _____	• _____
• _____	• _____

Leader #2 (name) _____

Task behaviors	Relationship behaviors
• _____	• _____
• _____	• _____
• _____	• _____
• _____	• _____

Questions

1. What differences did you observe between the two leaders?

2. What did you observe about the leader who was most task oriented?

3. What did you observe about the leader who was most relationship oriented?

4. How effective do you think you would be in each of these leadership positions?

 Visit **edge.sagepub.com/northouseintro4e** for a downloadable version of this exercise.

5.4 REFLECTION AND ACTION WORKSHEET

Task and Relationship

Reflection

1. As you reflect on what has been discussed in this chapter and on your own leadership style, how would you describe your own style in relation to task and relationship orientations? What are your strengths and weaknesses?

2. What biases do you maintain regarding task style and relationship style? How do your biases affect your leadership?

3. One of the most difficult challenges leaders face is to integrate their task and relationship behaviors. Do you see this as a challenge in your own leadership? How do you integrate task and relationship behaviors?

Action

1. If you were to change in an effort to improve your leadership, what aspect of your style would you change? Would you try to be more task oriented or more relationship oriented?

2. Identify three specific task or relationship changes you could carry out.

3. What barriers will you face as you try to make these changes?

4. Given that you believe this change will improve your overall leadership, what can you do (i.e., what strategies can you use) to overcome the barriers you cite in Action Item #3 above?

Visit **edge.sagepub.com/northouseintro4e** for a downloadable version of this worksheet.

REFERENCES

Blake, R. R., & McCanse, A. A. (1991). *Leadership dilemmas: Grid solutions.* Houston, TX: Gulf.

Blake, R. R., & Mouton, J. S. (1964). *The managerial grid.* Houston, TX: Gulf.

Bowers, D. G., & Seashore, S. E. (1966). Predicting organizational effectiveness with a four-factor theory of leadership. *Administrative Science Quarterly, 11*(2), 238–263.

Kahn, R. L. (1956). The prediction of productivity. *Journal of Social Issues, 12*(2), 41–49.

Misumi, J. (1985). *The behavioral science of leadership: An interdisciplinary Japanese research program.* Ann Arbor: University of Michigan Press.

Rohrlich, J. B. (1980). *Work and love: The crucial balance.* New York, NY: Summit Books.

Stogdill, R. M. (1974). *Handbook of leadership: A survey of theory and research.* New York, NY: Free Press.

Wilz, M. (2012, December 29). Don't just talk about change. Show it [as told to P. R. Olsen]. *The New York Times.* Retrieved from http://www.nytimes.com/2012/12/30/jobs/the-visual-workplace-and-how-to-build-it.html

Yukl, G., Gordon, A., & Taber, T. (2002). A hierarchical taxonomy of leadership behavior: Integrating a half century of behavior research. *Journal of Leadership & Organizational Studies, 9*(1), 15–32.

Developing Leadership Skills

INTRODUCTION

Whether it is playing the guitar, a video game, or the stock market, most of life's activities require us to have skills if we are to be successful. The same is true of leadership—skills are required. As discussed in the first chapter, leadership skills refer to learned competencies that leaders are able to demonstrate in performance (Katz, 1955). Leadership skills give people the capacity to influence others. They are a critical component in successful leadership.

Even though skills play an essential role in the leadership process, they have received little attention by researchers (Lord & Hall, 2005; T. Mumford, Campion, & Morgeson, 2007). Leadership traits rather than leadership skills have been the focus of research for more than 100 years. However, in the past 10 years a shift has occurred, and leadership skills are now receiving far more attention by researchers and practitioners alike (M. Mumford, Zaccaro, Connelly, & Marks, 2000; Yammarino, 2000).

ASK THE
AUTHOR

**What Types of
Skills Should Leaders
Seek to Develop?**

FIGURE 6.1   Model of Primary Leadership Skills

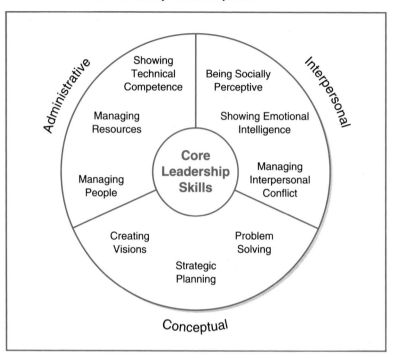

Developing Skills

Although there are many different leadership skills, they are often considered as groups of skills. In this chapter, leadership skills are grouped into three categories: *administrative skills, interpersonal skills,* and *conceptual skills* (see Figure 6.1). The next section describes each group of skills and explores the unique ways they affect the leadership process.

ADMINISTRATIVE SKILLS EXPLAINED

Administrative Skills

While often devalued because they are not glamorous or exciting, **administrative skills** play a primary role in effective leadership. Administrative skills help a leader to accomplish the mundane but critically important aspects of showing leadership. Some would even argue that administrative skills are the most fundamental of all the skills required of a leader.

What are administrative skills? Administrative skills refer to those competencies a leader needs to run an organization in order to carry out the organization's purposes and goals. These involve planning, organizing work, assigning the right tasks to the right people, and coordinating work activities (Mann, 1965).

Administrative Skills in Practice

For purposes of our discussion, administrative skills are divided into three specific sets of skills: (1) managing people, (2) managing resources, and (3) showing technical competence.

Managing People

Any leader of a for-profit or nonprofit organization, if asked what occupies the most time, will reply, "Managing people." Few leaders can do without the skill of being able to manage people. The phrase *management by walking around* captures the essence of managing people. An effective leader connects with people and understands the tasks to be done, those skills required to perform them, and the environment in which people work. The best way to know this is to be involved rather than to be a spectator. For a leader to deal effectively with people requires a host of abilities such as helping employees to work as a team, motivating them to do their best, promoting satisfying relationships among employees, and responding to their requests. The leader also needs to find time to deal with urgent staff matters. Staff issues are a daily fact of life for any leader. Staff members come to the leader for advice on what to do about a problem, and the leader needs to respond appropriately.

A leader must also pay attention to recruiting and retaining employees. In addition, leaders need to communicate effectively with their own board of directors, as well as with any external constituencies such as the public, stockholders, or other outside groups that have a stake in the organization.

Consider the leadership of Nate Parker, the director of an after-school recreation program serving 600 kids in a large metropolitan community. Nate's program is funded by an $800,000 government grant. It provides academic, fitness, and enrichment activities for underserved children and their families. Nate has managers who assist him in running the after-school program in five different public schools. Nate's own responsibilities include setting up and running staff meetings, recruiting new staff, updating contracts, writing press releases, working with staff, and establishing relationships with external constituencies. Nate takes great pride in having created a new and strong relationship between the city government and the school district in which he works. Until he came on board, the relationship between the schools and city government was tense. By communicating effectively across groups, Nate was able to bring the entire community together to serve the children. He is now researching the possibility of a citywide system to support after-school programming.

Managing Resources

Although it is not obvious to others, a leader is often required to spend a significant amount of time addressing resource issues. Resources, the lifeblood

Working in Teams

of an organization, can include people, money, supplies, equipment, space, or anything else needed to operate an organization. Managing resources requires a leader to be competent in both obtaining and allocating resources. Obtaining resources can include a wide range of activities such as ordering equipment, finding work space, or locating funds for special projects. For example, a middle school cross-country coach wanted to replace her team's outdated uniforms, but had no funds to do so. In order to buy new uniforms, the coach negotiated with the athletic director for additional funds. The coach also encouraged several parents in the booster club to sponsor a few successful fund-raisers.

Decision Making

In addition to obtaining resources, a leader may be required to allocate resources for new staff or new incentive programs, or to replace old equipment. While a leader may often engage staff members to assist in managing resources, the ultimate responsibility of resource management rests on the leader. As the sign on President Harry S. Truman's desk read, "The buck stops here."

Showing Technical Competence

Technical competence involves having specialized knowledge about the work we do or ask others to do. In the case of an organization, it includes understanding the intricacies of how an organization functions. A leader with technical competence has organizational know-how—he or she understands the complex aspects of how the organization works. For example, a university president should be knowledgeable about teaching, research, student recruitment, and student retention; a basketball coach should be knowledgeable about the basics of dribbling, passing, shooting, and rebounding; and a sales manager should have a thorough understanding of the product the salespeople are selling. In short, a leader is more effective when he or she has the knowledge and technical competence about the activities followers are asked to perform.

Technical competence is sometimes referred to as "functional competence" because it means a person is competent in a particular function or area. No one is required to be competent in all avenues of life. So, too, a leader is not required to have technical competence in every situation. Having technical skills means being competent in a particular area of work, the area in which one is leading.

The importance of having technical competence can be seen in the example of an orchestra conductor. The conductor's job is to direct rehearsals and performances of the orchestra. To do this, the conductor needs technical competence pertaining to rhythm, music composition, and all the many instruments and how they are played. Technical competence gives the conductor the understanding required to direct the many different musicians to perform together successfully.

INTERPERSONAL SKILLS EXPLAINED

In addition to administrative skills, effective leadership requires interpersonal skills (see Figure 6.1). **Interpersonal skills** are people skills—those abilities that help a leader to work effectively with followers, peers, and superiors to accomplish the organization's goals. While some people downplay the importance of interpersonal skills or disparage them as "touchy-feely" and inconsequential, leadership research has consistently pointed out the importance of interpersonal skills to effective leadership (Bass, 1990; Blake & McCanse, 1991; Katz, 1955).

Interpersonal Skills

Interpersonal Skills in Practice

Interpersonal skills are divided into three parts: (1) being socially perceptive, (2) showing emotional intelligence, and (3) managing interpersonal conflicts.

Being Socially Perceptive

To successfully lead an organization toward change, a leader needs to be sensitive to how her or his own ideas fit in with others' ideas. **Social perceptiveness** includes having insight into and awareness of what is important to others, how they are motivated, the problems they face, and how they react to change. It involves understanding the unique needs, goals, and demands of different organizational constituencies (Zaccaro, Gilbert, Thor, & Mumford, 1991). A leader with social perceptiveness has a keen sense of how employees will respond to any proposed change in the organization. In a sense, you could say a socially perceptive leader has a finger on the pulse of employees on any issue at any time.

Leadership is about change, and people in organizations often resist change because they like things to stay the same. Novel ideas, different rules, or new ways of doing things are often seen as threatening because they do not fit in with how people are used to things being done. A leader who is socially perceptive can create change more effectively if he or she understands how the proposed change may affect all the people involved.

One example that demonstrates the importance of social perceptiveness is illustrated in the events surrounding the graduation ceremonies at the University of Michigan in the spring of 2008. The university anticipated 5,000 students would graduate, with an expected audience of 30,000. In prior years, the university traditionally held spring graduation ceremonies in the football stadium, which, because of its size, is commonly known as "the Big House." However, because the stadium was undergoing major renovations, the university was forced to change the venue for graduation and decided to hold the graduation at the outdoor stadium of nearby Eastern Michigan University. When the university announced the change of location, the students, their families, and the university's alumni responded immediately and negatively. There was upheaval as they made their strong opinions known.

Clearly, the leadership at the university had not perceived the significance to seniors and their families of where graduation ceremonies were to be held. It was tradition to graduate in the Big House, so changing the venue was offensive to many. Phone calls came into the president's office, and editorials appeared in the press. Students did not want to graduate on the campus of another university. They thought that they deserved to graduate on their own campus. Some students, parents, and alumni even threatened to withhold future alumni support.

To correct the situation, the university again changed the venue. Instead of holding the graduation at Eastern Michigan University, the university spent $1.8 million to set up a temporary outdoor stage in the center of campus, surrounded by the University of Michigan's classroom buildings and libraries. The graduating students and their families were pleased that the ceremonies took place where their memories and traditions were so strong. The university ultimately was successful because it adapted to the deeply held beliefs of its students and their families. Clearly, if the university had been more socially perceptive at the outset, the initial dissatisfaction and upheaval that arose could have been avoided.

Showing Emotional Intelligence

Emotional Intelligence and Performance

Another important skill for a leader is being able to show emotional intelligence. Although emotional intelligence emerged as a concept less than 20 years ago, it has captivated the interests of many scholars and practitioners of leadership (Caruso & Wolfe, 2004; Goleman, 1995; Mayer & Salovey, 1995). Emotional intelligence is concerned with a person's ability to understand his or her own and others' emotions, and then to apply this understanding to life's tasks. Specifically, emotional intelligence can be defined as the ability to perceive and express emotions, to use emotions to facilitate thinking, to understand and reason with emotions, and to manage emotions effectively within oneself and in relationships with others (Mayer, Salovey, & Caruso, 2000).

The underlying premise of research on emotional intelligence is that people who are sensitive to their own emotions and the impact their emotions have on others will be more effective leaders. Since showing emotional intelligence is positively related to effective leadership, what should a leader do to enhance his or her emotional skills?

First, leaders need to work on *becoming aware* of their own emotions, taking their emotional pulse, and identifying their feelings as they happen. Whether

LEADERSHIP SNAPSHOT

Coquese Washington, Head Coach, Penn State Women's Basketball

© Jeff Golden/Contributor/Getty Images Sport/Getty Images

It was apparent early on that Coquese Washington had skills that would take her places. She grew up in Flint, Michigan, where she played seven musical instruments in high school, was an All-State selection for girls' basketball two years in a row, and was awarded a scholarship to attend Notre Dame. She finished Notre Dame in three years, earning a bachelor's degree in history. After taking a year off to be a high school special education teacher in her hometown, she returned to her alma mater to earn a juris doctorate from the Notre Dame Law School.

But where she ended up . . . well, not even she saw that coming.

Washington was a gifted basketball player, and although she excelled at the sport in high school and it is what brought her to play at Notre Dame, she says her dream was always to practice law.

But after law school, she took a left turn, being recruited and chosen to play for the Portland Power of the ABL (American Basketball League), a short-lived women's professional basketball league. A year later she joined the WNBA (Women's National Basketball Association), playing first for the New York Liberty and then moving to Houston, helping the Comets win the WNBA title. She was traded to the Indiana Fever and guided that team to its first ever playoff berth, becoming the first player in WNBA history to lead three different teams to the postseason tournament.

Former teammate Rebecca Lobo describes Washington as "a smart teammate who liked to learn. She could fit in with any crowd and had everyone's respect because she could blend without compromising who she was" (Haverbeck, 2007).

The WNBA season is in the summer, which allowed Washington to begin coaching at Notre Dame as an assistant under her former coach Muffet McGraw in the off-season. "She did not have any experience, but I thought she'd be great at it," McGraw says. "I wanted to give her that opportunity and just see if I could try to talk her into trying it out and she was just good at it. I think she found her passion" (McKenna, 2013).

It was also during this time that Washington's legal skills were called into action. She had been working as an attorney for a New York law firm, so when the WNBA players decided to form a union, she brought her litigation skills to the effort. She became the founding

(Continued)

(Continued)

president of the Women's National Basketball Players' Association and negotiated the players' first collective bargaining agreement. Lobo said that Washington was "a godsend" during the negotiations. "She was levelheaded and bright and also had her law degree" (Haverbeck, 2007).

It was in law school that she learned to research, analyze situations, and develop strategies, and Washington admits she always thought she would return to being a lawyer, but somewhere along the way that changed.

"I thought 'Man, I like coaching, you know. I like the relationships that I have with the players. I like being in the gym,'" Washington said. "I loved basketball. I love being around basketball. I never thought I would enjoy coaching as much as I have, but I really do enjoy it" (McKenna, 2013).

In 2007, Washington was tapped to be the head coach of Penn State's women's basketball team. Her success there has been steady; by 2013, she led the Lady Lions to three consecutive appearances at the National Collegiate Athletic Association Women's Division I Basketball Championships.

But the winning isn't what's keeping Washington on the court. It's the opportunity to be a mentor and leader to her players.

"Mentoring them and helping them learn to become powerful, dynamic women—that's the thing I love best of all.

"We use basketball as a vehicle, but I'm probably most proud of our kids' ability to achieve. I've learned over the years that that is a skill that's developed, not something you're born with. Perseverance, persistence, belief—there are so many skills that have to be nurtured to become an achiever" (Nilsen, 2009).

It's a philosophy her players respond to. "I think the biggest thing that coach does is not only tell us what to do, she does it herself," says Penn State player Alex Bentley. "She has been through the WNBA, she has been through coaching at the top institutions already. She knows the game and I have been picking her brain ever since I was a freshman stepping on the court.

"She is the epitome of a great woman. We just see that and want to be like that, she is a role model and a mentor. Us as women, we want to be like that one day" (McKenna, 2013).

it is mad, glad, sad, or scared, a leader needs to assess constantly how he or she is feeling and what is causing those feelings.

Second, a leader should train to become aware of the emotions of others. A leader who knows how to read others' emotions is better equipped to respond appropriately to these people's wants and needs. Stated another way, a leader needs to have empathy for others. He or she should understand the feelings of others as if those feelings were his or her own. Salovey and Mayer (1990) suggested that empathy is the critical component of emotional intelligence. Empathy, and how to demonstrate it, is discussed further in Chapter 10, "Listening to Out-Group Members."

Third, a leader needs to learn how to regulate his or her emotions and put them to good use. Whenever a leader makes a substantial decision, the leader's emotions are involved. Therefore, emotions need to be embraced and managed for the good of the group or organization. When a leader is sensitive to others and manages his or her own emotions appropriately, that leader increases the chances that the group's decisions will be effective. For example, a high school principal sensed that she was becoming extremely angry with some students who pulled a prank during an assembly. Instead of expressing her anger—"losing it"—she maintained her composure and helped to turn the prank into a learning experience. The key point here is that people with emotional intelligence understand emotions and incorporate these in what they do as leaders. To summarize, a leader with emotional intelligence listens to his or her own feelings and the feelings of others, and is adept at regulating these emotions in service of the common good.

Handling Conflict

A leader also needs to have skill in handling conflict. Conflict is inevitable. Conflict creates the need *for* change and occurs as the result *of* change. Conflict can be defined as a struggle between two or more individuals over perceived differences regarding substantive issues (e.g., the correct procedure to follow) or over perceived differences regarding relational issues (e.g., the amount of control each individual has within a relationship). When confronted with conflict, leaders and followers often feel uncomfortable because of the strain, controversy, and stress that accompany conflict. Although conflict is uncomfortable, it is not unhealthy, nor is it necessarily bad. If conflict is managed in effective and productive ways, the result is a reduction of stress, an increase in creative problem solving, and a strengthening of leader–follower and team-member relationships.

Because conflicts are usually very complex, and addressing them is never simple, Chapter 11, "Managing Conflict," provides a more thorough examination of the components of conflict and offers several practical communication approaches that a leader can take to constructively resolve differences.

CONCEPTUAL SKILLS EXPLAINED

Whereas administrative skills are about organizing work, and interpersonal skills are about dealing effectively with people, **conceptual skills** are about working with concepts and ideas. Conceptual skills involve the thinking or

Traits and Conceptual Skills

cognitive aspects of leadership and are critical to such things as creating a vision or strategic plan for an organization. A leader with conceptual skills is able to conceive and communicate the ideas that shape an organization from its goals and mission to how to best solve problems.

Conceptual Skills in Practice

Conceptual skills for leaders can be divided into three parts: (1) problem solving, (2) strategic planning, and (3) creating vision.

Problem Solving

Problem-Solving Skills

We all know people who are especially good at problem solving. When something goes wrong or needs to be fixed, they are the first ones to jump in and address the problem. Problem solvers do not sit idly by when there are problems. They are quick to ask, "What went wrong?" and they are ready to explore possible answers to "How can it be fixed?" Problem-solving skills are essential for effective leadership.

What are problem-solving skills? **Problem-solving skills** refer to a leader's cognitive ability to take corrective action in a problem situation in order to meet desired objectives. The skills include identifying the problem, generating alternative solutions, selecting the best solution from among the alternatives, and implementing that solution (see Table 6.1). These skills do not function in a vacuum, but are carried out in a particular setting or context.

TABLE 6.1   Steps in Problem Solving

1. Identify the problem
2. Generate alternative solutions
3. Select the best solution
4. Implement the solution

Step 1: Identify the problem. The first step in the problem-solving process is to identify or recognize the problem. The importance of this step cannot be understated. Seeing a problem and addressing it is at the core of successful problem solving. All of us are confronted with many problems every day, but some of us fail to see those problems or even to admit that they exist. Others may recognize that something is wrong but then do nothing about it. People with problem-solving skills see problems and address them.

Some problems are simple and easy to define, while others are complex and demand a great deal of scrutiny. Problems arise when there is a difference between what is expected and what actually happens. Identifying the problem requires awareness of these differences. The questions we ask in this phase of problem solving are "What is the problem?" "Are there multiple aspects to it?" and "What caused it?" Identifying the exact nature of the problem precedes everything else in the problem-solving process.

Step 2: Generate alternative solutions. After identifying the problem and its cause or causes, the next step in problem solving is to generate alternative solutions where there is more than one possible resolution to the problem. Because problems are often complex, there are usually many different ways of trying to correct them. During this phase of problem solving, it is important to consider as many solutions as possible and not dismiss any as unworthy. For example, consider a person with a major health concern (e.g., cancer or multiple sclerosis). There are often many ways to treat the illness, but before choosing a course of treatment it is important to consult a health professional and explore all the treatment options. Every treatment has different side effects and different probabilities for curing the illness. Before choosing an option, people often want to be sure that they have fully considered all of the possible treatment options. The same is true in problem solving. Before going forward, it is important to consider all the available options for dealing with a problem.

Step 3: Select the best solution. The next step in problem solving is to select the best solution to the problem. Solutions usually differ in how well they address a particular problem, so the relative strengths and weaknesses of each solution need to be addressed. Some solutions are straightforward and easy to enact, while others are complex or difficult to manage. Similarly, some solutions are inexpensive while others are costly. Many criteria can be used to judge the value of a particular solution as it applies to a given problem. Selecting the best solution is the key to solving a problem effectively.

The importance of selecting the best solution can be illustrated in a hypothetical example of a couple with marital difficulties. Having struggled in their marriage for more than two years, the couple decides that they must do something to resolve the conflict in their relationship. Included in the list of what they could do are attend marital counseling, receive individual psychiatric therapy, separate, date other people even though they are married, and file for divorce. Each of these solutions would have a different impact on what happens to the couple and their marital relationship. While not exhaustive, the list highlights the importance in problem solving of selecting the best solution to a given problem. The solutions we choose have a major impact on how we feel about the outcome of our problem solving.

Step 4: Implement the solution. The final step in problem solving is implementing the solution. Having defined the problem and selected a solution, it is time to put the solution into action. Implementing the solution involves shifting from thinking about the problem to doing something about the problem. It is a challenging step: It is not uncommon to meet with resistance from others when trying to do something new and different to solve a problem. Implementing change requires communicating with others about the change, and adapting the change to the wants and needs of those being affected by the change. Of course, there is always the possibility that the chosen solution will fail to address the problem; it might even make the problem worse. Nevertheless, there is no turning back at this phase. There is always a risk in implementing change, but it is a risk that must be taken to complete the problem-solving process.

To clarify what is meant by problem-solving skills, consider the following example of John and Kristen Smith and their troublesome dishwasher. The Smiths' dishwasher was five years old, and the dishes were no longer coming out clean and sparkling. Analyzing the situation, the Smiths determined that the problem could be related to several possible causes: their use of liquid instead of powdered dish detergent, a bad seal on the door of the dishwasher, ineffective water softener, misloading of the dishwasher, or a defective water heater. Not knowing what the problem was, John thought they should implement all five possible solutions at once. Kristen disagreed, and suggested they address one possible solution at a time to determine the cause. The first solution they tried was to change the dish detergent, but this did not fix the problem. Next, they changed the seal on the door of the dishwasher—and this solved the problem. By addressing the problem carefully and systematically, the Smiths were able to find the cause of the dishwasher malfunction and to save themselves a great deal of money. Their problem-solving strategy was effective.

Strategic Planning

Strategic Planning

A second major kind of conceptual skill is **strategic planning**. Like problem solving, strategic planning is mainly a cognitive activity. A leader needs to be able to think and consider ideas to develop effective strategies for a group or an organization. Being strategic requires developing careful plans of action based on the available resources and personnel to achieve a goal. It is similar to what generals do in wartime: They make elaborate plans of how to defeat the enemy given their resources, personnel, and the mission they need to accomplish. Similarly, athletic coaches take their knowledge of their players and their abilities to create game plans for how to best compete with the opposing team. In short, strategic planning is about designing a plan of action to achieve a desired goal.

In their analysis of research on strategic leadership, Boal and Hooijberg (2000) suggested that strategic leaders need to have the ability to learn, the capacity to adapt, and managerial wisdom. The *ability to learn* includes the capability to absorb new information and apply it toward new goals. It is a willingness to experiment with new ideas and even to accept failures. The *capacity to adapt* is about being able to respond quickly to changes in the environment. A leader needs to be open to and accepting of change. When competitive conditions change, an effective leader will have the capacity to change. Having *managerial wisdom* refers to possessing a deep understanding of the people with whom and the environment in which a leader works. It is about having the good sense to make the right decisions at the right time, and to do so with the best interests of everyone involved.

To illustrate the complexity of strategic planning, consider the following example of how NewDevices, a startup medical supply company, used strategic thinking to promote itself. NewDevices developed a surgical scanner to help surgical teams reduce errors during surgery. Although there were no such scanners on the market at that time, two companies were developing a similar product. The potential market for the product was enormous and included all the hospitals in the United States (almost 8,000 hospitals). Because it was clear that all hospitals would eventually need this scanner, NewDevices knew it was going to be in a race to capture the market ahead of the other companies.

NewDevices was a small company with limited resources, so management was well aware of the importance of strategic planning. Any single mistake could threaten the survival of the company. Because everyone at NewDevices, including the sales staff, owned stock in the company, everyone was strongly motivated to work to make the company succeed. Sales staff members were willing to share effective sales approaches with each other because, rather than being in competition, they had a common goal.

Every Monday morning the management team met for three hours to discuss the goals and directions for the company. Much time was spent on framing the argument for why hospitals needed the NewDevices scanner more than its competitors' scanners. To make this even more challenging, the NewDevices scanner was more expensive than the competition, although it was also safer. NewDevices chose to sell the product by stressing that it could save money in the long run for hospitals because it was safer and would reduce the incidence of malpractice cases.

Managers also developed strategies about how to persuade hospitals to sign on to their product. They contacted hospitals to inquire as to whom they should direct their pitch for the new product. Was it the director of surgical nursing or some other hospital administrator? In addition, they analyzed how they should allocate the company's limited resources. Should they spend more money on enhancing their website? Did they need a director of advertising? Should they hire more sales representatives? All of these questions were the subject of much analysis and debate. NewDevices knew the stakes were very high; if management slipped even once, the company would fail.

This example illustrates that strategic planning is a multifaceted process. By planning strategically, however, leaders and their employees can increase the likelihood of reaching their goals and achieving the aims of the organization.

Creating Vision

Similar to strategic planning, creating vision takes a special kind of cognitive and conceptual ability. It requires the capacity to challenge people with compelling visions of the future. To create vision, a leader needs to be able to set forth a picture of a future that is better than the present, and then move others toward a new set of ideals and values that will lead to the future. A leader must be able to articulate the vision and engage others in its pursuit. Furthermore, the leader needs to be able to implement the vision and model the principles set forth in the vision. A leader with a vision has to "walk the walk," and not just "talk the talk." Building vision is an important leadership skill and one that receives extensive discussion in Chapter 7, "Creating a Vision."

SUMMARY

In recent years, the study of leadership skills has captured the attention of researchers and practitioners alike. Skills are essential to being an effective leader. Unlike traits that are innate, leadership skills are *learned* competencies. Everyone can learn to acquire leadership skills. In this chapter, we considered three types of leadership skills: administrative skills, interpersonal skills, and conceptual skills.

Often thought of as unexciting, *administrative skills* play a primary role in effective leadership. These are the skills a leader needs to run the organization and carry out its purposes. These are the skills needed to plan and organize work. Specifically, administrative skills include managing people, managing resources, and showing technical competence.

A second type of skills is *interpersonal skills*, or people skills. These are the competencies that a leader needs to work effectively with followers, peers, and superiors to accomplish the organization's goals. Research has shown unequivocally that interpersonal skills are of fundamental importance to effective leadership. Interpersonal skills can be divided into being socially perceptive, showing emotional intelligence, and managing interpersonal conflict.

A leader also needs *conceptual skills.* Conceptual skills have to do with working with concepts and ideas. These are cognitive skills that emphasize the thinking ability of a leader. Although these cover a wide array of competencies, conceptual skills in this chapter are divided into problem solving, strategic planning, and creating vision.

In summary, administrative, interpersonal, and conceptual skills play a major role in effective leadership. Through practice and hard work, we can all become better leaders by improving our skills in each of these areas.

GLOSSARY TERMS

administrative skills   118

conceptual skills   125

interpersonal skills   121

problem-solving skills   126

social perceptiveness   121

strategic planning   128

technical competence   120

⑤SAGE edge™

Sharpen your skills with SAGE edge at **edge.sagepub.com/northouseintro4e**

SAGE edge for students provides a personalized approach to help you accomplish your coursework goals in an easy-to-use learning environment.

6.1 CASE STUDY

Sweet Caroline's

It started with cupcakes. As a teacher at Oak Park Elementary, Caroline would often make cupcakes for the school's teachers and staff. Everyone raved about her baking expertise, and a colleague asked Caroline to make cupcakes for her son's birthday party. The treats were such a hit that many of the parents at the party asked Caroline for her phone number, and she quickly found herself baking for multiple parties a week.

After a year of baking for private parties, an opportunity arose for Caroline to take her business to the next level. After a local coffee shop went out of business, Caroline signed a contract for its space and opened Sweet Caroline's, a bakery featuring her cupcakes, muffins, Danish, and other baked goods.

Starting small with birthday parties and graduations and growing to wedding receptions and banquets, Sweet Caroline's quickly became the most sought-after caterer in the city. As the demand for catering cupcakes and cakes outside of regular business hours grew, Caroline expanded her staff and the services they offered. In just five years, Sweet Caroline's morphed from a small bakery into a full-service restaurant and catering company.

Although Caroline had no plans of ever going into business, Sweet Caroline's has been very successful. Caroline is very personable and genuine, which has been instrumental in creating a large and loyal customer base. Furthermore, Caroline's intuitive sense for how to tailor her services to fit the needs of the community has fueled the company's growth. Despite her success, however, Caroline has struggled with certain aspects of running Sweet Caroline's.

Now five years after Sweet Caroline's opened, it has become a highly complex operation to keep organized. Caroline's staff has grown to 40 employees, some who work in the bakery, some in the restaurant, and some in both places. There are five drivers who deliver cupcakes, cakes, and other catered goods to private parties and businesses six days a week. In addition, Caroline runs weekly ads in the local media, on the radio, and on the Web. Her 22-year-old daughter manages the company's Facebook page and Twitter account, which boasts more than 3,000 followers.

Caroline is a skilled baker, but she is finding that the demands of her growing business and client base are creating challenges that are out of her area of expertise. Many of these fall into the administrative area where she hasn't the patience or knowledge to deal with detail-oriented aspects of managing her business.

For example, Dale, Sweet Caroline's delivery driver, is often frustrated because the company does not have a system for how orders are to be delivered throughout the city. Dale worked for another company that had a "zone system" so that each driver delivered all orders in one specific area on a given day. In addition, Caroline has opted not to use computers at her company, so all delivery orders are written by hand and then rewritten on clipboards for the drivers when the order is ready. There are often mistakes including duplicate deliveries or a delivery that gets missed completely.

Caroline also struggles with scheduling. Employees' work schedules are developed the weekend before the start of a workweek so that employees often are unaware of their upcoming shifts. As a result, Sweet Caroline's is constantly understaffed. The food and baked goods are so good that patrons rarely complain about the wait, but staff members get frustrated with the lack of notice regarding their schedules, the lack of staffing, and the stresses these issues cause.

When it comes to catering events, there is often chaos as Caroline chooses to work on food preparation, while leaving staff members, who are not trained to do so, to plan the events, manage client concerns and issues, and execute the event. While the quality of the food is consistently superb, clients are often surprised by the disorganized style of the catering staff. The staff feels it, too; many have commented that they feel like they are "running blind" when it comes to the events because Caroline gives very little direction and is often not around to help when issues arise.

Caroline, however, has a good working rapport with her staff, and they acknowledge that Sweet Caroline's can be a fun place to work. For her part, Caroline knows that working in a bakery can be difficult and demanding, and she consistently praises the efforts and dedication of her staff members. Caroline is also very good about pitching in and working with staff on the production of cupcakes, cakes, and food items, working side-by-side with them on big orders, while providing them with positive encouragement.

Caroline truly enjoys the novelty of being a business owner and handles all the accounting and payroll duties for the company. Unfortunately, this aspect of the job is becoming more demanding, and Caroline spends an increasing amount of time on these duties, leaving more and more of the day-to-day operations and catering to her staff.

Caroline has been approached about opening a second Sweet Caroline's in a neighboring town, and while she would like to build on her success, she already feels overwhelmed at times by her current operation and is not sure she can take on more. But she also knows the opportunity to expand won't last forever.

QUESTIONS

1. Based on the Model of Primary Leadership Skills (Figure 6.1), how would you describe Caroline's skills? In what skills is she strongest, and in what skills is she weakest?

2. Sweet Caroline's bakery and restaurant seemed to emerge out of nowhere. What role did Caroline play in this? Do you think Caroline could improve her business with more strategic planning?

3. Have you ever worked at a place that was very successful but felt quite chaotic and disorganized? How did you handle it?

4. If you were a consultant to Caroline, would you recommend she open a second location? If so, what three specific skills would you have Caroline develop in order to help manage her business better?

6.2 LEADERSHIP SKILLS QUESTIONNAIRE

Purpose

1. To identify your leadership skills
2. To provide a profile of your leadership skills showing your strengths and weaknesses

Directions

1. Place yourself in the role of a leader when responding to this questionnaire.
2. For each of the statements below, circle the number that indicates the degree to which you feel the statement is true.

Statements	Not true	Seldom true	Occasionally true	Somewhat true	Very true
1. I am effective with the detailed aspects of my work.	1	2	3	4	5
2. I usually know ahead of time how people will respond to a new idea or proposal.	1	2	3	4	5
3. I am effective at problem solving.	1	2	3	4	5
4. Filling out forms and working with details come easily for me.	1	2	3	4	5
5. Understanding the social fabric of the organization is important to me.	1	2	3	4	5
6. When problems arise, I immediately address them.	1	2	3	4	5
7. Managing people and resources is one of my strengths.	1	2	3	4	5
8. I am able to sense the emotional undercurrents in my group.	1	2	3	4	5
9. Seeing the big picture comes easily for me.	1	2	3	4	5
10. In my work, I enjoy responding to people's requests and concerns.	1	2	3	4	5
11. I use my emotional energy to motivate others.	1	2	3	4	5
12. Making strategic plans for my company appeals to me.	1	2	3	4	5
13. Obtaining and allocating resources is a challenging aspect of my job.	1	2	3	4	5
14. The key to successful conflict resolution is respecting my opponent.	1	2	3	4	5

Visit **edge.sagepub.com/northouseintro4e** for a downloadable version of this questionnaire.

6.2 LEADERSHIP SKILLS QUESTIONNAIRE

(Continued)

Statements	Not true	Seldom true	Occasionally true	Somewhat true	Very true
15. I enjoy discussing organizational values and philosophy.	1	2	3	4	5
16. I am effective at obtaining resources to support our programs.	1	2	3	4	5
17. I work hard to find consensus in conflict situations.	1	2	3	4	5
18. I am flexible about making changes in our organization.	1	2	3	4	5

Scoring

1. Sum the responses on items 1, 4, 7, 10, 13, and 16 (administrative skill score).

2. Sum the responses on items 2, 5, 8, 11, 14, and 17 (interpersonal skill score).

3. Sum the responses on items 3, 6, 9, 12, 15, and 18 (conceptual skill score).

Total Scores

Administrative skill: _____

Interpersonal skill: _____

Conceptual skill: _____

Scoring Interpretation

The Leadership Skills Questionnaire is designed to measure three broad types of leadership skills: administrative, interpersonal, and conceptual. By comparing your scores, you can determine where you have leadership strengths and where you have leadership weaknesses.

If your score is 26–30, you are in the very high range.

If your score is 21–25, you are in the high range.

If your score is 16–20, you are in the moderate range.

If your score is 11–15, you are in the low range.

If your score is 6–10, you are in the very low range.

Improve Your Leadership Skills

If you have the interactive eBook version of this text, log in to access the interactive leadership assessment. After completing this chapter's questionnaire, you will receive individualized feedback and practical suggestions for further strengthening your leadership based on your responses in this questionnaire.

APPLICATION

6.3 OBSERVATIONAL EXERCISE

Leadership Skills

Purpose

1. To develop an understanding of different types of leadership skills
2. To examine how leadership skills affect a leader's performance

Directions

1. Your task in this exercise is to observe a leader and evaluate that person's leadership skills. This leader can be a supervisor, a manager, a coach, a teacher, a fraternity or sorority officer, or anyone who has a position that involves leadership.
2. For each of the groups of skills listed below, write what you observed about this leader.

Name of leader: _____

Administrative skills	1	2	3	4	5
Managing people	Poor	Weak	Average	Good	Very good
Managing resources	Poor	Weak	Average	Good	Very good
Showing technical competence	Poor	Weak	Average	Good	Very good

Comments:

Interpersonal skills	1	2	3	4	5
Being socially perceptive	Poor	Weak	Average	Good	Very good
Showing emotional intelligence	Poor	Weak	Average	Good	Very good
Managing conflict	Poor	Weak	Average	Good	Very good

Comments:

Visit **edge.sagepub.com/northouseintro4e** for a downloadable version of this exercise.

6.3 OBSERVATIONAL EXERCISE

(Continued)

Conceptual skills	1	2	3	4	5
Problem solving	Poor	Weak	Average	Good	Very good
Strategic planning	Poor	Weak	Average	Good	Very good
Creating vision	Poor	Weak	Average	Good	Very good

Comments:

Questions

1. Based on your observations, what were the leader's strengths and weaknesses?

2. In what setting did this leadership example occur? Did the setting influence the kind of skills that the leader used? Discuss.

3. If you were coaching this leader, what specific things would you tell this leader about how he or she could improve leadership skills? Discuss.

4. In another situation, do you think this leader would exhibit the same strengths and weaknesses? Discuss.

APPLICATION

APPLICATION

6.4 REFLECTION AND ACTION WORKSHEET

Leadership Skills

Reflection

1. Based on what you know about yourself and the scores you received on the Leadership Skills Questionnaire in the three areas (administrative, interpersonal, and conceptual), how would you describe your leadership skills? Which specific skills are your strongest, and which are your weakest? What impact do you think your leadership skills could have on your role as a leader? Discuss.

2. This chapter suggests that emotional intelligence is an interpersonal leadership skill. Discuss whether you agree or disagree with this assumption. As you think about your own leadership, how do your emotions help or hinder your role as a leader? Discuss.

3. This chapter divides leadership into three kinds of skills (administrative, interpersonal, and conceptual). Do you think some of these skills are more important than others in some kinds of situations? Do you think lower levels of leadership (e.g., supervisor) require the same skills as upper levels of leadership (e.g., CEO)? Discuss.

Action

1. One unique aspect of leadership skills is that they can be practiced. List and briefly describe three things you could do to improve your administrative skills.

2. Leaders need to be *socially perceptive*. As you assess yourself in this area, identify two specific actions that would help you become more perceptive of other people and their viewpoints. Discuss.

3. What kind of problem solver are you? Are you slow or quick to address problem situations? Overall, what two things could you change about yourself to be a more effective problem solver?

 Visit **edge.sagepub.com/northouseintro4e** for a downloadable version of this worksheet.

REFERENCES

Bass, B. M. (1990). *Bass & Stogdill's handbook of leadership: Theory, research, and managerial applications* (3rd ed.). New York, NY: Free Press.

Blake, R. R., & McCanse, A. A. (1991). *Leadership dilemmas: Grid solutions.* Houston, TX: Gulf.

Boal, K. B., & Hooijberg, R. (2000). Strategic leadership research: Moving on. *Leadership Quarterly, 11*(4), 515–549.

Caruso, D. R., & Wolfe, C. J. (2004). Emotional intelligence and leadership development. In D. V. Day, S. J. Zaccaro, & S. M. Halpin (Eds.), *Leader development for transforming organizations: Growing leaders for tomorrow* (pp. 237–266). Mahwah, NJ: Erlbaum.

Goleman, D. (1995). *Emotional intelligence.* New York, NY: Bantam Books.

Haverbeck, M. J. (2007, December 19). The making of Coquese Washington: The Lady Lions' new coach goes from humble beginnings in Flint, Mich., to Happy Valley. *BlueWhite Illustrated.* Retrieved June 7, 2013, from http://www.personal.psu.edu/mjh11/CoqueseWashington.html

Katz, R. L. (1955). Skills of an effective administrator. *Harvard Business Review, 33*(1), 33–42.

Lord, R. G., & Hall, R. J. (2005). Identity, deep structure and the development of leadership skill. *Leadership Quarterly, 16*(4), 591–615.

Mann, F. C. (1965). Toward an understanding of the leadership role in formal organization. In R. Dubin, G. C. Homans, F. C. Mann, & D. C. Miller (Eds.), *Leadership and productivity* (pp. 68–103). San Francisco, CA: Chandler.

Mayer, J. D., & Salovey, P. (1995). Emotional intelligence and the construction and regulation of feelings. *Applied and Preventive Psychology, 4*(3), 197–208.

Mayer, J. D., Salovey, P., & Caruso, D. R. (2000). Models of emotional intelligence. In R. J. Sternberg (Ed.), *Handbook of intelligence* (pp. 396–420). Cambridge, MA: Cambridge University Press.

McKenna, K. (2013, March 1). Women's basketball: Coquese Washington transforms program with leadership. *The Daily Collegian.* Retrieved June 7, 2013, from http://collegian.psu.edu/archive/2013/03/01/WE_ARE_Coquese_Washington.aspx

Miller, C. C. (2010, October 10). Why Twitter's C.E.O. demoted himself. *The New York Times,* p. BU1.

Mumford, M. D., Zaccaro, S. J., Connelly, M. S., & Marks, M. A. (2000). Leadership skills: Conclusions and future directions. *Leadership Quarterly, 11*(1), 155–170.

Mumford, T. V., Campion, M. A., & Morgeson, F. P. (2007). The leadership skills strataplex: Leadership skill requirements across organizational levels. *Leadership Quarterly, 18*(2), 154–166.

Nilsen, D. (2009, November 13). Flint Hall inductee Coquese Washington followed folks' advice to explore, excel. *Flint Journal.* Retrieved June 7, 2013, from http://www.mlive.com/sports/flint/index.ssf/2009/11/flint_hall_inductee_coquese_wa.html#

Salovey, P., & Mayer, J. D. (1990). Emotional intelligence. *Imagination, Cognition, and Personality, 9*(3), 185–221.

Yammarino, F. J. (2000). Leadership skills: Introduction and overview. *Leadership Quarterly, 11*(1), 5–9.

Zaccaro, S. J., Gilbert, J., Thor, K. K., & Mumford, M. D. (1991). Leadership and social intelligence: Linking social perceptiveness and behavioral flexibility to leader effectiveness. *Leadership Quarterly, 2*(4), 317–331.

Creating a Vision

INTRODUCTION

An effective leader creates compelling visions that guide people's behavior. In the context of leadership, a **vision** is a mental model of an ideal future state. It offers a picture of what could be. Visions imply change and can challenge people to reach a higher standard of excellence. At the same time, visions are like a guiding philosophy that provides people with meaning and purpose.

In developing a vision, a leader is able to visualize positive outcomes in the future and communicate these to others. Ideally, the leader and the members of a group or an organization share the vision. Although this picture of a possible future may not always be crystal clear, the vision itself plays a major role in how the leader influences others and how others react to his or her leadership.

For the past 25 years, vision has been a major topic in writings on leadership. Vision plays a prominent role in training and development literature. For example, Covey (1991) suggested that vision is one of seven habits of highly

ASK THE
AUTHOR

Why Do I Have to Create a Vision to Become a Leader?

effective people. He argued that effective people "begin with the end in mind" (p. 42), that they have a deep understanding of their goals, values, and mission in life, and that this understanding is the basis for everything they do. Similarly, Loehr and Schwartz (2001), in their full-engagement training program, stressed that people are a mission-specific species, and their goal in life should be to mobilize their sources of energy to accomplish their intended mission. Kouzes and Posner (2003), whose Leadership Practices Inventory is a widely used leadership assessment instrument, identified vision as one of the five practices of exemplary leadership. Clearly, vision has been an important aspect of leadership training and development in recent years.

**Positive Visionary
Leadership**

Vision also plays a central role in many of the common theories of leadership (Zaccaro & Banks, 2001). For example, in transformational leadership theory, vision is identified as one of the four major factors that account for extraordinary leadership performance (Bass & Avolio, 1994). In charismatic leadership theories, vision is highlighted as a key to organizational change (Conger & Kanungo, 1998; House, 1977). Charismatic leaders create change by linking their vision and its values to the self-concept of followers. For example, through her charisma Mother Teresa linked her vision of serving the poor and disenfranchised to her followers' beliefs of personal commitment and self-sacrifice. Some theories are actually titled visionary leadership theories (see Nanus, 1992; Sashkin, 1988, 2004) because vision is their defining characteristic of leadership.

To better understand the role of vision in effective leadership, this chapter will address the following questions: "What are the characteristics of a vision?" "How is a vision articulated?" and "How is a vision implemented?" In our discussion of these questions, we will focus on how you can develop a workable vision for whatever context you find yourself in as a leader.

VISION EXPLAINED

Visionary Leadership

Given that it is essential for a leader to have a vision, how are visions formed? What are the main characteristics of a vision? Research on visionary leadership suggests that visions have five characteristics: a picture, a change, values, a map, and a challenge (Nanus, 1992; Zaccaro & Banks, 2001).

A Picture

A vision creates a **picture** of a future that is better than the **status quo**. It is an idea about the future that requires an act of faith by followers. Visions paint an ideal image of where a group or an organization should be going. It may be an image of a situation that is more exciting, more affirming, or more inspiring. As a rule, these mental images are of a time and place where people are working productively to achieve a common goal. Although it is easier for followers to comprehend a detailed vision, a leader's vision is not always fully developed. Sometimes a leader's vision provides only a general direction to followers or gives limited guidance to them. At other times, a leader may have only a bare-bones notion of where he or she is leading others; the final picture may not emerge for a number of years. Nevertheless, when a leader is able to paint a picture of the future that is attractive and inspiring, it can have significant impact on his or her ability to lead others effectively.

Vision and Organization Change

A Change

Another characteristic of a vision is that it represents a **change** in the status quo, and moves an organization or a system toward something more positive in the future. Visions point the way to new ways of doing things that are better than how things were done in the past. They take the best features of a prior system and strengthen them in the pursuit of a new goal.

Changes can occur in many forms: rules, procedures, goals, values, or rituals, to name a few. Because visions imply change, it is not uncommon for a leader to experience resistance to the articulated vision. Some leaders are even accused of "stirring the pot" when promoting visionary changes. Usually, though, visions are compelling and inspire others to set aside old ways of doing things and to become part of the positive changes suggested by a leader's vision.

Values

A third characteristic of a vision is that it is about **values**, or the ideas, beliefs, and modes of action that people find worthwhile or desirable. To advocate change within a group or an organization requires an understanding of one's own values, the values of others, and the values of the organization. Visions are about changes in those values. For example, if a leader creates a vision that emphasizes that everyone in the company is important, the dominant value being expressed is human dignity. Similarly, if a leader develops a vision that suggests that everyone in the company is equal, the dominant value being expressed is fairness and justice. Visions are grounded in values. They advocate a positive change and movement toward some new set of ideals. In so doing, they must address values.

Inspiring Action Through Values

LEADERSHIP SNAPSHOT

Rosalie Giffoniello, Cofounder, Empower the Children

© Rosalie Giffoniello

When New Jersey schoolteacher Rosalie Giffoniello decided to travel to India in the summer of 1999, she had no idea that one trip would propel her into a life dedicated to educating India's impoverished children.

In India, Giffoniello volunteered for a summer at Daya Dan, Mother Teresa's orphanage for children with disabilities in Kolkata. Using her special education background, she taught some children to feed themselves and walk for the first time. It was then that she made a life-changing decision. "When I went home, I took early retirement from my job, gave away my possessions and returned to Kolkata for good," Giffoniello says (O'Neil, 2004).

She returned to Daya Dan and spent two years working with the Missionaries of Charity to implement programs in language and teaching the children to feed, dress, and bathe themselves.

The next year, she and a friend, Janet Grosshandler, cofounded Empower the Children (ETC), a Jackson, New Jersey–based nonprofit, to raise funds for Daya Dan. At first Giffoniello's work and ETC's funds were channeled toward a number of efforts including an orphanage for boys, a school for the disadvantaged, a home for young adults with mental disabilities, and a tutorial center for teenage girls.

However, when Giffoniello observed that the children with disabilities in the Kolkata orphanages were fed each day and clothed while the homeless "street" children often went without food and the most basic necessities, she decided to broaden ETC's and her own efforts to address the city's poorest and most vulnerable citizens (Empower the Children, 2004).

She began working with Reena Das, a local woman who was educating homeless street urchins during her lunch hour on the steps of a nearby office building. Das provided her students with a healthy snack and introduction to the Bengali and English alphabets (Weir, 2012).

In January 2006, under the auspices of ETC, Giffoniello and Das opened their first school in a single-room slum building, which they named Preyrona, the Bengali word for inspiration. Four years later, they moved the school to a two-story building and incorporated vocational education including sewing instruction for teenage girls and neighborhood women.

Two years after Preyrona 1 opened, they opened a second school, Preyrona 2 School, in a one-room building with a leaky roof and no windows. For the 90 students who attended it, however, it was better than no school at all (Weir, 2012).

Within three years, they opened a third school, this time in a clean three-story building they were able to buy. Housed in this multistoried building, Preyrona 3 opened its doors in January 2009 and provides three separate educational programs for 60 children while also providing vocational programs for older students and their mothers.

Giffoniello teaches at the Preyrona schools, where she has instilled her teaching methodology of self-empowerment and love. In a nation where educators still discipline with a switch, her philosophy was a challenge for some teachers.

"I tell them 'If you love the children, then they'll work for you. They'll want to please you and make you proud. It's our responsibility to give them the right kind of attention,'" Giffoniello explains. "Happy children become smart children. That's why we give the children only love" (Weir, 2012).

ETC's work has attracted many volunteers from different countries and walks of life, who do everything from working on-site in Kolkata, to helping develop curriculum, to raising money in their home countries.

Giffoniello returns to the United States for six months each year, speaking around the country and raising money for ETC. Now more than a decade old, the organization donates funds for teachers' salaries, clothing and hot meals for children, and supplies, and sponsors cultural drama, dance, and art programs in more than a dozen different institutions, including some in the United States, Mexico, and Kenya.

The following example illustrates the centrality of values in visionary leadership. Chris Jones was a new football coach at a high school in a small rural community in the Midwest. When Jones started coaching, there were barely enough players to fill the roster. His vision was to have a strong football program that students liked and that instilled pride in the parents and school community. He valued good physical conditioning, self-discipline, skills in all aspects of the game, esprit de corps, and an element of fun throughout the process. In essence, he wanted a top-notch, high-quality football program.

Over a period of five years, the number of players coming out for football grew from 15 to 95. Parents wanted their kids to go out for football because Jones was such a good coach. Players said they liked the team because Coach Jones treated them as individuals. He was very fair with everyone. He was tough about discipline but also liked to have fun. Practices were always a challenge but seldom dull or monotonous. Because of his program, parents formed their own booster club to support team dinners and other special team activities.

Although Coach Jones's teams did not always win, his players learned lessons in football that were meaningful and long lasting. Coach Jones was an effective coach whose vision promoted individual growth, competence, camaraderie, and community. He had a vision about developing a program around these strong values, and he was able to bring his vision to fruition.

A Map

Vision as a Map

A vision provides a **map**—a laid-out path to follow—that gives direction so followers know when they are on track and when they have slipped off course. People often feel a sense of certainty and calmness in knowing they are on the right course, and a vision provides this assurance. It is also comforting for people to know they have a map to direct them toward their short- and long-term goals.

At the same time, visions provide a guiding philosophy for people that gives them meaning and purpose. When people know the overarching goals, principles, and values of an organization, it is easier for them to establish an identity and know where they fit within the organization. Furthermore, seeing the larger purpose allows people to appreciate the value of their contributions to the organization and to something larger than their own interests. The value of a vision is that it shows others the meaningfulness of their work.

A Challenge

Vision and Conflict

A final characteristic of a vision is that it **challenges** people to transcend the status quo to do something to benefit others. Visions challenge people to commit themselves to worthwhile causes. In his inaugural address in 1961, President John F. Kennedy challenged the American people by saying, "Ask not what your country can do for you—ask what you can do for your country." This challenge was inspiring because it asked people to move beyond self-interest to work for the greater good of the country. Kennedy's vision for America had a huge impact on the country.

An example of an organization that has a vision with a clear challenge component is the Leukemia and Lymphoma Society's Team In Training program. The primary goal of this program is to raise funds for cancer research, public education, and patient aid programs. As a part of Team In Training, participants who sign up to run or walk a marathon (26.2 miles) are asked to raise money for cancer research in return for the personalized coaching and fitness training they receive from Team In Training staff. Since its inception in the late 1980s, the program has raised more than $600 million for cancer research. A recent participant said of Team In Training, "I was inspired to find something I could do both to push myself a little harder and to accomplish something meaningful in the process." When people are challenged to do something good for others, they often become inspired and committed to the task. Whether it is to improve their own group, organization, or community, people like to be challenged to help others.

To summarize, a vision has five main characteristics. First, it is a mental *picture* or image of a future that is better than the status quo. Second, it represents a *change* and points to new ways of doing things. Third, it is grounded in *values*. Fourth, it is a *map* that gives direction and provides meaning and purpose. Finally, it is a *challenge* to change things for the better.

VISION IN PRACTICE

It is one thing for a leader to have a vision for an organization. But making that vision a reality requires communication and action. In this section, we explore how a leader can articulate a vision to others and what specific actions a leader can take to make the vision clear, understandable, and a reality.

Articulating a Vision

Although it is very important for a leader *to have* a vision, it is equally important for a leader to be able *to articulate*—explain and describe—the vision to others. Although some are better than others at this, there are certain ways all leaders can improve the way they communicate their visions.

First, a leader must communicate the vision by *adapting the vision* to his or her audience. Psychologists tell us that most people have a drive for consistency and when confronted with the need to change will do so only if the required change is not too different from their present state (Festinger, 1957). A leader needs to articulate the vision to fit within others' latitude of acceptance by adapting the vision to the audience (Conger & Kanungo, 1987). If the vision is too demanding and advocates too big a change, it will be rejected. If it is articulated in light of the status quo and does not demand too great a change, it will be accepted.

A leader also needs to *highlight the values* of the vision by emphasizing how the vision presents ideals worth pursuing. Presenting the values of the vision helps individuals and group members find their own work worthwhile. It also allows group members to identify with something larger than themselves, and to become connected to a larger community (Shamir, House, & Arthur, 1993).

Explaining a Vision
to Followers

Articulating a vision also requires *choosing the right language*. A leader should use *words and symbols* that are motivating and inspiring (Sashkin, 2004; Zaccaro & Banks, 2001). Words that describe a vision need to be affirming, uplifting, and hopeful, and describe the vision in a way that underscores its worth. The inaugural speech by President John F. Kennedy (see edge.sagepub.com/northouseintro4e) is an example of how a leader used inspiring language to articulate his vision.

Symbols are often adopted by leaders in an effort to articulate a vision and bring group cohesion. A good illustration of this is how, in 1997, the University of Michigan football team and coaching staff chose to use Jon Krakauer's book *Into Thin Air* and "conquering Mount Everest" as a metaphor for what they wanted to accomplish. Krakauer provided a firsthand account of a team's challenging journey up Mount Everest that was successful, although five climbers lost their lives in the process. One of the Michigan coaches said, "It's amazing how many similarities there are between playing football and climbing a mountain. . . . The higher you get on a mountain, the tougher it gets. The longer you play during the season, the harder it gets to keep playing the way you want to play." Throughout the season, the coaches frequently emphasized that achieving great feats required tremendous discipline, perseverance, strength, and teamwork. In the locker room, real climbing hooks and pitons were hung above the door to remind everyone who exited that the mission was to "conquer the mountain"—that is, to win the title. The imagery of mountain climbing in this example was a brilliant way to articulate the vision the coaches had for that season. This imagery proved to be well chosen: The team won the 1997 National Collegiate Athletic Association championship.

Visions also need to be described to others *using inclusive language* that links people to the vision and makes them part of the process. Words such as *we* and *our* are inclusive and better to use than words such as *they* or *them*. The goal of this type of language is to enlist participation of others and build community around a common goal. Inclusive language helps bring this about.

In general, to articulate a vision clearly requires that a leader *adapt the content* to the audience, emphasize the vision's *intrinsic value*, select *words and symbols* that are uplifting, and use language that is *inclusive*. If a leader is able to do these things, he or she will increase the chances that the vision will be embraced and the goal achieved.

Implementing a Vision

In addition to creating and articulating a vision, a leader needs to *implement* the vision. Perhaps the real test of a leader's abilities occurs in the implementation phase of a vision. Implementing a vision requires a great deal of effort by a leader over an extended period. Although some leaders can "talk the talk," leaders who implement the vision "walk the walk." Most important, in implementing a vision the leader must model to others the attitudes, values, and behaviors set forth in the vision. The leader is a living example of the ideals articulated in the vision. For example, if the vision is to promote a deeply humanistic organization, the leader needs to demonstrate qualities such as empathy and caring in every action. Similarly, if the vision is to promote community values, the leader needs to show interest in others and in the common good of the broader community. When a leader is seen *acting out the vision*, he or she builds credibility with others. This credibility inspires people to express the same kind of values.

Implementing a vision also requires a leader to set high performance expectations for others. Setting challenging goals motivates people to accomplish a mission. An example of setting high expectations and worthwhile goals is illustrated in the story of the Marathon of Hope (see Box 7.1). Terry Fox was

**Maintaining
High Standards**

BOX 7.1   Marathon of Hope

Photograph by Ian Muttoo, https://www.flickr.com/photos/20741443@N00/1416171954/CC BY-SA 2.0 https://creativecommons.org/licenses/by-sa/2.0/

Terry Fox was born in Winnipeg, Manitoba, and raised in Port Coquitlam, British Columbia, a community near Vancouver on Canada's west coast. An active teenager involved in many sports, Fox was only 18 years old when he was diagnosed with osteogenic sarcoma (bone cancer). In order to stop the spread of the cancer, doctors amputated his right leg 15 centimeters (6 inches) above the knee in 1977.

While in the hospital, Fox was so overcome by the suffering of other cancer patients—many of them young children—that he decided to run across Canada to raise money for cancer research. He called his journey the Marathon of Hope.

After 18 months and running more than 5,000 kilometers (3,107 miles) to prepare, Fox started his run in St. John's, Newfoundland, on April 12, 1980, with little fanfare. Although it was difficult to garner attention in the beginning, enthusiasm soon grew, and the money collected along his route began to mount. He ran 42 kilometers (26 miles) a day through Canada's Atlantic provinces, through Quebec, and through part of Ontario. It was a journey that Canadians never forgot.

On September 1, 1980, after 143 days and 5,373 kilometers (3,339 miles), Fox was forced to stop running outside Thunder Bay, Ontario, because cancer had appeared in his lungs. An entire nation was saddened when he passed away on June 28, 1981, at the age of 22.

The heroic Canadian was gone, but his legacy was just beginning. To date, more than $600 million has been raised worldwide for cancer research in his name through the annual Terry Fox Run, held in Canada and in countries around the world.

a cancer survivor and amputee who attempted to run across Canada to raise awareness and money for cancer research. Fox had a vision and established an extremely challenging goal for himself and others. He was courageous and determined. Unfortunately, he died before completing his journey, but his vision lives on. Today, the Terry Fox Foundation continues to thrive.

The process of carrying out a vision does not happen rapidly but takes continuous effort. It is a step-by-step process, and not one that occurs all at once. For this reason, it is imperative for a leader's eyes to stay on the goal. By doing so, the leader encourages and supports others in the day-to-day efforts to reach the larger goal. A leader alone cannot implement a vision. The leader must work with others and empower them in the implementation process. It is essential that leaders share the work and collaborate with others to accomplish the goal.

SUMMARY

A competent leader will have a compelling vision that challenges people to work toward a higher standard of excellence. A vision is a mental model of an ideal future state. It provides a *picture* of a future that is better than the present, is grounded in *values*, and advocates *change* toward some new set of ideals. Visions function as a *map* to give people direction. Visions also *challenge* people to commit themselves to a greater common good.

First, an effective leader clearly articulates the vision to others. This requires the leader to adapt the vision to the attitudes and values of the audience. Second, the leader highlights the *intrinsic values* of the vision, emphasizing how the vision presents ideals worth pursuing. Third, a competent leader uses language that is *motivating* and *uplifting* to articulate the vision. Finally, the leader uses *inclusive language* that enlists participation from others and builds community.

A challenge for a leader is to carry out the difficult processes of implementing a vision. To implement a vision, the leader needs to be a living *model* of the ideals and values articulated in the vision. In addition, he or she must *set high performance expectations* for others, and *encourage and empower* others to reach their goals.

GLOSSARY TERMS

challenge   146

change   143

map   146

picture   142

status quo   142

value   143

vision   141

$SAGE edge™

Sharpen your skills with SAGE edge at **edge.sagepub.com/northouseintro4e**

SAGE edge for students provides a personalized approach to help you accomplish your coursework goals in an easy-to-use learning environment.

7.1 CASE STUDY

A Clean Slate

Nick Gibbons was described by his classmates at Columbia University's prestigious School of Journalism as a "hard-core newshound with ink running in his blood." After working as a beat reporter for 10 years, Nick became city editor of a newspaper in a midsized Midwest town of about 100,000, overseeing a large staff of local reporters and writers.

So when the president of the large media group that owned his newspaper asked Nick to come to its headquarters for a meeting, he was excited. Until he heard what was said. The company was going to stop printing daily newspapers, instead publishing digital editions. Nick's newspaper would only be printed three days a week; the other days the news would be delivered in an electronic edition. As a result, 75% of the newspaper's workforce would lose their jobs. As the president witnessed Nick's shock and dismay, he said, "Nick, we think you are the only editor at your newspaper that can make this happen."

On the three-hour drive home, Nick realized that change at the newspaper was inevitable. Newspapers had been losing subscribers and revenue for a decade as readers turned to the Internet to get their news. Digital versions of newspapers were cheaper to produce and deliver. Although he did not like the idea of going digital, Nick knew in his heart that he still believed strongly in the importance of reporting the news and informing the community, no matter the format.

To succeed in taking the newspaper to a digital format, Nick was going to have to change an entrenched culture and belief system about newspapers, not only within his staff but among the public as well. To do this, he had to start from the ground up, creating something entirely new. This would require bringing aboard people who were energized about the future and not mourning the past.

His plan employed a three-prong approach. *First*, he informed the entire newspaper staff that they would lose their current jobs in three months and they would have to reapply for new jobs within the newspaper. The first required qualification was a willingness to "forge the future for local journalism and make a contribution to this movement." If you can't let go of the past, he told his coworkers, then you can't move forward. In the end, almost 80% of the new positions were filled by former staffers whom Nick believed to be the "best and brightest" people the newspaper had.

Second, Nick moved the company's offices out of the building it had been in for 120 years to a smaller, very public space on the first floor of a downtown building. The offices were located on a corner completely sided by windows, the inner workings of the newspaper on display to passersby. Nick wanted the newspaper's operations to be very visible so that it didn't seem like it had just "disappeared."

Nick's *third* approach was what he called a "high forgiveness factor." What they were creating was new and untried, and he knew there would be plenty of missteps along the way. He stressed to his new staffers that he didn't expect perfection, just dedication and determination. For example, one of those missteps was the elimination of the newspaper's exhaustive list of local events, which resulted in a huge community outcry. To correct this, staffers determined they could satisfy the community's frustrations by creating a dedicated website for a local events calendar with event organizers submitting the information electronically. A staff member would oversee college interns in editing the submissions and updating the website.

When the newspaper announced its change to a digital format, the reaction was harsh: Readers canceled subscriptions, and advertisers dropped away like flies. It's been four years since the change, and the newspaper is slowly gaining back readers and experiencing more visits to its website. The sales staff is starting to be successful teaching advertisers how to create digital ads that can reach the right audiences by using behavioral targeting and social media.

QUESTIONS

1. What is Nick Gibbons's vision in this case study? How is it similar to or different from the vision of the owners of the paper? Discuss the unique challenges a leader faces when required to implement a vision of his or her superiors.

2. Why do you think Nick wanted to open the workings of the paper up to the public? How is this related to his vision?

3. Visions usually require changing people's values. What desired changes in values are highlighted by this case study?

4. How well did Nick Gibbons articulate his vision for the paper? If you were in Nick's shoes, how would you articulate your vision in this case?

5. Do you think the newspaper will thrive under Nick's leadership? Why?

7.2 LEADERSHIP VISION QUESTIONNAIRE

Purpose

1. To assess your ability to create a vision for a group or an organization
2. To help you understand how visions are formed

Directions

1. Think for a moment of a work, school, social, religious, musical, or athletic organization of which you are a member. Now, think what you would do if you were the leader and you had to create a vision for the group or organization. Keep this vision in mind as you complete the exercise.
2. Using the following scale, circle the number that indicates the degree to which you agree or disagree with each statement.

Statements	Strongly disagree	Disagree	Neutral	Agree	Strongly agree
1. I have a mental picture of what would make our group better.	1	2	3	4	5
2. I can imagine several changes that would improve our group.	1	2	3	4	5
3. I have a vision for what would make our organization stronger.	1	2	3	4	5
4. I know how we could change the status quo to make things better.	1	2	3	4	5
5. It is clear to me what steps we need to take to improve our organization.	1	2	3	4	5
6. I have a clear picture of what needs to be done in our organization to achieve a higher standard of excellence.	1	2	3	4	5
7. I have a clear picture in my mind of what this organization should look like in the future.	1	2	3	4	5
8. It is clear to me what core values, if emphasized, would improve our organization.	1	2	3	4	5
9. I can identify challenging goals that should be emphasized in my group.	1	2	3	4	5
10. I can imagine several things that would inspire my group to perform better.	1	2	3	4	5

Visit **edge.sagepub.com/northouseintro4e** for a downloadable version of this questionnaire.

7.2 LEADERSHIP VISION QUESTIONNAIRE

(Continued)

Scoring

Sum the numbers you circled on the questionnaire (visioning ability skill).

Total Scores

Visioning ability skill: _____

Scoring Interpretation

The Leadership Vision Questionnaire is designed to measure your ability to create a vision as a leader.

> If your score is 41–50, you are in the very high range.

> If your score is 31–40, you are in the high range.

> If your score is 21–30, you are in the moderate range.

> If your score is 10–20, you are in the low range.

Improve Your Leadership Skills

If you have the interactive eBook version of this text, log in to access the interactive leadership assessment. After completing this chapter's questionnaire, you will receive individualized feedback and practical suggestions for further strengthening your leadership based on your responses in this questionnaire.

APPLICATION

7.3 OBSERVATIONAL EXERCISE

Leadership Vision

Purpose

1. To understand the way visions are constructed by leaders in ongoing groups and organizations

2. To identify strategies that leaders employ to articulate and implement their visions

Directions

1. For this exercise, select two people in leadership positions to interview. They can be leaders in formal or informal positions at work, at school, or in society. The only criterion is that the leader influences others toward a goal.

2. Conduct a 30-minute interview with each leader, by phone or in person. Ask the leaders to describe the visions they have for their organizations. In addition, ask, "How do you *articulate* and *implement* your visions?"

Leader #1 (name) _____

Vision content   Vision articulation   Vision implementation

Leader #2 (name) _____

Vision content   Vision articulation   Vision implementation

Questions

1. What differences and similarities did you observe between the two leaders' visions?

2. Did the leaders advocate specific values? If yes, what values?

3. Did the leaders use any unique symbols to promote their visions? If yes, what symbols?

4. In what ways did the leaders' behaviors model their visions to others?

Visit **edge.sagepub.com/northouseintro4e** for a downloadable version of this exercise.

7.4 REFLECTION AND ACTION WORKSHEET

Leadership Vision

Reflection

1. Stephen Covey (1991) contended that effective leaders "begin with the end in mind." These leaders have a deep understanding of their own goals and mission in life. How would you describe your own values and purpose in life? In what way is your leadership influenced by these values?

2. Creating a vision usually involves trying to change others by persuading them to accept different values and different ways of doing things. Are you comfortable influencing people in this way? Discuss.

3. As we discussed in this chapter, effective visions can be articulated with strong symbols. How do you view yourself as being able to do this? Are you effective at generating language and symbols that can enhance a vision and help make it successful?

Action

1. Based on your score on the Leadership Vision Questionnaire, how do you assess your ability to create a vision for a group? Identify specific ways you could improve your abilities to create and carry out visions with others.

2. Good leaders *act out the vision.* Describe what ideals and values you act out or could act out as a leader.

3. Take a few moments to think about and describe a group or an organization to which you belong presently or belonged in the past. Write a brief statement describing the vision you would utilize if you were the leader of this group or organization.

 Visit **edge.sagepub.com/northouseintro4e** for a downloadable version of this worksheet.

REFERENCES

Bass, B. M., & Avolio, B. J. (1994). *Improving organizational effectiveness through transformational leadership.* Thousand Oaks, CA: Sage.

Conger, J. A., & Kanungo, R. N. (1987). Toward a behavioral theory of charismatic leadership in organizational settings. *Academy of Management Review, 12*(4), 637–647.

Conger, J. A., & Kanungo, R. N. (1998). *Charismatic leadership in organizations.* Thousand Oaks, CA: Sage.

Covey, S. R. (1991). *Principle-centered leadership.* New York, NY: Simon & Schuster.

Empower the Children. (2004). *How one person made a difference.* Retrieved June 8, 2013, from http://www.etc-empowerchildren.org/Organization.htm#OnePerson

Festinger, L. (1957). *A theory of cognitive dissonance.* Stanford, CA: Stanford University Press.

House, R. J. (1977). A 1976 theory of charismatic leadership. In J. G. Hunt & L. L. Larson (Eds.), *Leadership: The cutting edge* (pp. 189–207). Carbondale: Southern Illinois University Press.

Kouzes, J. M., & Posner, B. Z. (2003). *The leadership challenge* (3rd ed.). San Francisco, CA: Jossey-Bass.

Loehr, J., & Schwartz, T. (2001). *The power of full engagement: Managing energy, not time, is the key to high performance and personal renewal.* New York, NY: Simon & Schuster.

Nanus, B. (1992). *Visionary leadership: Creating a compelling sense of direction for your organization.* San Francisco, CA: Jossey-Bass.

O'Neil, J. (2004, February 1). Going global: Want to see the world—and help kids read at the same time? These NEA-Retired members are continuing a lifetime of public service—while seeing the world with new eyes. *NEA Today.* Retrieved August 21, 2013, from http://www.accessmylibrary.com/coms2/summary_0286-20297851_ITM

Sashkin, M. (1988). The visionary leader. In J. A. Conger & R. N. Kanungo (Eds.), *Charismatic leadership: The elusive factor in organizational effectiveness* (pp. 122–160). San Francisco, CA: Jossey-Bass.

Sashkin, M. (2004). Transformational leadership approaches: A review and synthesis. In J. Antonaki, A. T. Cianciolo, & R. J. Sternberg (Eds.), *The nature of leadership* (pp. 171–196). Thousand Oaks, CA: Sage.

Shamir, B., House, R. J., & Arthur, M. B. (1993). The motivational effects of charismatic leadership: A self-concept based theory. *Organization Science, 4*(4), 577–594.

Weir, R. M. (2012, February). Empowering Calcutta's children. *Encore Magazine,* pp. 35–37.

Zaccaro, S. J., & Banks, D. J. (2001). Leadership, vision, and organizational effectiveness. In S. J. Zaccaro & R. J. Klimoski (Eds.), *The nature of organizational leadership: Understanding the performance imperatives confronting today's leaders* (pp. 181–218). San Francisco, CA: Jossey-Bass.

Establishing a Constructive Climate

INTRODUCTION

As discussed in earlier chapters, a leader needs to attend to tasks and to people. A leader also has to have a vision that he or she can express and implement. Equally important, a leader must be able to *establish a constructive climate* for the people in a group or an organization.

ASK THE
AUTHOR

What Is a Climate and What Does It Mean for Leadership?

CONSTRUCTIVE CLIMATE EXPLAINED

Climate refers to the atmosphere of a team or an organization. It is defined as people's shared perceptions of the way things are in an organization (Reichers & Schneider, 1990). Related to climate are the rituals, values, procedures, and underlying assumptions of a group (Schein, 2010). It is the shared perception individuals have about the activities, procedures, and assumptions of a group. A positive climate is shaped by the degree to which people feel they are supported, appreciated, and encouraged for their roles in the organization. A constructive climate is just that: an atmosphere that promotes group members' satisfaction and achieving their personal best.

Establishing a constructive climate demands that a leader provide structure, clarify norms, build cohesiveness, and promote standards of excellence. By establishing a constructive climate for the group, a leader ensures that members work more effectively together.

When a leader creates a constructive climate, he or she helps group members perform at their highest levels of excellence (Larson & LaFasto, 1989).

Transformational Leadership in Groups

CLIMATE IN PRACTICE

In order to create a constructive climate, a leader needs to consider four factors: providing structure, clarifying norms, building cohesiveness, and promoting standards of excellence.

Providing Structure

Because working in groups can be chaotic and challenging, it is helpful when a leader provides a sense of **structure** for group members. Providing structure is much like giving group members an architectural blueprint for their work. The drawing gives form and meaning to the purposes of the group's activities. Instilling structure into the organization provides people with a sense of security, direction, and stability. It helps them to understand where they fit in and what goals they need to accomplish. For example, it would be frightening to be in a group climbing Mount Everest if team members did not know their roles and follow a clear plan for the ascent. Working in a group *without* structure is more difficult for everyone involved.

How does a leader give structure to a group? First, a leader needs to communicate to the group the group's goals. When a leader gives a clear picture of assignments and responsibilities, group members gain a better sense of direction. For example, soldiers in the military are given orders to carry out a specific **mission**. The mission is the goal toward which they are working, and it provides organization to the rest of their activities. Another example is a group meeting where the leader provides an agenda.

In most college classrooms on the first day of class, professors hand out and discuss syllabi. Going over the syllabus is important to students because it provides information about the structure of the class. The syllabus also gives details about the professor, the course objectives, reading and writing assignments, tests, attendance requirements, and exam schedules. Some professors even include a calendar of lecture topics for each week to help students prepare more effectively. The syllabus sets the tone for the class by giving a structure for what will be accomplished. Students usually leave the first class feeling confident about what the class is going to be like and what will be required of them.

A leader also provides structure by identifying the unique ways that each individual member can contribute to the group. The leader helps followers understand their roles within the group and how to be productive group members. Effective groups use the talents of each individual and, as a result, accomplish a great deal. This is known as **synergy**, when the group outcome is greater than the sum of the individual contributions. The challenge for a leader is to find how each individual group member can contribute to the group's mission, and to encourage the group to recognize these contributions. For example, some people are good at generating ideas, while others are skilled at building consensus. Additionally, some people are good at setting agendas, and others are adept at making sure the proper supplies are available at meetings. Each person has a distinctive talent and can make a unique contribution. Effective leaders know how to discover these talents to benefit the entire group. (See Chapter 3, "Engaging Strengths," for an extended discussion of how leaders can help followers capitalize on their strengths.)

Clarifying Norms

In addition to structuring the group, a leader needs to clarify group norms. **Norms** are the rules of behavior that are established and shared by group members. Social psychologists have argued for years that norms play a major role in the performance and effectiveness of groups (Cartwright & Zander, 1968; Harris & Sherblom, 2007; Napier & Gershenfeld, 2004). Norms are like a road map for navigating how we are supposed to behave in a group. They tell us what is appropriate or inappropriate, what is right or wrong, and what is allowed or not allowed (Schein, 1969). Norms do not emerge on their own—they are the outcome of people interacting with each other and with the leader. For example, in a daylong training seminar, the participants and seminar leader might mutually decide that everyone will turn off their cell phones and no one will leave early. Or staff members in an insurance agency might determine that a "business casual" dress code is appropriate during the week and jeans are OK on Fridays. Norms emerge as a result of how leaders treat followers and followers treat each other.

The reason norms are important is because they have such a strong impact on how the group functions and whether the group is successful or not. For

Structure

example, a classroom setting with an established norm that students do not raise their hands or offer comments to the discussion can be very boring. A weekly staff meeting where people are allowed to constantly whisper with the person next to them will create an atmosphere that lacks cohesiveness and most likely be very unproductive. On the positive side, when a norm of helping others with their work develops in a small business setting, it can be very helpful and inspiring. Leaders need to be aware that norms always exist, and even when they are subtle or not verbally expressed, they do impact the productivity of the group.

Understanding Norms

A leader can have a significant impact on establishing group norms as well as recognizing norms and working to make them constructive. When a leader brings about constructive norms, it can have a positive effect on the entire group. The following example illustrates how a leader positively influences group norms. Home from college for the summer, Matt Smith was asked to take over as coach of his little brother's baseball team because the previous coach was leaving. Before taking over coaching the team, Matt observed several practices and became aware of the norms operating on the team. Among other things, he observed that team members frequently arrived 15 to 30 minutes late for practice, they often came without their baseball shoes or gloves, and they goofed off a lot during drills. Overall, Matt observed that the kids did not seem to care about the team or have much pride in what they were doing. Matt knew that coaching this team was going to be a real challenge.

After Matt had coached for a few weeks, the team's norms gradually changed. Matt continually stressed the need to start practice on time, encouraged players to "bring their stuff" to practice, and complimented players when they worked hard during drills. By the end of the summer, they were a different team. Players grew to enjoy the practice sessions, they worked hard, and they performed well. Most important, they thought their baseball team was "the greatest."

In this situation, the norms the players were operating under with the old coach interfered with the team and its goals. Under Matt's leadership, the players developed new norms that enabled them to function better.

Norms are an important component of group functioning. They develop early in a group and are sometimes difficult to change. A leader should pay close attention to norm development and try to shape norms that will maximize group effectiveness.

Building Cohesiveness

The third way a leader establishes a constructive climate is to build cohesiveness. Cohesiveness is often considered an elusive but essential component of highly functioning groups. **Cohesiveness** is described as a sense of "we-ness," the cement that holds a group together, or the esprit de corps that exists within a group. Cohesiveness allows group members to express their personal viewpoints, give and receive feedback, accept opinions different from their own, and feel comfortable doing meaningful work (Corey & Corey, 2006). When a group is cohesive, the members feel a special connection with each other and with the group as a whole. Members appreciate the group, and in turn are appreciated by the group. Group members identify with the group and its goals and find satisfaction in being an accepted member of the group.

Cohesiveness has been associated with a number of positive outcomes for groups (see Table 8.1) (Cartwright, 1968; Shaw, 1976). First, high cohesiveness is frequently associated with *increased participation* and *better interaction* among members. People tend to talk more readily and listen more carefully in cohesive groups. They also are more likely to express their own opinion and be open to listening to the opinions of others.

Second, in highly cohesive groups, membership tends to be more *consistent*. Members *develop positive feelings toward one another* and *are more willing to attend* group meetings. For example, in an Alcoholics Anonymous group that is cohesive, members often express strong support for each other, and attendance at meetings is very consistent.

Third, highly cohesive groups are able to exert a *strong influence* on group members. Members *conform more closely to group norms* and *engage in more goal-directed behavior* for the group. On a highly successful cross-country track team, all the members support each other and push one another to do their personal best.

Fourth, *member satisfaction is high* in cohesive groups; members tend to feel more secure and find enjoyment participating in the group. Think of the best

Team Cohesiveness

TABLE 8.1   Positive Outcomes of Cohesive Groups

- There is increased participation from members.
- There is better interaction among members.
- Group membership is more consistent.
- Members develop positive feelings toward one another.
- Members are more willing to attend group meetings.
- Members influence each other.
- Members conform more closely to group norms.
- Group behavior is more goal directed.
- Member satisfaction is high.
- Members are more productive.

Sources: Cartwright, 1968; Shaw, 1976.

class you have ever been in as a student. It was probably very cohesive, and you probably enjoyed it so much that you were sorry when the semester ended.

Finally, members of a cohesive group usually are *more productive* than members of a group that is less cohesive. Members of groups with greater cohesion can direct their energies toward group goals without spending a lot of time working out interpersonal issues and conflicts. For example, when a project team is cohesive, there are no social loafers. Everyone is together in pursuit of the team goals.

As described by Daniel Brown in his book, *Boys in the Boat*, the University of Washington rowing team is a good example of how a group of disparate individuals built a cohesive climate and experienced success because of it. Rowing is a sport in which every member of the nine-member team must be in perfect synergy with his teammates as they oar in and move across the water. The sons of loggers, shipyard workers, and farmers, the UW team defeated elite rivals first from eastern and British universities and finally the German crew rowing for Adolf Hitler in the 1936 Olympic Games in Berlin, Germany. Pivotal to their success was that each member of the team had a role and adapted to those roles in sync with one another. "All were merged into one smoothly working machine; they were, in fact, a poem of motion, a symphony of swinging blades" (Brown, 2013, p. 249).

In addition, the team members shared a common goal, which led them to abandon their own self-interest in pursuit of the unified goal of winning. But ultimately it was the trust they had in each other that made them a victorious team.

Given the positive outcomes of cohesiveness, how can a leader help groups become cohesive? Group cohesiveness does not develop instantaneously, but is created gradually over time. A leader can assist a group in building cohesiveness by incorporating the following actions in his or her leadership:

Cohesiveness in Multicultural Organizations

- Help groups to create a climate of trust
- Invite group members to become active participants
- Encourage passive or withdrawn members to become involved
- Be willing to listen and accept group members for who they are
- Help group members to achieve their individual goals
- Promote the free expression of divergent viewpoints in a safe environment
- Allow group members to share the leadership responsibilities
- Foster and promote member-to-member interaction instead of only leader-to-follower interaction (Corey & Corey, 2006)

When a leader is able to do some of the things described on this list, it increases the chance that the group will build a sense of cohesiveness.

Consider the following example of a service-learning group of five students who had a goal of raising money for Special Olympics by sponsoring a rock concert. The group included *John*, a student who was hard of hearing, and who felt alienated and excluded from college life; *Emily*, an energetic student with high hopes of earning an A in the class; *Bill*, an older student with very definite opinions; *Abby*, a free spirit with a strong interest in rock bands; and *Dane*, a talented student who resented having to work with others on a group project.

During its initial meetings, the group was very disjointed and had low group cohesion. The two people in the group with musical talent (Emily and Abby) thought they would have to do all of the work to put on the concert to raise $200. John never spoke, and Bill and Dane had attitudes that put them on the sidelines. During these early meetings, the group members were unenthusiastic and had negative feelings about each other. However, after the professor for the class encouraged Emily to reach out to John and try to include him in the group, a gradual change started to take place, and the group began moving in a more positive direction. Emily found it difficult to communicate with John because he could only hear if people spoke directly into a special hand-held microphone. Emily spent an hour or so with John outside the group and soon established a meaningful association with him. At the same time, Bill, who initially was certain that John could not contribute to the group, started to change his mind when he saw how well Emily and John were getting along. Since Emily was talking to John through the microphone, Bill thought he should try it, too.

Because Abby knew people in three local bands, she put her energies into finding a good band to play for their concert. When John, who was an engineering student, came up with the idea of making posters and handing out flyers to advertise the concert, the energies in the group became focused. Within two weeks of John's offer, the group had completed a massive promotion throughout the community. The rekindled energies of John, Bill, and Dane were put to good use, and the group far exceeded its previous expectations.

By the end of the project, the group had raised $450 for Special Olympics, and walked away as friends. John claimed that this group project was one of the most meaningful experiences in his college education. Dane wanted to take credit for knowing the most people who came to the concert. Bill was ecstatic that the group had far exceeded his expectations. Abby was pleased to have hired the band and that the concert was a great hit, and Emily was proud of her leadership and the success of the group.

The service-learning group in the above example was a group with low cohesion when it started, but was highly cohesive by the end of the project. Cohesiveness was created because group members developed trust, and withdrawn and passive members were encouraged to participate and become involved. Group members learned to listen and respect one another's opinions, and to accept each other as unique people. From this example, the lesson for leaders is to help their group to build cohesiveness. When they do, the results can far exceed expectations.

Promoting Standards of Excellence

Leading a High-Performance Team

Finally, a leader establishes a constructive climate by promoting **standards of excellence**. In a classic study, Larson and LaFasto (1989) analyzed the characteristics of 75 highly successful teams. Included in their study were famous teams such as the DeBakey-Cooley cardiac surgery team, the *Challenger* disaster investigation team, the 1966 Notre Dame championship football team, and even the McDonald's Chicken McNugget team. In their analysis, researchers found that standards of excellence were a crucial factor associated with team success.

What are standards of excellence? These standards are the expressed and implied expectations for performance that exist within a group or an organization. Standards of excellence include six factors that are essential for members to function effectively:

1. What group members need to know and what skills they need to acquire

2. How much initiative and effort they need to demonstrate

3. How group members are expected to treat one another

4. The extent to which deadlines are significant

5. What goals they need to achieve

6. What the consequences are if they achieve or fail to achieve these goals (Larson & LaFasto, 1989, p. 95)

In essence, standards of excellence refer to the established benchmarks of desired performance for a group. A good example of standards of excellence can be seen in the slogan (see Figure 8.1) of The Upjohn Company, a pharmaceutical manufacturing firm in Kalamazoo, Michigan. Founded in 1885, Upjohn was known for revolutionizing the drug industry through its invention of the "friable pill," which can crumble under the pressure of a person's thumb. In addition to this innovation, over the years Upjohn made many other drug discoveries, and grew to become one of the largest pharmaceutical companies

FIGURE 8.1   Standard of Excellence Slogan

Sources: Used as Courtesy of the WMU Archives and Regional History Collections

in the world. For many years, the internal slogan promoted throughout the company was "Keep the quality up."

"Keep the quality up" captures the essence of what standards of excellence are all about. This slogan is clear, direct, and forceful. It puts responsibility on employees to work toward maintaining quality—a standard of excellence. The slogan strongly suggests that employees should work consistently toward these standards over time. In addition, "Keep the quality up" stresses a positive expectation that has value for both employees and the company; quality is the valued benchmark of the company's desired performance for its employees.

Based on studies of more than 600 team leaders and 6,000 team members, LaFasto and Larson (2001) identified several specific ways that a leader can influence performance and promote standards of excellence. To influence performance, the authors contend that a leader must stress the "three *R*s": (1) *Require* results, (2) *Review* results, and (3) *Reward* results.

1.   Require results. A leader needs to articulate clear, concrete expectations for team members. Working together, a leader and team members should establish mutual goals and identify specific objectives for achieving the results associated with those goals. Without clear expectations, team members flounder and are uncertain about what is required of them. They are unsure what results they are expected to achieve. Requiring results is the critical first step in managing performance (LaFasto & Larson, 2001).

Requiring Results

For example, students in a research course were expected to form a group with four or five of their classmates and work together to complete a "utilization project" by the end of the course. Although the professor had a clear idea of what she wanted students to accomplish, students had no idea what

LEADERSHIP SNAPSHOT

Meg Whitman, CEO, Hewlett Packard Enterprise

© epa european pressphoto
agency b.v. / Alamy Stock Photo.

When Meg Whitman took over as CEO of Hewlett-Packard (HP) in 2011, she was walking into a company that could best be described as "a complete mess" (Winkler, 2012).

HP was once the undisputed ruler of Silicon Valley, rising from its humble beginnings in a one-car garage to becoming a technology giant that produced computers, software, printers, and other information technology services and products. Even though it is the world's largest tech company with $120 billion in annual revenue and 330,000 employees, the company has spiraled downward in the past decade, creating a revolving door of CEOs that began in 1999.

Whitman was the fourth new CEO for HP in less than a decade. A graduate of both Princeton and Harvard universities, she has an impressive track record. As eBay's CEO, she marshaled its growth into an online auction giant that went from sales of $86 million her first year to $7.7 billion a decade later, when Whitman stepped down as CEO. After an unsuccessful run for the California governor's office in 2010, Whitman, who was serving on

HP's board of directors, was asked to run the struggling company.

Described as blunt, folksy, and persistent, Whitman's leadership style harkens back to that of HP's original founders, William Hewlett and David Packard. During their reign, the company created a culture known as The HP Way, which emphasized integrity, teamwork, and innovation and resulted in the deep employee loyalty. But after the founders left and subsequent leadership changes, that revered culture slipped away.

While Whitman knows in today's competitive tech world she can't re-create the culture that was, she is intent on reviving the integrity, innovation, and loyalty from those earlier days. Known as being informal, she is the antithesis of the executive. Her first move was to remove the barbed wire and locked gates that separated executive parking from the general employee lot. "We should enter the building the same way everyone else does," she says (Anders, 2013). Inside, Whitman removed executive vice presidents from their plush offices, including herself, and placed them in cubicles. "This is not a fancy pants kind of company," she says (Vance & Ricadela, 2013).

Described as a being "decisive without being abrasive, persuasive without being slick," Whitman is a team builder who is aiming to fix the hundreds of small problems that riddle the company rather than looking for one miracle acquisition or cure. "Problems are good, as long as you solve them quickly," she says (Anders, 2013).

Inside her organization, she preaches frugality and humility. When HP rival Dell was awarded a $350 million order for Microsoft Bing, Whitman was on the phone to the Microsoft CEO to ask why. "Tell me where we came up short," Whitman asked. "Don't sugarcoat it, I'd like to know so we can do better next time." What resulted was a multipage memo that listed nine ways HP had fallen short. Whitman didn't take that as an insult—she saw it as a battle plan (Anders, 2013).

"Run to the fire, don't hide from it," she tells employees.

Externally, Whitman has personally reached out to the company's customers and partners, traveling to more than 300 one-on-one meetings and 42 roundtable chats in one year alone. At those meetings she heard complaints and problems, and worked quickly to solve a number of those back in Silicon Valley. "She's made herself more available than her predecessor ever did," said one customer (Anders, 2013). "There's quite a bit of pride in being part of something that means so much to the Valley and this country. It's a nice company. Nice people," she says (Anders, 2013).

Whitman admits that what attracted her to the job was the opportunity to revive an iconic company. And while many felt she achieved that, Whitman now sees the company's future in innovating its services, which harkens back to the company's early days of leading the computer revolution. In 2014, she split the company into two companies: HP Inc., which is the printer and PC side of the business, and Hewlett Packard Enterprise (HPE), an information technology unit catering to business customers. Whitman is now the head of HPE, leading the company in a new direction.

a utilization project was or how to go about developing it. After a number of students expressed frustration at the lack of clear guidelines, the professor explained that a utilization project involved taking findings from a research study and applying them to a real-world situation. She developed evaluation criteria for the project that outlined what students were supposed to do, the level of depth required for the project, and the key elements of the project that needed to be reported in the evaluation paper. With these explicit instructions, students' anxiety about the utilization project decreased, and they were able to work more effectively in their groups.

In this example, the professor initially required results that were unclear. When she clarified her expectations, the students were able to produce the results. Giving clear objectives and instructions is the first step to high-quality performance.

Reviewing Performance

2. Review results. In addition to requiring results, a leader needs to review results. According to LaFasto and Larson (2001), a leader does this by giving constructive feedback and resolving performance issues.

Giving constructive feedback is a must for a leader if he or she is going to help group members maintain standards of excellence (see Table 8.2). Constructive feedback is honest and direct communication about a group member's performance. It is not mean-spirited or paternalistic, nor is it overly nice or patronizing. Constructive feedback helps group members know if they are doing the right things, in the right way, at the right speed. Although it is not easy to do, giving constructive feedback is a skill that everyone can learn. When done correctly, constructive feedback allows group members to look at themselves honestly and know what they need to maintain or improve (LaFasto & Larson, 2001).

Consider the following example of two restaurant managers (Managers A and B) and their waitstaff. Manager A was known for being very blunt and sometimes even mean. Although he wanted the best for the restaurant, his performance reviews were always disasters. Manager A was brutally honest; he did not know how to be diplomatic. If a server was slow or inefficient, he let the person know it in no uncertain terms. In fact, staff members often thought Manager A was attacking them. Although Manager A wanted people to perform well, he did not know how to make that behavior happen. As he frequently told his employees, "Around this place, I don't sugarcoat anything. If your performance is poor, you're going to hear about it!"

In contrast, Manager B was very careful in how she treated the waitstaff. Manager B cared about staff, and it showed in how she did performance reviews. If waitstaff did something wrong, Manager B would always comment on it, but never in a mean way. When giving praise or criticism, the feedback was always objective and never extreme; the feedback never attacked the person. Manager B consistently evaluated her staff, but always in a way that made them feel better about themselves and that made them want to try harder.

Manager A and Manager B were very different in how they gave feedback to their staff. Manager A's feedback was destructive and debilitating, while Manager B's feedback was constructive and helped to improve performance. As a result, the waitstaff liked working for Manager B and disliked working for Manager A. Staff performed better when Manager B was in charge and worse when Manager A was in charge.

Resolving performance issues is the second part of reviewing results. LaFasto and Larson (2001) found that, more than anything else, the distinguishing characteristic of effective leaders was their willingness to confront and

TABLE 8.2   Tips for Giving Constructive Feedback

People benefit greatly from feedback that is delivered in a nonconfrontational, constructive manner. Unfortunately, not many of us have the innate skill for delivering feedback this way. There are, however, some simple communication methods that can improve your ability to provide constructive feedback.

1. Address behaviors.
Use facts to describe the behavior that is problematic, rather than focusing on personal traits. For example, a leader might say, "Jane, I have noticed that you have been late for the past three mornings. Can you explain why?" rather than "Why aren't you able to arrive on time?"
2. Describe specifically what you have observed.
Observations are what you have seen occur; an interpretation is your analysis or opinion of what has occurred. By telling the person what you have seen and not what you think of what you have seen, you provide observations that are more factual and less judgmental. For example, a leader might say, "Dan, I noticed and highlighted several factual and grammatical errors in the report you submitted," rather than "Dan, all these mistakes make me wonder if you were doing this report at the last minute."
3. Use "I" language.
Employing "I" statements rather than "you" statements will help reduce the defensiveness of the person you are addressing. For example, if you say, "Joe, because our cubicles are so close together I have a hard time concentrating when you play music on your computer," rather than "It is really inconsiderate of you to play music when other people are trying to work," you are more likely to elicit the change you would like.
4. Give the feedback in calm, unemotional language.
Avoid "need to" phrases (e.g., "You need to improve this . . .") or using a tone that implies anger, frustration, or disappointment. Rather than saying, "If you'd just learn the software, you'd do a better job," a leader should say, "I am sure you will be much faster now that you understand how to use this software."
5. Check to ensure clear communication has occurred.
Solicit feedback from the other person to ensure he or she understands what you have been trying to communicate to him or her. For example, a leader might say, "Ann, do you know the procedure for ordering the supplies? Can you go over it to be sure I covered everything?" rather than "Ann, you got all that, didn't you?"

resolve inadequate performance by team members. Clearly, individuals in groups want their leaders to keep other group members "on track." If some group members are slacking off, or not doing their part, the leader needs to address the situation.

Giving Feedback

Working in groups is a collective effort—everyone must be involved. Group members are interdependent, and all members share the responsibility of trying to achieve group goals. When some members do not pull their own weight, it affects everyone in the group. This is why a leader must address the inadequate performance of any group members. If the leader fails to do so, contributing group members will feel angry and slighted, as if their work does not really matter.

Confronting inadequate performance by group members is a challenging and emotionally charged process that requires much of leaders (LaFasto & Larson, 2001). It is not easy, but it is a necessary part of leadership. An effective leader is proactive and confronts problems when they occur. In problem situations, a leader has to communicate with low-performing group members and explain how their behaviors hinder the group from meeting its goals. The leader also has to explain what needs to be done differently. After the changes have been clearly identified, the leader needs to monitor the behaviors of the low-performing group members. If the group members make satisfactory changes, they can remain in the group. If a group member refuses to change, the leader needs to counsel him or her about leaving the group. When a leader addresses behavioral problems in a timely fashion, it is beneficial both to the person with the performance problem and to the entire group.

An example of a performance review can be seen in the story of Sam Wilson, a principal at a private, suburban high school. Sam is a highly effective leader who is respected by students, teachers, and parents of his school. As principal, he is responsible for hiring all the teachers at the school. During one fall semester, Sam noticed that Michelle Long, a teacher he had hired to teach geometry, appeared to be slacking off in her work. Michelle was coming to work late, was skipping faculty meetings, and did not seem very excited about teaching. Seeing that she was underperforming, Sam called Michelle into his office to discuss his concerns. During the meeting, Sam described thoroughly his concerns about Michelle's work and asked Michelle to give her point of view on these concerns. After a long discussion, Sam identified several changes Michelle needed to make if she wanted to continue to teach at the high school.

Following the meeting, Michelle temporarily changed her behavior. She came to school on time, attended some of the faculty meetings, and improved her teaching plans. This positive behavior lasted for about a month, and then she fell back into her old habits. In March, when Sam gave Michelle her annual performance review, he told her that her teaching contract would not be renewed for the following year. Although Michelle was not pleased, she understood why she was being let go.

In the ensuing months, Michelle finished the school year and then found a job at another school. While letting Michelle go was not easy, Sam was comfortable with what he had done. Although some teachers at the school were surprised that Michelle had been let go, they also expressed some relief because they realized that her work was not up to the standards of the school.

3. Reward results. Finally, an effective leader rewards group members for achieving results (LaFasto & Larson, 2001). Many of the behaviors required to be an effective leader are abstract (such as establishing norms) and challenging (such as building group cohesion). However, that is not the case when it comes to rewarding results. Rewarding results is a very practical, straightforward process. It is something that every leader can do.

In their well-known consulting work on leadership effectiveness, Kouzes and Posner (2002) claimed that rewarding results is one of the five major practices of exemplary leaders. They argued that a leader needs to recognize the contributions of group members and express appreciation for individual excellence. This includes paying attention to group members, offering them encouragement, and giving them personalized appreciation. These expressions can be dramatic, such as a dinner celebration, or simple, such as a short email of praise. When a leader recognizes group members and gives encouragement, members feel valued, and there is a greater sense of group identity and community spirit.

A good example of how to effectively reward performance can be seen in how the leader of a nonprofit organization rewarded one of its members, Christopher Wolf. Christopher was an active member of the board who willingly shared his insights and expertise for 15 consecutive years. To show appreciation for his work, the board president had T-shirts made that characterized Christopher's contributions. On the front of the shirt was a caricature of a wolf in sheep's clothing symbolizing Christopher's many positive contributions to the board. On the back of the shirt were the words "The Wolf Pack" and a list of the names of each of the other board members. Both Christopher and each member of the board were given a shirt, which was a big hit with everyone. Although the shirts were simple and inexpensive, they were a unique way of positively recognizing Christopher and all his fellow board members.

SUMMARY

Establishing a constructive climate is a subtle but essential aspect of effective leadership that plays a major role in whether groups or organizations function effectively. Establishing a constructive climate is similar to creating a positive climate for workers in a company. It requires that a leader *provide structure, clarify norms, build cohesiveness,* and *promote standards of excellence.*

A leader *provides structure* by establishing concrete goals, giving explicit assignments, and making responsibilities clear. Helping each group member feel included and know that he or she contributes to the overall goals of the group also provides structure.

Facilitative Leadership

A leader plays a significant role in helping to develop positive *group norms.* Effective groups establish positive norms that allow them to work productively. When norms for a group are negative or unproductive, the leader needs to help group members to change and develop new norms. By assisting groups in establishing positive norms, a leader facilitates the group in maximizing its performance.

Building cohesiveness is the third facet of establishing a constructive climate. Cohesiveness is a special quality of high-functioning groups that feel a strong sense of connectedness and esprit de corps. Associated with many positive outcomes, cohesiveness is established by a leader who assists group members in trusting each other, listening to and respecting one another's opinions, and accepting each other as unique people.

Finally, to establish a constructive climate a leader *promotes standards of excellence.* Highly effective teams have strong standards of excellence—they have established benchmarks for desired performance. Standards of excellence are best achieved when the leader *requires results, reviews results,* and *rewards results.*

To summarize, establishing a constructive climate is a complex process that involves a great deal of work by a leader. A leader who sets a positive tone will find payoffs in remarkable group performance.

GLOSSARY TERMS

cohesiveness   163   standards of excellence   166

mission   160   structure   160

norms   161   synergy   161

⑤SAGE edge™

Sharpen your skills with SAGE edge at **edge.sagepub.com/northouseintro4e**

SAGE edge for students provides a personalized approach to help you accomplish your coursework goals in an easy-to-use learning environment.

8.1 CASE STUDY

A Tale of Two Classes

Ebony Ellis has two communication classes back-to-back in the same room, but they couldn't be more different.

The first, a class on interpersonal communication, is taught by Steve Gardner, an older professor who has taught at the university for 20 years. The first day of class he verbally explained the rules for class conduct, which were also distributed in a printed handout—cell phones off, no texting, and, unless a student needs to use one for taking notes, laptops closed. Class starts on time and ends on time, and students should try not to leave early.

Ebony's second class, an organizational communication course taught by Marissa Morgan, a younger professor in her 40s, has different rules. There aren't any. This professor doesn't care if the students use their laptops during class. Texting and talking are unrestrained. Professor Morgan announced on the first day that all students are responsible for their own learning in the class, and she trusts them to know how they learn best. When students walk in late or leave early, she always says hello or goodbye to them.

Ebony likes her interpersonal communication class a lot. Professor Gardner's manner has succeeded in getting the class of 75 students to engage with him and listen to one another. Personal disclosures by students and the professor alike are frequent, and there is often much humor and laughter. Even though it is a large class, most people know each other's names, as does Professor Gardner. Many of the students do things with each other outside of class. In his course, students write a reflection paper every other week, and they have a midterm and final exams.

The atmosphere in the organizational communication class is strikingly different to Ebony. It is spontaneous and uncontrolled. Sometimes professor Morgan lectures, but most of the time she just comes to class and invites students to discuss whatever they want to talk about. Students do not know each other's names and seldom connect with each other outside of class. Professor Morgan also assigns papers, but they are short, personal observation papers that aren't given grades but are marked as turned in or not. Students' final grades for the class are dependent on a presentation each student must give on an interpersonal communication topic of his or her choice.

Ebony thinks the two differing styles of the professors would make a great topic for her organizational communication class presentation. To get more information, she interviews both instructors to learn why their classroom management styles are so different.

Professor Gardner describes his teaching philosophy this way: "I want students to think that this class is unique and the subject is

(Continued)

(Continued)

important and has value. I know all students by name, and I allow them to call me by my first name or my title. I really want them to be on board with the direction the train is going from the start. I try to build a community by getting the students to listen to one another. The fun and spirit of the class comes from the camaraderie they establish. In order to listen to one another, however, they have to be fully present. To be fully present, they have to be paying full attention. Texting and open laptops suggest to me that the students are disassociated and disconnected from the group. The attention is on self, rather than the community."

Professor Morgan says her goal is to be sure to cover the required course content and still enjoy the teaching experience. "I give the students just enough freedom in class that they will either sink or swim. This freedom allows me to present my ideas, and then they are free to discuss them as they wish. I think today's students are so multifaceted that they can find their own way to learn, even if it involves texting or using their laptops during class. Many times a student will bring up something valuable that he or she has found while surfing the Internet during class that really adds to our discussions. As I see it, my role as a professor is to present the material to be learned, while the students are responsible for how much of it they can absorb."

Ebony also interviewed two students, like herself, who are enrolled in both classes. Ian said he is very pleased with Professor Gardner's class because he knows what is expected of him and what the norms for class behavior are, noting "He's the only prof at the U who knows my name." Professor Gardner's grading structure is similar to that of most other classes Ian has had, and he likes that there are several graded assignments that allow him to know how he is doing through the course of the semester. As for Professor Morgan's class, he thinks it is "OK" but finds it distracting when people are texting in class. Ian is also stressed about his grade being dependent on one big assignment.

Professor Gardner's class is also BreeAnn's favorite. She says that Professor Morgan's class feels "a little wild," the discussions are not controlled by the professor so the class does not stay on topic, and you learn very little. While Professor Morgan writes thoughtful comments on each of their papers, it is unclear how the papers are related to her lectures and more importantly the student's final grade. BreeAnn finds the final presentation assignment to be an interesting challenge but irrelevant to the class and her major.

"They are both good," Ian says, "just very, very different."

QUESTIONS

1. In establishing a constructive climate for his or her class, what kind of structure has each professor put in place?

2. How would you describe the group norms for each class?

3. What actions has each professor taken to establish cohesiveness in his or her class?

4. What standards of excellence has each professor established for his or her course?

5. Which class atmosphere would you do best in? Why?

8.2 ORGANIZATIONAL CLIMATE QUESTIONNAIRE

Purpose

1. To develop an understanding of how your leadership affects others
2. To help you understand your strengths and weaknesses in establishing the climate for a group or an organization

Directions

1. For each of the statements below, indicate the frequency with which you engage in the behavior listed.
2. Give your immediate impressions. There are no right or wrong answers.

When I am the leader . . .	Never	Seldom	Sometimes	Often	Always
1. I give clear assignments to group members.	1	2	3	4	5
2. I emphasize starting and ending group meetings on time.	1	2	3	4	5
3. I encourage group members to appreciate the value of the overall group.	1	2	3	4	5
4. I encourage group members to work to the best of their abilities.	1	2	3	4	5
5. I make the goals of the group clear to everyone.	1	2	3	4	5
6. I model group norms for group members.	1	2	3	4	5
7. I encourage group members to listen and to respect each other.	1	2	3	4	5
8. I make a point of recognizing people when they do a good job.	1	2	3	4	5
9. I emphasize the overall purpose of the group assignment to group members.	1	2	3	4	5
10. I demonstrate effective communication to group members.	1	2	3	4	5
11. I encourage group members to respect each other's differences.	1	2	3	4	5
12. I promote standards of excellence.	1	2	3	4	5
13. I help group members understand their purpose for being in the group.	1	2	3	4	5
14. I encourage group members to agree on the rules for the group.	1	2	3	4	5
15. I encourage group members to accept each other as unique individuals.	1	2	3	4	5
16. I give group members honest feedback about their work.	1	2	3	4	5

(Continued)

Visit **edge.sagepub.com/northouseintro4e** for a downloadable version of this questionnaire.

8.2 ORGANIZATIONAL CLIMATE QUESTIONNAIRE

(Continued)

When I am the leader . . .	Never	Seldom	Sometimes	Often	Always
17. I help group members understand their roles in the group.	1	2	3	4	5
18. I expect group members to listen when another group member is talking.	1	2	3	4	5
19. I help group members build camaraderie with each other.	1	2	3	4	5
20. I show group members who are not performing well how to improve the quality of their work.	1	2	3	4	5

Scoring

1. Sum the responses on items 1, 5, 9, 13, and 17 (providing structure).

2. Sum the responses on items 2, 6, 10, 14, and 18 (clarifying norms).

3. Sum the responses on items 3, 7, 11, 15, and 19 (building cohesiveness).

4. Sum the responses on items 4, 8, 12, 16, and 20 (promoting standards of excellence).

Total Scores

Providing structure: _____

Clarifying norms: _____

Building cohesiveness: _____

Promoting standards of excellence: _____

Scoring Interpretation

This questionnaire is designed to measure four factors related to establishing a constructive climate: providing structure, clarifying norms, building cohesiveness, and promoting standards of excellence. By comparing your scores, you can determine your strengths and weaknesses in establishing a constructive climate as a leader.

If your score is 20–25, you are in the high range.

If your score is 15–19, you are in the high moderate range.

If your score is 10–14, you are in the low moderate range.

If your score is 5–9, you are in the low range.

Improve Your Leadership Skills

If you have the interactive eBook version of this text, log in to access the interactive leadership assessment. After completing this chapter's questionnaire, you will receive individualized feedback and practical suggestions for further strengthening your leadership based on your responses in this questionnaire.

APPLICATION

8.3 OBSERVATIONAL EXERCISE

Establishing a Constructive Climate

APPLICATION

Purpose

1.   To develop an understanding of how leaders establish a constructive climate for a group or an organization

2.   To identify how specific factors contribute to effective group performance

Directions

1.   For this exercise, you will observe a leader running a meeting, a practice, a class, or some other group-related activity.

2.   Attend a full session of the group and record your observations below.

Name of the leader: _____

Name of the group: _____

Observations about the structure (organization) of the group:

Observations about the group's norms:

Observations about the cohesiveness of the group:

Observations about the group's standards of excellence:

Questions

1.   In what ways did the leader make the goals of the group clear to group members?

2.   How did the leader utilize the unique talents of different group members?

3.   What were some of the positive and negative norms of this group? How did the leader reinforce these norms?

4.   How would you evaluate, on a scale from 1 (*low*) to 5 (*high*), the cohesiveness of this group? In what ways did the leader promote or fail to promote the esprit de corps in the group?

5.   A key factor in promoting standards of excellence is rewarding results. How did the leader reward group members for achieving results?

 Visit **edge.sagepub.com/northouseintro4e** for a downloadable version of this exercise.

8.4 REFLECTION AND ACTION WORKSHEET

Establishing a Constructive Climate

Reflection

1. Based on the scores you received on the Organizational Climate Questionnaire, what are your strengths and weaknesses regarding establishing a constructive climate for a group or an organization? Discuss.

    –   Strengths:

    –   Weaknesses:

2. How did you react to the example in this chapter (pp. 167–168) of the service-learning group that developed cohesiveness? In what way do you think cohesiveness plays an important role in groups? Have you ever experienced cohesiveness in a group yourself? Discuss.

3. In this chapter, group rules and norms are stressed as being very important to effective teams. Do you agree with this? Explain your answer. Briefly comment on your own desire and ability to adapt to the rules of a group.

4. An important aspect of establishing a constructive climate is giving recognition to others. Is rewarding or praising others something that would come easily for you as a leader? Discuss.

Action

1. Imagine that you have been chosen to lead a group project for your class and are preparing for the first meeting. Based on what you have read in this chapter, identify five important actions you could take to help establish a constructive climate for the group.

2. This chapter argues that establishing a constructive climate demands that the leader be a role model for how group members should act. What three values are important to you in a group? How would you demonstrate these values to group members?

3. High-performing teams have strong standards of excellence. Discuss your level of comfort with encouraging others to "keep the quality up." What leadership behaviors could you strengthen to encourage others to work to the best of their ability?

Visit **edge.sagepub.com/northouseintro4e** for a downloadable version of this worksheet.

REFERENCES

Anders, G. (2013, June 10). The reluctant savior of Hewlett-Packard. *Forbes, 191*(8), 64–76.

Brown, D. J. (2013). *The boys in the boat: Nine Americans and their epic quest for gold at the 1936 Berlin Olympics.* New York, NY: Viking.

Cartwright, D. (1968). The nature of group cohesiveness. In D. Cartwright & A. Zander (Eds.), *Group dynamics: Research and theory* (3rd ed., pp. 91–109). New York, NY: Harper & Row.

Cartwright, D., & Zander, A. (Eds.). (1968). *Group dynamics: Research and theory* (3rd ed.). New York, NY: Harper & Row.

Corey, M. S., & Corey, G. (2006). *Groups: Process and practice* (7th ed.). Pacific Grove, CA: Brooks/Cole.

Harris, T. E., & Sherblom, J. C. (2007). *Small group and team communication* (4th ed.). Boston, MA: Pearson.

Kouzes, J. M., & Posner, B. Z. (2002). *The leadership challenge* (3rd ed.). San Francisco, CA: Jossey-Bass.

LaFasto, F. M. J., & Larson, C. E. (2001). *When teams work best: 6,000 team members and leaders tell what it takes to succeed.* Thousand Oaks, CA: Sage.

Larson, C. E., & LaFasto, F. M. J. (1989). *Teamwork: What must go right/what can go wrong.* Newbury Park, CA: Sage.

Napier, R. W., & Gershenfeld, M. K. (2004). *Groups: Theory and experience* (7th ed.). Boston, MA: Houghton Mifflin.

Reichers, A. E., & Schneider, B. (1990). *Organizational climate and culture.* San Francisco, CA: Jossey-Bass.

Schein, E. H. (1969). *Process consultation: Its role in management development.* Reading, MA: Addison-Wesley.

Schein, E. H. (2010). *Organizational culture and leadership* (4th ed.). San Francisco, CA: Jossey-Bass.

Shaw, M. E. (1976). *Group dynamics: The psychology of small group behavior* (2nd ed.). New York, NY: McGraw-Hill.

Vance, A., & Ricadela, A. (2013, January 10). Can Meg Whitman reverse Hewlett-Packard's free fall? *Bloomberg Businessweek.* Retrieved from http://www.businessweek.com/articles/2013-01-10/can-meg-whitman-reverse-hewlett-packards-free-fall#p1

Winkler, R. (2012, November 20). Another fine mess for H-P. *The Wall Street Journal.* Retrieved from http://online.wsj.com/article/SB10001424127887324712504578131252852902768.html

Embracing Diversity and Inclusion

INTRODUCTION

Leadership requires skill, a clear vision, and a strong commitment to establishing a constructive organizational climate. It also requires that leaders understand diversity and inclusion, and the essential role these play in organizational outcomes. While many of the leadership concepts discussed in this text so far (e.g., task behavior, goal setting, and strengths) involve rather straightforward leadership efforts, addressing diversity and inclusion is a multilayered process that requires a wider range of leadership practices. Although the terms *diversity* and *inclusion* seem to represent distinctly different concepts, they are actually interrelated processes, and while not usually discussed as core leadership concepts, diversity and inclusion play a seminal role in effective leadership.

Hearing the word *diversity* conjures up a multitude of different reactions in people. To some, the word *diversity* suggests being enriched by the different perspectives, attitudes, and life experiences that people bring to a situation.

ASK THE AUTHOR

Why Should Leaders Embrace Diversity?

For others, the word stirs up feelings of unfairness, injustice, and exclusion. Furthermore, some people embrace the positive outcomes of diversity, while others resent the burden of having to adapt to those who are different from themselves. Whatever your reaction is to the word *diversity*, when you are in a leadership role, you must be prepared to address diversity. How you approach diversity and inclusion will have an impact on your success as a leader.

In this chapter, we explore how embracing diversity and inclusion can make you a more effective leader. First, we define *diversity* and *inclusion* and discuss common usages for these terms. Next, we provide a brief history of how these concepts have become more important in society over time. Additionally, we provide a framework to conceptualize inclusion and a model of inclusive practices. Last, we discuss communication practices to improve inclusion and the barriers that can be encountered when trying to embrace diversity and inclusion.

DIVERSITY AND INCLUSION EXPLAINED

Definitions

Diversity and *inclusion* are general terms that represent complex processes. A closer look at each of the terms will help explain why they are closely related and why leaders need to be aware of both concepts when addressing diversity within their group or organization.

Understanding Diversity

Diversity. In the most general sense, **diversity** is about variety or difference. Researchers have defined diversity in a multitude of ways (Mor Barak, 2014). For example, *diversity* is often used to refer to the mixture of races, genders, or religions that make up a group of people. Harrison and Sin (2006) define diversity as "the collective amount of differences among members within a social unit" (p. 196). Ferdman (2014), a diversity scholar, suggests that diversity is the representation of multiple groups of individuals with different identities and cultures within a group or organization. Similarly, Herring and Henderson (2015) suggest that diversity refers to policies and practices that are designed to include people who are different in some way from the traditional group members. From this perspective, diversity means creating an organizational culture that embraces the values and skills of all of its members. Herring and Henderson contend that diversity is about more than valuing differences between groups; it includes addressing issues of parity, equity, and inequality.

According to a study by Deloitte and the Billie Jean King Leadership Initiative (Dishman, 2015), of 3,700 individuals from a variety of backgrounds, Millennials (born 1980–2000) define diversity differently than Boomers (born 1946–1964) and Gen-Xers (born 1965–1979). Millennials look at diversity as the mixing of different backgrounds and perspectives within a group. Boomers and Gen-Xers, on the other hand, see diversity as a process of fairness and protection for all group members, regardless of gender, race, religion, ethnicity, or sexual orientation. Millennials are more likely than non-Millennials to focus on the unique experiences of individuals, team-work, and collaboration than issues of justness.

In this chapter, we define diversity *as the amount of difference among members of a group or organization*. As set forth by Loden (1996), the core dimensions of diversity include age, ethnicity, gender, mental/physical abilities and char-acteristics, race, and sexual orientation (see Table 9.1). Secondary dimensions include communication style, education, family status, military experience, organizational role and level, religion, first language, geographic location, income, work experience, and work style. The primary dimensions of diver-sity are more powerful and less changeable, while the secondary dimensions can change, are less visible, and are less influential in how they impact our lives.

Inclusion. **Inclusion** is the process of incorporating differing individuals into a group or organization. It is creating an environment where people who are different feel they are part of the whole. For example, inclusion is repre-sented by making accommodations so that a student with disabilities can feel involved and accepted in regular school classes. Similarly, inclusion is about the *majority* incorporating the opinions of the *minority* and giving voice to the people who are seldom heard. Booysen (2014) suggests that when

TABLE 9.1   Dimensions of Diversity

Primary Dimensions	Secondary Dimensions
Age	Geographic Location
Gender	Military and Work Experience
Race	Family Status
Mental and Physical Abilities	Income
Ethnicity	Religion
Sexual Orientation	Education
	First Language
	Organizational Role and Level
	Communication and Work Style

Source: Based on Loden (1996).

inclusion exists in a workplace, "all people from diverse backgrounds will feel valued, respected, and recognized" and "no one will feel that he or she . . . does not have a place in the organization; no one will ask: 'What about me?'" (p. 299). Furthermore, Ferdman (2014) suggests that people experience inclusion not only when they feel they are treated well individually but also when groups of people who share their identity are respected and valued.

The Importance of Inclusion

The underpinnings of inclusion are described in the work of Schutz (1958), who posited that inclusion (along with control and affection) is a basic human need that people experience in their interpersonal relationships. It is our need to belong, feel accepted, and be connected to others, but not to the extent that we lose a sense of ourselves as unique individuals. Inclusion means feeling like you are a full member of the group but at the same time maintaining your own identity. It requires a balance between belonging and uniqueness (Shore et al., 2011).

Schutz (1958) argued that we express our need to be included by how we communicate with others and we experience less anxiety if our need to be "in the group" matches the degree to which we want others to "include us." This suggests that leaders should open their arms to include others, but not so much that the individual differences of others get smothered or lost.

In short, diversity focuses on recognizing differences, and inclusion is concerned with embracing those differences. As Myers (2012) aptly suggests, diversity is about "being invited to the party," and inclusion is about "being asked to dance" (p. 13). Leaders often recognize the value of diversity but struggle with creating supportive, inclusive environments. It is one thing to have a diverse group or organization, but another to make sure each individual is included in the group or organization in a positive manner. Later in the chapter, we provide an inclusion framework to help leaders understand how to approach diversity in different settings.

Brief Historical Perspective

Approaches to Diversity

To better understand the complexity of diversity, it is useful to briefly describe how diversity has been addressed in the past, and then to discuss how these descriptions influence the meaning of diversity today. Addressing issues of diversity is not unique; it has been a central challenge for leaders of every generation.

In the United States, diversity was at the foundation of the country's democratic system. The United States was originally formed by people seeking to escape religious persecution elsewhere. This ideal of seeking freedom drove to the country many groups of immigrants, all of whom had different values, traditions, and religions. As the country evolved, diversity also came to mean addressing the needs of people who are marginalized in the United States, including African Americans whose descendants originally came as slaves as well as Native Americans who were already living in the country. Even today, the diversity of the country continues to shift and change as waves of new-comers enter the United States and continue to alter the social landscape of the nation (Healey & Stepnick, 2017). Building a democratic nation is only possible by acknowledging and addressing issues of diversity.

While there is a lot written on **multiculturalism**, intergroup relations, and diversity in society, much of the information we present in this chapter comes from diversity and inclusion research as it has occurred in the realm of the workplace. While this research may be workplace specific, it is salient to leaders of any organization. This is especially true of the research on the historical development of workplace diversity in the United States as it reflects how perspectives on diversity evolved in wider society. Harvey (2015) suggests that the approach to diversity in the workplace has changed and evolved over three periods: the early years of diversity (1960s and 1970s), the era of valuing diversity (1980s and 1990s), and diversity management and inclusion in the 21st century (2000 to present) (see Table 9.2).

Moving Beyond an Exclusionary Culture

Early years—1960s and 1970s. This was the period of the civil rights movement in the United States. During this time, efforts were made to end discrimination against African Americans and to secure their legal rights as spelled out in the U.S. Constitution. It was also a time when the federal

TABLE 9.2 Changing Perspectives on Diversity

Time Period	Perspective	Metaphor	Emphasis
1960s and 1970s	Government Addresses Inequalities	Melting Pot	Assimilation
1980s and 1990s	Advantages of Accepting Differences Recognized	Salad	Differentiation (Multiculturalism)
2000 to present	Different Opinions and Insights Valued	Smorgasbord	Inclusion (Integration)

Source: Adapted from Harvey, C. P. (2015). Understanding workplace diversity: Where have we been and where are we going? In C. P. Harvey & M. J. Allard (Eds.), *Understanding and managing diversity: Readings, cases, and exercises* (pp. 1–7). Boston, MA: Pearson; Thomas, D. A., & Ely, R. J. (1996, September–October). Making differences matter: A new paradigm for managing diversity. *Harvard Business Review.*

government passed a series of landmark equal employment opportunity laws: (1) the *Equal Pay Act* (1963), which stated that women and men must receive equal pay for equal work; (2) the *Civil Rights Act* (1964), which prohibited discrimination in employment based on race, sex, national origin, religion, and color; (3) the *Executive Orders* (1961–1965), which required organizations that accepted federal funds to submit affirmative action plans that demonstrated their progress in hiring and promoting groups of people who had been discriminated against previously; and (4) the *Age Discrimination Act* (1975), which protected workers over 40 years of age from being discriminated against at work because of their age.

During these early years, the focus of diversity was on "righting the wrongs" experienced by people who were perceived as different because of their race or gender (Harvey, 2015) and who were also the targets of discrimination and exclusion. It was also a time when the government began forcing organizations to confront inequities between individuals and groups in the workplace. Thomas and Ely (1996) contend that these early years were focused on discrimination and fairness. Because of prejudice, certain demographic groups were not treated the same as other groups. To comply with federal mandates, it was important for organizations to ensure that all people were treated equally and that no one was given an unfair advantage over another person.

Assimilation

It was common during the early years to think of diversity using the term *melting pot*, a metaphor for a blending of many into one, or a heterogeneous society becoming homogeneous. Sociologically, diversity was thought of as an assimilation process where those from different cultures were expected to adapt to and, in many cases, adopt the customs of the majority group (Blaine, 2013). **Assimilation** focused on the process of making people from diverse cultures come together to create one American culture. Healey and Stepnick (2017) point out that while assimilation is often thought of as a gradual and fair blending of diverse cultures, in fact it requires different cultures to blend in with the predominant English language and British cultural style. Although assimilation helps to bring diverse individuals together, it requires that those in the minority culture give up many, if not most, of their own values and traditions in order to adopt the dominant culture.

Era of valuing diversity—1980s and 1990s. This period was marked by a new approach to diversity that emphasized the acceptance and celebration of differences (Thomas & Ely, 1996). The approach to diversity at this time broadened beyond an emphasis on race and gender to include many dimensions (sexual orientation, age, physical and mental abilities, etc. [see Table 9.1]). In addition to stressing fairness and equality, organizations recognized that society was becoming more multicultural and that supporting diversity in the workforce could have competitive advantages. Research focused on how diversity in the workplace was related to positive outcomes for an organization, such as reduced turnover, better creative thinking, enhanced problem solving, and improved decision making. Organizations found that diversity was not just about fairness; it made economic sense (Thomas & Ely, 1996).

Rather than a melting pot, the metaphor for diversity during this time was more of a salad composed of different ingredients, made by mixing different individuals or cultures and their unique characteristics into one. A multicultural approach acknowledges and accepts differences. The emphasis was on the individual unique contributions that each person or culture brings to an organization, rather than blending ("melting") differences into a single whole (Harvey, 2015). Furthermore, diversity during this period emphasized **pluralism**, the recognition that people of different cultures did not need to sacrifice their own traditions and values to become a part of one society. Pluralism means that people of all races, classes, religions, and backgrounds can coexist in one society without giving up their identities, customs, or traditions. A pluralistic society appreciates and celebrates differences.

Diversity management and inclusion in the 21st century—2000 to present. Diversity during this period continues to be a major concern for organizations and society in general. Inequities between individuals and groups in regard to differences in race, gender, ethnicity, sexual orientation, and other dimensions remain unresolved. The laws of the 1960s and 1970s still occupy an important role in trying to achieve diversity in the workplace. At the same time, multiculturalism is more widely accepted and celebrated today.

What is new in the last 20 years regarding diversity is an emphasis on creating inclusive organizations. Harvey (2015) points out that people today are recognizing that both organizations and individuals can benefit from diversity. Furthermore, she points out that diversity today is broader in scope and harder to manage because of a changing composition of workers, the need to acknowledge multiple social identities, and the challenge of trying to establish and maintain an inclusive organizational culture. The new way of approaching diversity acknowledges differences among people and values those differences, integrating them into the organization. People feel they are all on the same team because of their differences, not despite their differences (Thomas & Ely, 1996).

As opposed to being like a melting pot that blends many into one or a salad that mixes differences together, diversity today could be thought of as a smorgasbord that celebrates the unique qualities of a variety of different dishes. Diversity from this perspective means that people's unique qualities are accepted and enjoyed, and that people do not need to downplay their own unique characteristics for the benefit of others. It also means that people do not need to deny their own cultural identities to be a part of the larger group or organization. Diversity means that an organization is composed of many unique elements and, when taken together, these elements make the organization unique.

Emotional and Cultural Intelligence

Diversity Management

While our perspectives on diversity have changed over the last 50 years, society's need to address matters of diversity has remained constant. The current approach to diversity places the inclusion process at center stage as the pathway to addressing concerns about diversity. Inclusion means allowing people with different cultural characteristics to have a voice and feel integrated and connected with others (Ferdman, 2014). In the next section, we describe a framework for understanding the inclusion process.

INCLUSION FRAMEWORK

Inclusion, Diversity, and Leadership

Social psychologist Brewer (1991) argued that individuals have two opposing needs in regard to being a part of a group. First, they have a desire to assimilate and be included; second, they have a need to differentiate themselves from the group. Similar to Schutz's (1958) early work on inclusion, people seek an optimal balance between inclusion and differentiation.

To better understand how people balance these needs, Shore and colleagues (2011) developed an inclusion framework. The framework, depicted in Table 9.3, illustrates how varying levels of belongingness (i.e., the desire to be included) interact with uniqueness (i.e., the desire to maintain one's own identity) and result in the four quadrants shown below.

The *Exclusion quadrant* (top left) represents individuals in a group or organization who feel left out and excluded; they do not feel a part of things, and they do not feel valued. Exclusion occurs when organizations fail to see and value the unique qualities of diverse employees and fail to accept them as organizational insiders. An example might be a female vice president of a bank whose ideas are discounted by her male counterparts and who is seldom invited to corporate planning meetings. In effect, exclusion represents a complete failure to deal with matters of diversity.

The *Differentiation quadrant* (lower left) describes individuals who feel unique and respected but who also feel left out and not a part of the in-group. **Differentiation** occurs when organizations accept and value the unique qualities of members who are different but then fail to let these individuals become full members of the organization. For example, this might occur when a customer service center hires several Spanish-speaking representatives because the center is working with more Spanish-speaking customers. But those representatives are not asked for their input on organizational issues such as the scripting they use for complaint calls. In terms of diversity, differentiation goes halfway—it recognizes different individuals, but does not fully accept them.

TABLE 9.3   Inclusion Framework

	Low Belongingness	High Belongingness
Low Value in Uniqueness	**Exclusion** Individual is not treated as an organizational insider with unique value in the work group, but there are other employees or groups who are insiders.	**Assimilation** Individual is treated as an insider in the work group when he or she conforms to organizational/dominant culture norms and downplays uniqueness.
High Value in Uniqueness	**Differentiation** Individual is not treated as an organizational insider in the work group, but his or her unique characteristics are seen as valuable and required for group/organization success.	**Inclusion** Individual is treated as an insider and also allowed/encouraged to retain uniqueness within the work group.

Source: Shore, L. M., Randel, A. E., Chung, B. G., Dean, M. A., Holcombe Ehrhard, K., & Singh, G. (2011). Inclusion and diversity in work groups: A review and model for future research. *Journal of Management, 37*(4), 1266.

The *Assimilation quadrant* (top right) represents people who feel they are insiders and in the organizational in-group but whose unique characteristics are not really valued by the organization. An example of assimilation could be a Native American college student who is 100% involved and accepted in the classroom but whose unique heritage is not acknowledged by the others, who expect him to give up that heritage to blend into the dominant group. In terms of diversity, assimilation represents an attempt by organizations to open their arms and bring everyone in; however, the same organizations can be faulted for failing to acknowledge the uniqueness of their members—they accept different individuals, but do not fully value them.

The *Inclusion quadrant* (lower right) describes individuals who feel they belong and are valued for their unique beliefs, attitudes, values, and background. This quadrant represents the optimal way to address diversity. It means, in short, accepting others and at the same time valuing them for who they are without requiring them to give up valued identities or cultural features (Ferdman, 1992). For example, inclusion occurs when students at a small rural high school welcome three new students who are Arabic refugees who have come to live with families in the area. The students establish an "international club" in which they learn Syrian from the new students while helping the Syrian students with their English and discuss one another's culture. The social sciences teacher incorporated a research project on Syria for all his students based on a presentation that one of the Syrian students gave about his experiences. Another of the Syrian students is a gifted singer and is in the choir, and the choir teacher asked her to pick out a song from her native country that the choir is

LEADERSHIP SNAPSHOT
Xerox Corporation

When Xerox named Ursula Burns its CEO in 2009, it became the first Fortune 500 company to have a successive female CEO. Burns's ascendency to the top position at the $22 billion company is evidence of the diversity and inclusion efforts that began at Xerox more than 40 years before.

In 1964, as race riots were occurring near Xerox's Rochester, New York, headquarters, the company's founder, Joe Wilson, met with Black leaders and learned people were rioting because they didn't have access to jobs. Xerox pledged to change that, sending out a company-wide directive, condemning racial discrimination, mandating minority recruitment, and holding managers responsible for the success of the minorities they hired ("Xerox a Success," 1991). In addition, Xerox funded and provided consulting to a minority-owned and -operated plant in Rochester's Black community, which made parts for Xerox, to provide jobs for the community's unemployed (Friedman & Deinard, 1990).

Xerox's program was about more than recruitment; it was about a company-wide commitment to diversity and inclusion on all levels from the manufacturing floor to the executive offices. By 1974, Xerox had increased its minority workforce from 3% to 14.6% (Friedman & Deinard, 1990).

It wasn't as simple as hiring more Black employees however. Despite the company-wide mandate, Black employees at Xerox still experienced unequal treatment, especially when it came to promotions. In addition, Black employees weren't part of the informal networks that White employees enjoyed where they shared support, information, and mentoring, which often inhibited the Black employees' knowledge of job openings and promotion opportunities. Because of this, Black Xerox workers in various company locations began meeting together at one another's homes as informal support groups. These Black caucuses not only advocated and fought for equal treatment for Black employees within the company, but they also created what would become a hallmark of the company's Managing for Diversity program: minority caucus groups.

Caucus groups engage in self-advocacy, informing management on issues that keep minorities from progressing within the company. The company now has 6 caucus groups to meet the needs of employees who are Black, Hispanic, Asian, women, Black women, and LGBT.

By 1991, the company's efforts had succeeded in increasing the minority ranks of Xerox's U.S. workforce to 25.7%. Among its senior executives, 17% were minorities. But even though the program had been effective, there was more to be done. Only 8.5% of the company's senior executives were women, and more minorities and women were employed in lower- and middle-level jobs than upper-level jobs. Burns, who is African American and was recruited by Xerox in 1980 as part of its summer minority internship program, said that back then the diversity efforts "didn't extend to gender.

"We looked up one day, and all the African American men were doing better . . . they were leaders of the company. But there were very few women of any race. So we said, 'Oh my God,' then we have to do something about women," says Burns. "What we've learned during that time is this idea of inclusion can't be inclusion of one group. Because as soon as you focus on one group only, then you actually exclude the other groups" (Solman, 2014).

It was through a woman's caucus group that Xerox management learned one obstacle in the way of women obtaining and retaining top positions in its manufacturing divisions was the rigid hours of shift schedules. These schedules made it difficult for women who were also primary caregivers to their children to work in manufacturing. Executives learned that "women weren't dumb in manufacturing, [but] they need more flexibility" than the company allowed them, says Burns (Solman, 2014).

Today, Xerox has 140,000 employees and does business in more than 180 countries. In the United States, minorities make up 30.2% of the company's workforce. Among company officials and managers, 22% are minorities, and minorities hold 18% of the company's vice president positions. Women make up nearly 30% of the company's vice presidents while the company's U.S. workforce is 36% female (Xerox, 2016).

Xerox rose to dominance as maker of copy machines, but watched that market shrivel with competition from digital imaging. As a result, Xerox dramatically changed its business model. It is now in the business of client services and has become more globally oriented. In doing so, the company found that its suppliers, customers, and partners came from diverse cultures, backgrounds, and experiences. In order to be able to connect with them, Xerox had to connect with the diversity within its own ranks.

Xerox officials contend that its diversity has allowed the company to successfully shift to new markets because it is able to approach issues and challenges from different perspectives. "Xerox found out a while ago that including more of the resources of the world to attack problems or address opportunities is better than including fewer," says Burns.

"The entire approach here is not to have diversity just because we think it's a nice thing to do. It's a good business result. The way to stay in front, if you are a tech company, is to engage as much difference and as much breadth as you can in thinking and approach and background and language and culture" (Solman, 2014) learning to sing for its winter program. Most important of all, students at the school feel accepted, engaged, and comfortable. The camaraderie they have has produced a new sense of community.

The inclusion framework presented in Table 9.3 is useful for understanding ways to address diversity because it illustrates inclusion as an integration of two factors: (1) an individual's connectedness (i.e., belonging) to others and (2) a person's individuality (i.e., uniqueness). In addition, the inclusion framework is helpful because it underscores that *differentiation* focuses primarily on people's differences and *assimilation* focuses primarily on people's connectedness to the whole.

DIVERSITY AND INCLUSION IN PRACTICE

Model of Inclusive Practices

Benefits of Diverse Leadership

Since inclusion is essential for integrating everyone into a group or organization, the next question is, how does the inclusion process work in practice?

To understand this process, Ferdman (2014) suggests treating inclusion as a multilevel process centered on each individual's experience of inclusion. Simply put, inclusion exists when individuals experience it. This occurs as a result of inclusion practices on many levels, including interpersonal, group, leader, organizational, and societal (see Figure 9.1). Ferdman's framework illustrates how inclusion at one level is related to the way inclusion is practiced at other levels.

As shown at the top of the model in Figure 9.1, the way a society or community thinks about and addresses inclusion affects the way an individual experiences it. For example, if the city commission in a community such as Dearborn, Michigan, which has a large percentage of Arab Americans, were to promote the recognition of the Muslim holy month of Ramadan, then Dearborn residents of Middle Eastern descent might feel that their Muslim heritage is being valued and recognized.

Moving down the model, organizational policies and practices also influence the inclusion experience. For instance, if a new employee training program at a retail store fosters acceptance of customers who are lesbian, gay, bisexual, or transgender, it may help these customers feel welcome shopping at the store.

At the leadership level, which is indispensable to promoting inclusion at all levels, leaders need to set the tone for inclusion and hold followers

FIGURE 9.1 Systems of Inclusion: A Multilevel Analytic Framework

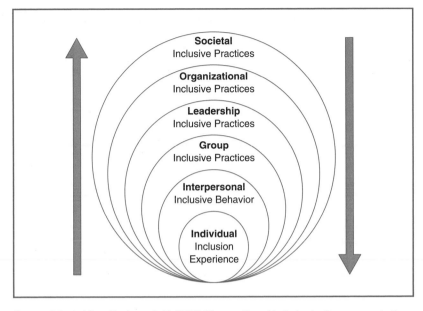

Source: Adapted from Ferdman, B. M. (2014). The practice of inclusion in diverse organizations. In B. M. Ferdman, & B. R. Deane (Eds.), *Diversity at work: The practice of inclusion* (pp. 3–54). San Francisco, CA: Wiley.

accountable for inclusion practices. For example, if, during a staff meeting of a department that is predominantly male, the department head gives a disgruntled female staff member time to voice her opinions to the others, that staff member will feel that her opinions matter. It will also model to the group's members how to listen to others and value their opinions, even if those opinions are different from their own.

Another form of inclusion occurs at the group level. Groups promote inclusion when they establish enabling norms that give everyone in the group an equal chance to voice his or her opinion, acknowledge and respect individuals' differences, promote collaborative work on tasks, and address conflicts productively. There is an old axiom regarding people in groups: "By the group are you sickened, by the group are you healed." When a group is functioning inclusively, it is positive to group members, not toxic. The members feel accepted, comfortable, unique, valued, and inspirited. This is the strength of inclusive group practices.

The interpersonal level is perhaps the most common place where inclusive practices are played out. Through our interpersonal communication with others, we let them know our need to be included, our willingness to include

Challenges for Women in Leadership

others, and our willingness to have others include us. For example, a first-year foreign student living on campus may want her roommate to invite her to parties, but when the roommate does invite her, the student makes an excuse for not being able to attend. The student expresses a need to be included, but when she is included, the student becomes uncomfortable and wants to pull back. Interpersonal inclusion happens when we ask others for their opinions and are interested in who they are, but still enable them to maintain their personal space as individuals.

The individual inclusion experience is the foundation of the framework illustrated in Figure 9.1. Ferdman, Barrera, Allen, and Vuong (2009) describe this experience "as the degree to which individuals feel safe, trusted, accepted, respected, supported, valued, fulfilled, engaged, and authentic in their working environment, both as individuals and as members of particular identity groups" (p. 6). The experience of individual inclusion is affected by the inclusion practices at other levels, and individual inclusion can also impact these other levels (see Figure 9.1).

To understand how the different levels of inclusion in the framework can influence the other levels, consider, for example, in the United States, same-sex marriage has been legalized, giving same-sex couples the same legal rights as those in heterosexual marriages. This can influence other inclusive practices down the line. At the organizational level, this new legal status allows same-sex couples the same benefits as heterosexual couples, such as health insurance and family leave. If the leader of an organization engages in inclusive practices of same-sex couples, such as encouraging same-sex couples to openly attend organizational events together and inviting them to dinner with other staff members and their spouses, that leader is modeling inclusive behavior for his followers. At the group level, the coworkers of same-sex spouses host a baby shower when the same-sex couple welcomes a child into their family. On the interpersonal level, coworkers will talk with the same-sex spouse about her partner, and establish bonds the same as they would with another coworker. Finally, you can see how this inclusion would lead to the same-sex spouse feeling that her sexual orientation and her marriage are accepted and respected by those with whom she works every day. As a result, she feels her opinions and input are valued because she is not regarded in a negative way or as different by others because of her sexual orientation. Inclusion comes from the top down—starting with society and community and ending with the individual.

As shown in Figure 9.1, Ferdman's framework also identifies that the influence of inclusion travels back up the levels from individual to societal. The same-sex couple example from above also works to show this upward influence of inclusion. Because the individual described above feels accepted and respected, she is more likely to engage in inclusive behaviors with others who are different from her. Through their example, same-sex couples inclusive behaviors can help foster acceptance and respect for others among the members of groups to which the individuals belong. If a group's majority is engaged in inclusive behaviors, it can influence its leaders to adopt those same inclusive practices. To illustrate this, we will again use an example of an individual in a same-sex relationship who wants to have the same health and leave benefits as her married coworkers. This coworker talks about her desires with other members of her department, who are accepting of her relationship. As a result, at a department meeting, the employees approach their leader about changing the company's benefit policy to include same-sex couples. The boss takes the matter to his superiors, and ultimately the issue is put before the company's owners, who adopt the policy. As a result of the company's acceptance of same-sex couples, the community in which the company operates is influenced by the company's inclusive practices. Because of the company's inclusive practices, more gay and lesbian employees may choose to join the company, which will bring more same-sex couples into the community. As same-sex couples become engaged in the community as neighbors, friends, and community members, the society around them will become more accepting and respecting of same-sex relationships.

While this example shows that inclusion can and should happen at many levels, as a leader, the challenge is to foster that sense of inclusion among one's followers as well as influence the organization's approach to diversity and inclusion. In the next section, we discuss some practices leaders can engage in that help to do just that.

Leader Practices That Advance Diversity and Inclusion

A questionnaire to measure inclusion in work groups developed by Ferdman and his colleagues (Ferdman, 2014; Ferdman et al., 2009; Hirshberg & Ferdman, 2011) identified six key components of the experience of inclusion (see Table 9.4). Components are like the ingredients of inclusion. When followers experience these components, they feel included. These components provide a good blueprint for actions and behaviors and communication that leaders should engage in to provide inclusion for others.

1. Feeling Safe

To help individuals feel safe, it is important for leaders to treat followers in nonthreatening ways. In situations where one person feels different from others, the leader plays a fundamental role in letting that person know that he or she will not be hurt physically or psychologically if his or her ideas differ from others and that he or she will not be ridiculed or criticized for expressing these

Feeling Safe

TABLE 9.4   Components of the Inclusion Experience

Components	Examples
1 **Feeling Safe**	• Do I help others feel physically and psychologically safe? • Do I help others feel like they are a full member of the group? • Do I help others express opposing opinions without fear of negative repercussion?
2 **Feeling Involved and Engaged**	• Do I treat others as full participants—as insiders? • Do I give others access to information and resources to do their work? • Do I help others feel like they are part of our team?
3 **Feeling Respected and Valued**	• Do I treat others as I would like to be treated myself? • Do I let others know I trust and care about them? • Do I treat others like they are a valued group member?
4 **Feeling Influential**	• Do I let others' ideas and perspectives influence the group? • Do I let others participate in decision making? • Do I listen to others' perspectives on substantive issues?
5 **Feeling Authentic and Whole**	• Do I allow others to be truly themselves in the group? • Do I let others know they can be completely open with the group? • Do I encourage others to be honest and transparent?
6 **Recognizing, Attending to, and Honoring Diversity**	• Do I treat everyone fairly without discrimination? • Do I let others know I trust and care about them? • Do I encourage others to be honest and transparent?

Source: Adapted from Ferdman, B. M. (2014). The practice of inclusion in diverse organizations. In B. M. Ferdman & B. R. Deane (Eds.), *Diversity at work: The practice of inclusion* (pp. 3–54). San Francisco, CA: Wiley.

ideas. Even if a person's opinions go directly against the majority opinion, that individual can feel safe that he or she will not experience negative repercussions. Leaders need to communicate with each of their followers in such a way that all of them feel they are a part of the whole. It is a safe feeling for individuals to know they will not be rejected by the group for their uniqueness.

2. Feeling Involved and Engaged

In addition to a feeling of safety, inclusion comes from feeling involved and engaged. Helping followers find this feeling is a challenge for leaders, but worthwhile because engaged and involved followers are more productive and satisfied. It is inspiriting to be around them. Leaders must find ways to help individuals become involved and immersed in the larger group's efforts. When an individual likes her work, participates freely in it, and enjoys being a part of the team, she is more likely to feel involved and engaged. As discussed in Chapter 3, "Engaging Strengths," recognizing people's strengths is a wonderful way for leaders to help followers feel engaged. In addition, leaders should treat followers as if they are insiders, as people who are important and deserve to know what is going on within the organization. Leaders need to share information freely so that followers feel like full participants in the workings of the group or organization. People feel involved and engaged when they know they are full-fledged group members and that their participation matters.

3. Feeling Respected and Valued

Practicing the Golden Rule—"Treat others as you would like to be treated"— is at the core of how leaders can help followers feel respected and valued. When leaders put themselves in the shoes of their followers, they can get in touch with what it means to be well thought of, worthy, and wanted. None of us like to be judged, stereotyped, ridiculed, singled out, disconfirmed, ignored, or belittled. Followers want to feel that they belong and are connected to the group, that the leader trusts and cares about them, and that they are intrinsic to the group.

4. Feeling Influential

Another component contributing to the inclusion experience is a feeling of having influence. All of us have unique ideas and positions on issues. When people express their ideas and are heard, they feel like they exist and that they are meaningful. When an individual is in a staff meeting and others listen to his or her ideas, it makes that individual feel significant. If that person's comments influence the direction of the group, it really makes the person feel significant. We all want to be influential, to put our stamp on things, to touch the world and have our efforts mean something.

It is critically important for leaders to recognize that followers have a need to have an impact—to express themselves in a way that affects others. Effective leaders help followers feel influential when they recognize that followers want to be heard and have an impact. Letting followers participate in important organizational discussions and acknowledging their comments and suggestions as substantive and valuable makes those followers feel influential. Another way of allowing followers to feel influential is by including them in the decision making of a group. When followers are able to participate in decisions, they feel a sense of significance; they feel agency. To have agency is to affect the process, to feel alive, to feel influential. It is having agency that helps followers to feel included.

Women in Leadership

5. Feeling Authentic and Whole

In any group or organization, there is always a certain amount of pressure to assimilate to that group or organization's mission, norms, and values. This pressure creates tension within individuals because in order to be accepted with the larger group, they often find it necessary to hide or downplay unique characteristics of themselves or the group with whom they identify. For example, to be accepted as an autoworker at a Ford plant in Detroit, an individual might try to hide the fact that he or she drives a foreign-made car. Or, if your partner's parents are quite liberal and against the National Rifle Association's stance on gun rights, you might not want to disclose to them that you are an avid hunter and longtime NRA member.

This tension between wanting to be yourself while also wanting to be a part of the group can be counterproductive to one's feeling authentic and whole. Leaders can address this tension for followers by creating an atmosphere where individuals feel free to be as honest and transparent as they are comfortable being. To be transparent and authentic, followers need to feel trust from the leader. Leaders need to establish environments where being fully transparent with one another is rewarded and not punished. When you are in this kind of group or organization, you feel unique and connected at the same time. It is a situation where assimilating to the larger entity does not require losing one's own sense of self.

For example, Angie is a multiracial college student at a small private university who, because of her very light skin color, knows that most of her fellow students assume she is White. Even though she is very involved in campus activities, the topic of her race rarely comes up, and Angie doesn't feel a need to discuss it with other students. However, she often wants to speak up when she hears students making biased or stereotypical comments based on ethnicity, but doesn't do so. The college's president recently asked Angie to join the school's antiracism committee representing students of color on the campus. Angie is hesitant to do so because it would mean being open about her race, which could change how some of the other students treat her. However, she also knows that she would be more true to herself if she did participate on the committee, because she could effect change in some of the racist attitudes on campus. The president has talked with her at length about the importance of being acknowledged by others for her unique multiracial perspective, encouraging her to be authentic and transparent with others. He has expressed that he believes because she is already a very respected and active member of the campus community, she would be influential in helping the other students to embrace change regarding racism.

6. Recognizing, Attending to, and Honoring Diversity

The last component of the inclusion experience is directly related to leaders and diversity. In any group or organization, people want to be treated fairly;

they do not want to be discriminated against because of their social identity or the identity of their social groups. As a leader, each of us has the responsibility to be fair-minded and open-minded toward all of our followers. But dealing with diversity is not just about fairness. It is also about acknowledging differences and fully embracing them even if it produces conflict. Leaders need to work through conflicts related to differences in mutually beneficial ways. Last, leaders need to be attentive to recognizing the ways people differ and honoring the individuality of each of them.

Barriers to Embracing Diversity and Inclusion

Unfortunately, in the effort to successfully embrace diversity and inclusion, a leader can run into four common barriers—both on an individual level and on an organizational level—that can hinder this: ethnocentrism, prejudice, stereotypes, and privilege. Leaders must confront these barriers head-on in order to effectively address diversity and develop inclusion in their organization.

Ethnocentrism

As the word suggests, **ethnocentrism** is the tendency for individuals to place their own group (ethnic, racial, or cultural) at the center of their observations of others and the world. Ethnocentrism is the perception that one's own culture is better or more natural than the culture of others. Because people tend to give priority and value to their own beliefs, attitudes, and values over and above those of other groups, they often fail to recognize the unique perspectives of others. Ethnocentrism is a universal tendency, and each of us is ethnocentric to some degree.

Ethnocentrism is a perceptual window through which people make subjective or critical evaluations of people from cultures other than their own (Porter & Samovar, 1997). For example, some Americans think that the democratic principles of the United States are superior to the political beliefs of other countries; they often fail to understand the complexities of other cultures. Ethnocentrism accounts for our tendency to think our own cultural values and ways of doing things are right and natural (Gudykunst & Kim, 1997).

Ethnocentrism can be a major obstacle to effective leadership because it prevents people from fully understanding or respecting the viewpoints of others. For example, if a person's culture values individual achievement, it may be difficult for that person to understand someone from a culture that emphasizes collectivity (i.e., people working together as a whole). Similarly, if a person believes strongly in respecting authority, that person may find it difficult to understand someone who challenges authority or does not easily defer to authority figures. The more ethnocentric we are, the less open or tolerant we are of other people's cultural traditions or practices.

A skilled leader cannot avoid issues related to ethnocentrism. A leader must recognize his or her own ethnocentrism, as well as understand—and to a degree tolerate—the ethnocentrism of others. In reality, it is a balancing act for leaders. On the one hand, leaders need to promote and be confident in their own ways of doing things; on the other, they need to be sensitive to the legitimacy of the ways of other cultures. Skilled leaders are able to negotiate the fine line between trying to overcome ethnocentrism and knowing when to remain grounded in their own cultural values.

Prejudice

Prejudice

Closely related to ethnocentrism is prejudice. **Prejudice** is a largely fixed attitude, belief, or emotion held by an individual about another individual or group that is based on faulty or unsubstantiated data. Prejudice refers to judgments we make about others based on previous decisions or experiences and involves inflexible generalizations that are resistant to change or evidence to the contrary (Ponterotto & Pedersen, 1993).

Prejudice often is thought of in the context of race or ethnicity (e.g., European American vs. African American), but it also applies in areas such as gender, age, sexual orientation, and other independent contexts. Although prejudice can be positive (e.g., thinking highly of another culture without sufficient evidence such as "the Swiss are the best skiers"), it is usually negative (e.g., "women are too emotional").

As with ethnocentrism, we all hold prejudices to some degree. Sometimes our prejudices allow us to keep our partially fixed attitudes undisturbed and constant. Sometimes prejudice can reduce people's anxiety because it gives them a familiar way to structure their observations of others. One of the main problems with prejudice is that it is self-oriented rather than other-oriented. It helps us to achieve balance for ourselves at the expense of others. Moreover, attitudes of prejudice inhibit understanding by creating a screen that limits one's ability to see multiple aspects and qualities of other people. Prejudice is often expressed in crude or demeaning comments that people make about others. Both ethnocentrism and prejudice interfere with our ability to understand and appreciate the human experience of others.

In addition to fighting their own prejudices, leaders face the challenge of dealing with the prejudice of their followers. These prejudices can be toward the leader or the leader's culture. Furthermore, it is not uncommon for a leader to have followers who represent several culturally different groups that have their own prejudices toward each other. Prejudice can result in advantages for some groups over others and in **systemic discrimination**, which occurs when patterns of discriminatory behavior, policies, or practices become a part of an organization and continue to perpetuate disadvantage to those being discriminated against. Systemic discrimination can have a broad impact on an industry, profession, or geographic area.

A skilled leader needs to think about, recognize, and address when systemic discrimination exists within his or her organization and find ways to create inclusion with followers and groups who exhibit a multitude of differences.

Stereotypes

A **stereotype** is a fixed belief held by an individual that classifies a group of people with a similar characteristic as alike. Stereotypes allow people to respond to complex information and make meaning from it by either generalizing it or putting a blanket category around it. It is a way of processing information quickly.

Stereotypes label a group of individuals as the same at the expense of recognizing the uniqueness of each individual. Labeling everyone the same results in assuming things about some individuals that are not true. Stereotypes provide a way to generalize information, but during the process, "overgeneralizing" can occur, and individuals may get labeled with characteristics or qualities that do not apply to them. For example, if you say, "Nightshift workers are lazy," you are characterizing every worker who works that shift as lazy, when in fact it may be only one or two workers. If you stereotype the members of a certain ethnic or cultural group as terrorists, you may be correct for some individuals in that group, but not all of them.

In a small way, stereotypes can be useful. Stereotypes can reduce uncertainty in some situations because they provide partial information to us about others. For example, if you see some people wearing jerseys for the New England Patriots and you are also a Patriots fan, you will feel comfortable sitting next to them at a Patriots football game. You already assume, based on their clothing, that they have beliefs similar to yours. Similarly, if you tell your parents, who are of Dutch heritage, that they'll like your new partner because she is a "good Dutch woman," you are using a positive stereotype that will give your parents some information about your partner. This kind of stereotype provides limited information and begs to be challenged with phrases such as "What else can you tell me about this person?" Each individual is much more than a stereotype, so we must constantly challenge our mental assessments to look for the unique qualities of every person.

For leaders, stereotypes are a barrier to diversity and inclusion because stereotypes categorize individual followers into a single classification, which prevents the leader from seeing each individual's unique merits and qualifications. Because stereotypes are a mental shortcut, leaders can avoid thinking more deeply about individual followers. For example, if a college professor who teaches three classes labels one class as "a good class" and the other two as "bad classes" based on experiences he has had with some students in those classes, the stereotype will prevent him from seeing the many good qualities of individuals in the "bad" classes and also the negative qualities of the students in the "good" class.

Stereotypes have a significant impact on how leaders treat followers. To include followers and embrace them fully, leaders need to be attentive and open to the individual nuances of each of their followers. For Jane Doe to be included requires more than recognition of her gender. It requires understanding that she is a single mom with four kids, a part-time college student, a wife who lost her husband in the Iraq War, and a woman who is struggling with breast cancer. Calling Jane Doe a woman classifies her, but fails completely in accurately describing the uniqueness of her situation. When leaders stereotype followers, they box them in and trap them under simplistic and empty labels.

Privilege

A final barrier to inclusion is privilege. **Privilege** is an advantage held by a person or group that is based on age, race, ethnicity, gender, class, or some other cultural dimension, which gives those who have it power over those who don't. Privilege has been described as an unfair advantage that some people have in comparison to others. In situations where it exists, privilege excludes others and puts them at a disadvantage. For example, in many countries around the world, privileged people in the ruling class have political, economic, and social power over the poor, who are exploited and lack opportunities to transcend their circumstances. Or, to consider another example, during the Jim Crow period in the United States, privileged White citizens had power over Black citizens, and as a result, Black citizens suffered tremendously on all levels from employment and economics to education. Privilege is something that often goes unrecognized by those who have it, but usually is very apparent to those who do not have it.

Because privilege is a barrier to inclusion, leaders need to be introspective and determine if they are privileged in some way in comparison to others, including their followers. Because leadership involves a power differential between the leader and followers, leaders can often be blinded to the privilege they have. In addition, privilege can be very difficult for those without it to address because leaders may deny they have privilege or not acknowledge it because they do not want to weaken their power.

Those with privilege sometimes argue that the status and power they have is *not* privilege. Rather, they believe it is the result of their hard work, competence, and experience. For example, individuals who are born to affluent parents and go to good schools are likely to land good jobs when they graduate from college (Rivera, 2015). If one were to challenge privileged individuals about their privilege, they might say they obtained a good job because they worked hard and put in long hours. Rivera (2015) points out that it is often the connections that privileged individuals have with others of influence that lead them to find better jobs.

Unfortunately, those with privilege are many times unaware of how that privilege makes their lives different from the lives of those without privilege. Some people may believe that those in poverty are lazy and undeserving because they have not worked hard enough to pull themselves out of their circumstances. They may not be aware that poverty is a difficult condition to transcend. For example, imagine being the mother of two children, and as the result of a car accident, your spouse has developed a chronic health condition that keeps him from working and requires he have constant care. His medical bills wipe out any extra money you have. Even with welfare and disability income, it's a struggle to make rent and utility payments and buy enough food to feed your family. You want to work, but you can only work during school hours on weekdays when your children are in school. You do not have a car, so you must walk or take public transportation, which limits how far away your job can be from your home. Any small thing can upset the fragile balance you have established: a trip to the doctor, an unexpected bill, an increase in expenses. The road out of poverty for this mother and her family seems nearly impossible. Her situation seems so intractable that no amount of motivation or hard work could resolve it.

Having privilege blinds individuals to the experience of the underprivileged. Without the ability to understand, without judgment, individuals and their unique situations, leaders end up excluding rather than including them.

Collectively, the barriers to embracing diversity and inclusion (i.e., ethnocentrism, prejudice, stereotypes, and privilege) underscore the difficulty in accepting and confirming those who are different from ourselves. Leaders must not only address these barriers as they occur with their followers, but must also take a critical look at their own biases regarding diversity and work to eliminate these barriers in their own lives. As we have learned from Ferdman's framework, inclusion is a fluid process and must occur at the individual as well as societal level.

Privilege

SUMMARY

This chapter discusses how leaders can embrace diversity and inclusion in their organizations. *Diversity* plays a seminal role in effective leadership; it is defined as the *differing individuals in a group or organization. Inclusion* is defined as the process of *incorporating others who are different into a group or organization* in a way that allows them to feel they are part of the whole.

Diversity focuses on recognizing differences, and inclusion is concerned with embracing those differences.

The historical development of workplace diversity in the United States has emerged over three periods. The *early years* (1960s and 1970s), which included the creation of landmark equal employment laws, focused on discrimination and fairness. Second, the *era of valuing diversity* (1980s and 1990s) emphasized pluralism and the competitive advantages of diversity in the workplace. Third, the *era of diversity management and inclusion in the 21st century* (2000 to present) emphasizes acknowledging, valuing, and integrating people's differences into the organization and places inclusion at center stage in addressing concerns about diversity.

An inclusion framework was developed by researchers to describe how the process of inclusion works. This framework illustrates inclusion as an interaction of an individual's levels of belongingness (i.e., the desire to be connected) and uniqueness (i.e., the desire to maintain one's own identity). For leaders, managing diversity is about managing the tension followers experience between connectedness and individuality. The individual experience of inclusion occurs as a result of inclusion practices on many levels, including interpersonal, group, leader, organizational, and societal. Inclusion travels from the societal level down to the individual and back up the levels from the individual to societal.

Researchers have identified six components of the inclusion experience that provide a blueprint of how leaders should behave and communicate to provide inclusion for followers. To help followers *feel safe*, leaders need to treat them in nonthreatening ways. To help followers *feel involved and engaged*, leaders should recognize followers' strengths and let them know they are full-fledged members of the organization. To help followers *feel respected and valued*, leaders should practice the Golden Rule and show trust and care for followers. To help followers *feel influential*, leaders should recognize followers' need to have an impact on others and enable them to participate in decision making. To help followers feel *authentic and whole*, leaders should create an atmosphere where followers can feel free to be as honest and transparent as they are comfortable being. Finally, to help followers feel *recognized, attended to, and honored*, leaders should exhibit open-mindedness toward all followers, honoring the individuality of each of them.

Barriers that can inhibit leaders and followers from embracing diversity are *ethnocentrism, prejudice, stereotypes,* and *privilege*. The challenge for leaders is to remove or mitigate these barriers. Although addressing diversity is an interactive process between leaders and followers, the burden of effectively addressing diversity and building inclusion rests squarely on the shoulders of the leader. Effective leaders recognize the importance of diversity and make it a focal point of their leadership.

GLOSSARY TERMS

assimilation   188

differentiation   190

diversity   184

ethnocentrism   201

inclusion   185

melting pot   188

multiculturalism   187

pluralism   189

prejudice   202

privilege   204

stereotypes   203

systemic discrimination   202

ⓈSAGE edge™

Sharpen your skills with SAGE edge at **edge.sagepub.com/northouseintro4e**

SAGE edge for students provides a personalized approach to help you accomplish your coursework goals in an easy-to-use learning environment.

9.1 CASE STUDY

What's in a Name?

Springfield High School's athletic teams have been called the Redskins since the school opened in 1944. The small town of 7,000, which is roughly 95% White, is located in an area of the Midwest that once had thriving Native American tribes, a fact the community is proud to promote in its tourism brochures. So when the members of a local family with Native American ancestry came before the school board to ask that the name of Springfield High School's athletic teams be changed because they found the use of the word *Redskins* to be offensive, it created a firestorm in the town.

The school's athletic teams had competed as Redskins for 70 years, and many felt the name was an integral part of the community. People personally identified with the Redskins, and the team and the team's name were ingrained in the small town's culture. Flags with the Redskins logo flew outside homes and businesses, and decals with the image of the smiling Redskins mascot adorned many car windows.

"Locals would come before the board and say, 'I was born a Redskin and I'll die a Redskin,'" recalls one board member. "They argued that the name was never intended to be offensive, that it was chosen for the teams before 'political correctness' was a thing, and that it honored the area's relatively strong Native American presence."

But several other local Native American families and individuals also came forward in support of changing the name. One pointed out that "the use of the word *Redskin* is essentially a racial slur, and as a racial slur, it needs to be changed." The issue drew national attention, and speakers came in from outside the state to discuss the negative ramifications of Native American mascots.

However, the opposition to change was fierce. T-shirts and bumper stickers started appearing around town sporting the slogans "I'm a Redskin and Proud" and "Don't tell me I'm not a Redskin." At board meetings, those in favor of keeping the name would boo and talk over those speaking in favor of changing it, and argue that speakers who weren't from Springfield shouldn't even be allowed to be at the board meetings.

The board ultimately approved a motion, 5-2, to have the students at Springfield High School choose a new name for their athletic teams. The students immediately embraced the opportunity to choose a new name, developing designs and logos for their proposed choices. In the end, the student body voted to become the Redhawks.

There was still an angry community contingent, however, that was festering over the change. They began a petition to recall the school board members and received enough signatures for the recall to be put up for an election.

"While the kids are going about the business of changing the name and the emblem, the community holds an election and proceeds to recall the five members of the board who voted in favor of it," one of the recalled board members said.

The remaining two board members, both of whom were ardent members of the athletic booster organization, held a special meeting of the board (all two of them) and voted to change the name back to the Redskins.

That's when the state Department of Civil Rights and the state's Commission for High School Athletics stepped in. They told the Springfield School Board there could not be a reversal of the name change and that the high school's teams would have to go for four years without one, competing only as Springfield.

Over the course of those four years, new school board members were elected, and the issue quieted down. At the end of that period, the students again voted to become the Springfield Redhawks. "You know, the kids were fine with it," says one community member. "It's been ten years, and there's an entire generation of kids who don't have a clue that it was ever different. They are Redhawks and have always been Redhawks.

"It was the adults who had the problem. There's still a small contingent today that can't get over it. A local hardware store still sells Springfield Redskins T-shirts and other gear. There is just this group of folks who believe there was nothing disrespectful in the Redskins name."

QUESTIONS

1. Do you agree with the assertion the athletic team name should be changed?

2. Describe how Ferdman's model of inclusion practices (Table 9.4) worked in this case. Did the influence for inclusive practices travel both up and down the model?

3. What barriers to embracing diversity and inclusion did the school board and community experience in this case?

4. Using the inclusion framework in Table 9.3, where would you place the Native American residents in the town of Springfield? What about Native American students at Springfield High School?

5. By changing the name of the athletic teams, do you believe the school board was showing inclusive practices? If so, which ones?

6. What role does privilege play in the resistance of community members to change the athletic teams' name?

APPLICATION

9.2 CULTURAL DIVERSITY AWARENESS QUESTIONNAIRE

Purpose

1. To identify your attitudes and perspectives regarding cultural diversity
2. To help you become aware of and understand your prejudices and biases
3. To help you understand the potential consequences of your approach to diversity in the workplace

Directions

1. Read each statement and circle the number that best describes your belief or behavior.
2. Be as candid as possible with your responses; there are no right or wrong answers.

		Almost Never	Never	Sometimes	Almost Always	Always
1.	I am aware of my own biases and how they affect my thinking.	1	2	3	4	5
2.	I can honestly assess my strengths and weaknesses in the area of diversity and try to improve myself.	1	2	3	4	5
3.	I assume good intent and ask for clarification when I don't understand what was said or implied.	1	2	3	4	5
4.	I challenge others when they make racial/ethnic/sexually offensive comments or jokes.	1	2	3	4	5
5.	I speak up if I witness another person being humiliated or discriminated against.	1	2	3	4	5
6.	I do not participate in jokes that are derogatory to any individual group.	1	2	3	4	5
7.	I don't believe that my having a friend of color means that I'm culturally competent.	1	2	3	4	5
8.	I understand why a lack of diversity in my social circle may be perceived as excluding others.	1	2	3	4	5
9.	I realize that people of other cultures have a need to support one another and connect as a group.	1	2	3	4	5
10.	I do not make assumptions about a person or individual group until I have verified the facts on my own.	1	2	3	4	5
11.	I have multiple friends from a variety of ethnicities and abilities.	1	2	3	4	5
12.	I connect easily with people who look different than me and am able to communicate easily with them.	1	2	3	4	5
13.	I'm interested in the ideas and beliefs of people who don't think and believe as I do, and I respect their opinions even when I disagree.	1	2	3	4	5

Visit **edge.sagepub.com/northouseintro4e** for a downloadable version of this questionnaire.

9.2 CULTURAL DIVERSITY AWARENESS QUESTIONNAIRE

(Continued)

		Almost Never	Never	Sometimes	Almost Always	Always
14.	I work to make sure people who are different from me are heard and accepted.	1	2	3	4	5
15.	I recognize and avoid language that reinforces stereotypes.	1	2	3	4	5
16.	I know others' stereotypes associated with my ethnicity.	1	2	3	4	5
17.	I encourage People culturally different from myself to speak out on their issues and concerns and I validate their issues and concerns.	1	2	3	4	5
18.	I avoid assuming that others will have the same reaction as me when discussing or viewing an issue.	1	2	3	4	5
19.	I understand that I'm a product of my upbringing and believe there are valid beliefs other than my own.	1	2	3	4	5
20.	I do not take physical characteristics into account when interacting with others or when making decisions about others' competence or ability.	1	2	3	4	5
21.	I recognize that others stereotype me and I try to overcome their perceptions.	1	2	3	4	5
22.	I include people culturally different from myself in team decision-making processes that impact them.	1	2	3	4	5
23.	I actively seek opportunities to connect with people different than me and seek to build rapport with them.	1	2	3	4	5
24.	I believe "color blindness" is counterproductive and devalues a person's culture or history.	1	2	3	4	5
25.	I avoid generalizing behaviors or attitudes of one individual in a group to others.	1	2	3	4	5
26.	I actively convey that employees or students of varying backgrounds are as skilled and competent as others.	1	2	3	4	5
27.	I do not try to justify acts of discrimination to make the victim feel better. I validate his/her assessment of what occurred.	1	2	3	4	5
28.	I try to learn about and appreciate the richness of other cultures and honor their holidays and events.	1	2	3	4	5
29.	I believe there are policies and practices in place that negatively impact people outside the majority culture.	1	2	3	4	5
30.	I understand the definition of internalized racism and how it impacts people of color.	1	2	3	4	5
31.	I believe that race is a social construct, not a scientific fact.	1	2	3	4	5
32.	I know and accept that [people's] experiences and background impact how they interact and trust me.	1	2	3	4	5

Source: Adapted from Special Populations and CTE Illinois Leadership Project. (2016). Cultural Diversity Self-Assessment. Retrieved from http://illinoiscte.org/index.php/resources/cultural-competency-module

APPLICATION

(Continued)

9.2 CULTURAL DIVERSITY AWARENESS QUESTIONNAIRE
(Continued)

Scoring

Sum the numbers you circled on the questionnaire. This number is your cultural diversity awareness score.

Total Score

Cultural diversity awareness score: _____

Scoring Interpretation

This self-assessment is designed to measure your beliefs and behavior regarding cultural diversity and inclusion. A *higher score* on the assessment indicates that you are acutely aware of prejudice and bias, and that you are very aware of the impact of your behavior on others. Individuals who score high relate to others in ways that value diversity. A *lower score* on the assessment suggests that you are unaware of prejudice and bias, and that you are not fully aware of the impact of your biased behavior on others. Individuals who score low communicate with others in ways that do not value diversity.

If your score is 130–160, you are in the very high range.

If your score is 100–129, you are in the high range.

If your score is 70–99, you are in the moderate range.

If your score is 40–69, you are in the low range.

If your score is 0–39, you are in the very low range.

Improve Your Leadership Skills

If you have the interactive eBook version of this text, log in to access the interactive leadership assessment. After completing this chapter's questionnaire, you will receive individualized feedback and practical suggestions for further strengthening your leadership based on your responses in this questionnaire.

9.3 Observational Exercise

Diversity and Inclusion

Purpose

1.   To become aware of the dimensions of diversity and inclusion

2.   To develop an understanding of how leaders address diversity and inclusion in the workplace

Directions

1.   Your task in this exercise is to interview a leader about her or his views on diversity and inclusion. The individual you interview should have a formal position of authority in a company (e.g., supervisor, manager), a school (e.g., teacher, principal), or the community (e.g., director of social work, bank vice president, small business owner).

2.   Conduct a 30-minute semistructured interview with this individual by phone or in person.

3.   Develop your own interview questions. If necessary, you may incorporate ideas from the following questions:

   •   Tell me about your job. How long have you held this position, and how did you get it?
   •   What comes to your mind when you hear the word *diversity*? How is diversity addressed within your organization? How important do you think diversity is in your place of work? Why?
   •   Are there areas within your organization that have less diversity than other areas? Do you think the organization should address this?
   •   What challenges do you face regarding diversity among those whom you supervise?
   •   How do you treat employees/followers who are different from others? Do you allow everyone to participate in decision making?
   •   What is the best way to make an employee/follower who is a minority feel genuinely included with others?

Questions

1.   Based on your observations, how important is diversity and inclusion to the leader you interviewed?

2.   Which metaphor in Table 9.2 (i.e., melting pot, salad, or smorgasbord) would you use to describe the way the leader approaches his or her followers? Give examples to illustrate this metaphor.

3.   Do you think the leader holds any stereotypes about others? In what way do these affect his or her leadership?

4.   In what way does the leader try to make individuals who are different feel a part of the organization? Give specific examples where relevant.

5.   Do you think privilege is in any way related to how this person leads? Defend your answer.

Visit **edge.sagepub.com/northouseintro4e** for a downloadable version of this exercise.

9.4 REFLECTION AND ACTION WORKSHEET

Diversity and Inclusion

Reflection

1. What is your response to the word *diversity*? Do you think it is a significant problem in our society, or do you think it is overemphasized? Explain your thoughts on diversity.

2. Reflect on the six primary dimensions of cultural diversity shown in Table 9.1 (i.e., age, gender, race, mental and physical abilities, ethnicity, and sexual orientation). Which type of diversity is easiest for you to embrace, and which is hardest for you to embrace? Why? Explain your answers.

3. One way to explore the concept of *inclusion* is to reflect on your own personal feelings about inclusion. In a group situation, how much do you want to be included by others? Using a personal example, discuss a time when you were in a group or on a team when you felt included by others and a time when you felt excluded. Why did you feel included in one situation and not the other? Elaborate and discuss.

4. Think about what circumstances got you to where you are today. Do you have a past that some would describe as privileged? Or, would you say you are not privileged? Do you see your colleagues or coworkers as having privilege? Discuss your thoughts on privilege.

Action

1. Explore your answers on the Cultural Diversity Awareness Questionnaire. Select three items on which you chose *almost never* or *never*. Based on your responses to these items, discuss what you could do in your own leadership to be more inclusive toward others.

2. Imagine for a moment that you have been selected to lead a group service-learning project. What will you say to make others in your group feel psychologically safe? In what way will you let them participate in decision making? How will you encourage those individuals who are most different from the group to feel like insiders yet still unique? Discuss.

3. As discussed in the chapter, stereotypes often get in the way of including others who differ from us. What common stereotypes do you sometimes attribute to others (e.g., a White male police officer, a Muslim woman wearing a hijab, or a transgender man)? How can you change these stereotypes? What messages will you give yourself to eliminate these stereotypes? Discuss.

 Visit **edge.sagepub.com/northouseintro4e** for a downloadable version of this worksheet.

REFERENCES

Blaine, B. E. (2013). *Understanding the psychology of diversity* (2nd ed.). Thousand Oaks, CA: Sage.

Booysen, L. (2014). The development of inclusive leadership practice and processes. In B. M. Ferdman & B. R. Deane (Eds.), *Diversity at work: The practice of inclusion* (pp. 296–329). San Francisco, CA: Wiley.

Brewer, M. B. (1991). The social self: On being the same and different at the same time. *Personality and Social Psychology Bulletin, 17*(5), 475–482.

Dishman, L. (2015, May 18). Millennials have a different definition of diversity and inclusion. *Fast Company*. Retrieved from http://www.fastcompany.com/3046358/the-new-rules-of-work/millennials-have-a-different-definition-of-diversity-and-inclusion

Ferdman, B. M. (1992). The dynamics of ethnic diversity in organizations: Toward integrative models. In K. Kelly (Ed.), *Issues, Theory, and Research in Industrial/Organizational Psychology* (pp. 339-384). Amsterdam, The Netherlands: Elsevier Science Publishers.

Ferdman, B. M. (2014). The practice of inclusion in diverse organizations. In B. M. Ferdman & B. R. Deane (Eds.), *Diversity at work: The practice of inclusion* (pp. 3–54). San Francisco, CA: Wiley.

Ferdman, B. M., Barrera, V., Allen, A., & Vuong, V. (2009, August). Inclusive behaviors and the experience of inclusion. In B. G. Chung (Chair), *Inclusion in organizations: Measures, HR practices, and climate*. Symposium presented at the 69th Annual Meeting of the Academy of Management, Chicago.

Ferdman, B. M., & Deane, B. R. (Eds.). (2014). *Diversity at work: The practice of inclusion*. San Francisco, CA: Wiley.

Friedman, R. A. & Deinard, C. (1990). *Black Caucus Groups at Xerox Corporation (A)*. HBS No. 9-491-047. Boston, MA: Harvard Business School Publishing.

Gudykunst, W. B., & Kim, Y. Y. (1997). *Communicating with strangers: An approach to intercultural communication* (3rd ed.). New York, NY: McGraw-Hill.

Harrison, D. A., & Sin, H. (2006). What is diversity and how should it be measured? In A. M. Konrad, P. Prasad, & J. K. Pringle (Eds.), *Handbook of workplace diversity* (pp. 191–216). Thousand Oaks, CA: Sage.

Harvey, C. P. (2015). Understanding workplace diversity: Where have we been and where are we going? In C. P. Harvey & M. J. Allard (Eds.), *Understanding and managing diversity: Readings, cases, and exercises* (pp. 1–7). Boston, MA: Pearson.

Harvey, C. P., & Allard, M. J. (2015). *Understanding and managing diversity: Readings, cases, and exercises*. Boston, MA: Pearson.

Healey, J. P., & Stepnick, A. (2017). *Diversity and society: Race, ethnicity, and gender* (5th ed.). Thousand Oaks, CA: Sage.

Herring, C., & Henderson, L. (2015). *Diversity in organizations: A critical examination*. New York, NY: Routledge.

Hirshberg, J. J., & Ferdman, B. M. (2011, August 16). Leader-member exchange, cooperative group norms, and workplace inclusion in workgroups. In M. Shuffler, S. Burke, & D. Diaz-Granados (Chairs), *Leading across cultures: Emerging research trends from multiple levels*. Symposium presented at the 71st Annual Meeting of the Academy of Management, San Antonio, TX.

Loden, M. (1996). *Implementing diversity*. Boston, MA: McGraw-Hill.

Mor Barak, M. E. (2014). *Managing diversity: Toward a globally inclusive workplace* (3rd ed.). Thousand Oaks, CA: Sage.

Myers, V. A. (2012). *Moving diversity forward: How to go from well-meaning to well-doing*. Washington, DC: American Bar Association.

Ponterotto, J. G., & Pedersen, P. B. (1993). *Preventing prejudice: A guide for counselors and educators*. Newbury Park, CA: Sage.

Porter, R. E., & Samovar, L. A. (1997). An introduction to intercultural communication. In L. A. Samovar &

R. E. Porter (Eds.), *Intercultural communication: A reader* (8th ed., pp. 5–26). Belmont, CA: Wadsworth.

Rivera, L. A. (2015) *Pedigree: How elite students get elite jobs*. Princeton, NJ: Princeton University Press.

Schutz, W. C. (1958). *FIRO: A three dimensional theory of interpersonal behavior*. New York, NY: Holt, Rinehart & Winston.

Shore, L. M., Randel, A. E., Chung, B. G., Dean, M. A., Holcombe Ehrhard, K., & Singh, G. (2011). Inclusion and diversity in work groups: A review and model for future research. *Journal of Management, 37*(4), 1262–1289.

Solman, P. (2014, September 15). How Xerox became a leader in diversity—and why that's good for business. *PBS Newshour* [Television broadcast]. New York, NY: Newshour Productions.

Special Populations and CTE Illinois Leadership Project. (2016). *Cultural Diversity Self-Assessment*. Retrieved from http://illinoiscte.org/index.php/resources/ cultural-competency-module

Thomas, D. A., & Ely, R. J. (1996, September–October). Making differences matter: A new paradigm for managing diversity. *Harvard Business Review*. Retrieved from https://hbr.org/1996/09/making-differences -matter-a-new-paradigm-for-managing-diversity

Xerox. (2016). *Xerox diversity: Different ideas. Diverse people. Dramatic results*. Retrieved from https://www .xerox.com/assets/pdf/Xerox_Diversity_Brochure.pdf

Xerox a success in diversifying its work force. (1991, November 3). *Boston Globe*. Retrieved from http://articles.sun-sentinel.com/1991-11-03/ business/9102140547_1_affirmative-action-xerox -minorities

Listening to Out-Group Members

INTRODUCTION

In general, humans do not like conflict. And so when there are individuals in a group or an organization who do not identify with the larger group—an out-group—we tend to look at them as "troublemakers" or "malcontents." But in fact, all of us have been out-group members at one time or another. The term itself is descriptive, not derogatory. Out-groups are common and inevitable, and listening and responding to out-group members is one of the most difficult challenges facing a leader. When a leader fails to meet this challenge, out-group members feel devalued, and their unique contributions go unexpressed for the common good. Good leaders know the importance of listening to *all* members of a group, especially the out-group members.

It is common to find out-groups in any context where a group of individuals is trying to reach a goal. Out-groups are a natural occurrence in everyday life. They exist in all types of situations at the local, community, and national

ASK THE AUTHOR

Why is it Important for Leaders to Listen to Out-Group Members?

levels. In nearly all of these situations, when one or more individuals are *not* "on board," the performance of the group is adversely affected. Since out-group members are so common, it is important for anyone who aspires to be a leader to know how to work with them.

Out-group members can be identified in many everyday encounters. At school, out-group members are often those kids who do not see themselves as a part of the student body. For instance, they may want to participate in music, clubs, sports, and so on, but for a host of reasons do not do so. At work, there are out-groups comprising people who are at odds with management's vision, or who are excluded from important decision-making committees. On project teams, some out-group members are those who simply refuse to contribute to the activities of the larger group. On a broader scale, in the United States, the Tea Party is an out-group representing people who are disenchanted with taxes and big government.

Using Inclusive Language

The important thing to remember about out-group members is that, in spite of their seeming opposition to the larger group, they often have valuable contributions to make, and effort should be made to create an inclusive environment that will facilitate their contributions. As we discussed in Chapter 9, "Embracing Diversity and Inclusion," inclusion is the process of incorporating others into a group or organization by helping people who are different feel they are part of the whole. Rather than being viewed as "difficult," out-group members should be seen as being "different" than the whole, with different values and skills that can be recognized—and embraced—by other group members. Admittedly, this can be hard, but it starts with listening to out-group members.

This chapter will examine why it is important for a leader to listen to out-group members. The questions it will address are "Who is in the out-group?" "Why do out-groups form?" "What is the impact of out-groups?" and "How should a leader respond to out-groups?" This discussion of out-groups will emphasize specific strategies that leaders can employ to build a sense of belonging and community, and advance the goals of the larger group. And despite the negativity that is often associated with out-groups, there is a value implied in the direction taken in this chapter that out-groups aren't evil and that leaders have an obligation and a responsibility to *listen to out-group members and "bring them in"* to the efforts of the larger group. Some will argue with this position, and others will say it is naïve; but the unique inherent value of every single member of a group or an organization cannot go understated. Although there will be times when out-group members need to be abandoned because they are too extreme, it is inefficient to deal with them, or they just simply do not want to be included, this chapter will argue that in most situations leaders have a duty to listen to and include out-group members.

OUT-GROUP MEMBERS EXPLAINED

There are many different ways to define out-group members. For our purposes, the term **out-group members** refers to those individuals in a group or an organization who do not identify themselves as part of the larger group. They are individuals who are disconnected and not fully engaged in working toward the goals of the group. They may be in opposition to the will of a larger group or simply disinterested in the group's goals. They may feel unaccepted, alienated, and even discriminated against such as the class "bully" who acts out because she feels left out. In addition, they may think they are powerless because their potential resources have not been fully accepted by the larger group.

Out-groups come in many forms: They can be minorities who think their voice is not being heard, or people who think their ideas are unappreciated. They can be those who simply do not identify with the leader or other members of the primary group. Sometimes out-group members are social loafers—group members who are inclined to goof off or work below their capacity when they are in a group. In short, out-group members sense themselves to be at odds with the larger group. For example, the single female on an all-male board of trustees might feel that the other board members do not take her ideas seriously or appreciate her perspective on issues.

How Out-Groups Form

There are many different reasons that out-groups form. First, some out-groups form because people disagree with the social, political, or ethical position of the majority—they sense that they are in *opposition* to the larger group. When decisions need to be made in organizational settings, consensus is often difficult to achieve because of time constraints and the need to move forward. Without consensus, individuals align themselves either with the majority viewpoint or with the minority. This minority is often seen as an out-group. Even when decisions are made by taking a vote, the results often produce winners and losers, and the losers frequently perceive themselves as members of the out-group. Although voting on a decision is often seen as a desirable democratic approach to reaching an outcome, the downside is that it always results in individuals feeling they are not in concert with the rest of the group.

A second reason that out-groups form is explained by **social identity theory**. This theory suggests that out-groups come about because some individuals *cannot identify* with the beliefs, norms, or values of the dominant group members. Research on groups (Hogg & Abrams, 1988; Tajfel & Turner, 1979, 1986) indicates that individuals in groups often share a social

Group Identity

identity and act toward each other in terms of that identity (Abrams, Frings, & Randsley de Moura, 2005). In group settings, members embrace the social identity of other group members and make the group's concerns their own. For example, in a support group for people with cancer, group members are likely to embrace a common identity—as cancer survivors who are coping with the disease. People find meaning in belonging to the group and sharing their experiences with others. They see one another as having a shared experience. However, if one of the members is struggling with a more serious form of cancer and does not feel like a survivor, then that person may become an out-group member. Out-groups are created when individuals in a group cannot identify with the group and, as a result, do not embrace the dominant group's reality.

Closely related to the identity issue, a third reason out-groups form is because people sense that they are being *excluded* by the larger group. They do not know where they fit in or whether they are needed by others in the group. Group members may think they are too old, too young, too conservative, too liberal, or just plain different from the larger group. For example, on a college soccer team, freshman players might wonder how they fit in with the upperclassmen. Similarly, in a college nursing class made up mostly of women, a male student might feel different from the other nursing students and wonder how he fits in the program. In situations such as these, people often sense that they are alienated from the larger group. In addition, they may think of themselves as powerless and weak. It is no fun to think you are not a part of the group and to feel excluded from it. We all have a need for inclusion, and when those needs go unmet, we feel anxiety.

Understanding Out-Group Members

A fourth reason for out-group development is that some people *lack communication skills* or *social skills* that are needed to relate to a larger group. In any group of people, there are often one or two people who set themselves apart from the group through their actions. For example, in an undergraduate group project team, there may be a student who talks excessively or dominates group discussions and consequently alienates himself from the rest of the group. Or there could be a student who acts very dogmatic, or another who consistently makes off-the-wall remarks. These types of individuals distinguish themselves as different from the rest of the group by how they talk or act. It is as if they are unable to adapt to the norms of the group. As much as they try, these people often find themselves on the outside looking in. Even though they may want to join the larger group, they have difficulty doing so because they do not know how to fit in. In these situations, their lack of communication and social skills often leads them to becoming out-group members. In reality, there are many possible reasons for out-groups. Any one reason is as legitimate as another. Developing an understanding of these reasons is the first step in trying to resolve out-group issues.

The Impact of Out-Group Members

Out-group members can have many adverse effects on others. Some of the downsides of out-groups are relatively insignificant, such as causing minor inefficiencies in organizational productivity. Other downsides are more important, such as creating conflict or causing a strike to be called.

So why should a leader be concerned about the negative impact of out-group members? First, *out-group members run counter to building community.* The essence of community is encouraging everyone to be on the same page and moving everyone in the same direction. Community brings people together and provides a place where they can express similar ideas, values, and opinions, and where they can be heard by members of their team. Community allows people to accomplish great things. It enables people to work hand in hand in pursuit of a shared vision that supports the common good. Through community, people can promote the greater good of everyone in the group.

However, by their very nature, out-group members are either in conflict with or avoiding community. Because the community may seem threatening, unfamiliar, or uninteresting to them, some people have a need to pull away from community. Their action detracts from the community being able to use all of its resources to reach a common goal.

The following example occurred in a college social work class; it illustrates how out-groups can have a negative impact on community. Introduction to Social Work is a popular class with a good reputation on campus. Every semester, the major assignment in the class is a group service project in which everyone is required to participate.

One semester a few months after Hurricane Katrina had wreaked havoc in the South, several members of the class proposed a service project doing relief work in New Orleans over spring break. Clearly, there was a need for the project, and the project would utilize everyone's talents and skills. To pull it off, the class would need to do a lot of planning and fund-raising. Committees were to be formed and T-shirts designed. There seemed to be agreement that a good theme would be "Together—We Can Make Things Better."

Problems arose for the class when some of the students did not want to participate. One student pointed out that he thought it was the government's job to provide relief, not the private sector's. Another student argued that there were already many volunteers in New Orleans, and maybe the class could better serve others by doing cleanup work on the south side of their own city. Two others in the class did not like the idea of working for the poor over spring break because they wanted to go to Cancún, Mexico.

These students could not find common ground. The trip to New Orleans was canceled, there were no T-shirts printed, and the students ended up doing 40 hours each of tutoring at the local grade school as their service project. The class could not come to an agreement with the out-group members, whose wants and needs prevented the rest of the class from pursuing the project in New Orleans. The interests of the out-group prevented the class from experiencing community and all its benefits.

A second reason that leadership should be concerned with out-groups is that *out-groups have a negative impact on group synergy.* Group synergy is the positive energy created by group members who are working toward a common goal. It is an additive kind of energy that builds on itself. Group synergy is one of the most miraculous features of effective groups and of highly functioning teams. Groups with synergy accomplish far more than groups without it. Group synergy is not just the sum of each person's contribution; it is the sum of each person's contribution *and then some.* It is the "plus more" that allows high-functioning groups to achieve far beyond what would be expected.

Unfortunately, out-groups prevent groups from becoming synergistic. Out-groups take energy *away from* the group rather than *adding energy to* the group. If out-group members are upset and demanding, they take even more energy from the group. This energy is not directed toward the goals of the group and so has a negative impact on productivity. Rather than working together to accomplish a common goal, out-group members stand alone and seek to do their own thing. This is harmful for the group because the unique contributions of out-group members are not expressed, discussed, or utilized for the common good. Every person in a group brings singular talents and abilities that can benefit the group. When out-groups form, the individual contributions of some group members are not utilized, and group synergy is compromised.

This example about a team of marketing executives at a publishing company may help to illustrate this issue. The team was charged with developing concepts for a new publication on food and dining in their city. Two of the team members had worked on magazines before and had some strong ideas about the content for the new publication. Another team member worked in the restaurant industry for a number of years and had a different idea for the magazine's content based on his experience. A marketing executive who had neither magazine nor food industry experience had been put in charge of the team based on her seniority with the company. The fifth team member was a new hire who had just started at the agency.

Unfortunately, there were strained relationships between different groups on the committee from the outset. The two former magazine executives wanted the publication to be a dining guide with reviews of local area restaurants and

**Relationships Among
Group Members**

a detailed listing of every eatery in town. The writer from the food industry felt it should be more upscale, a glossy publication with feature stories on food trends and local chefs and beautiful, mouth-watering photographs created by a food stylist. The new hire, still learning the company's culture, was hesitant to offer an opinion, instead saying he would support what the team leader thought best. The team leader, who was four months from retirement, believed that the group members should work things out among themselves and come to a consensus on the best concept with which to move forward. The two magazine executives took the new hire to lunch several times, trying to convince him to come to their side. After several weeks of meetings, the team had to present a concept to the publishing company's board of directors. Because the team could not agree on a direction for the new publication, each side presented its concept to the board. The company president became incensed that the team was unable to put together a solid plan for a magazine and released all members from the project.

In the above example, the team leader failed to pull the divergent out-group members together into a single group. She needed to recognize the unique contributions of each of the out-group members (e.g., previous magazine experience, food industry knowledge, marketing expertise) and use those contributions for the benefit of the entire group. Because the leader was not successful in responding to the out-group members, group synergy was diminished, and the project was placed on hold.

A third reason out-groups are of concern to a leader is that *out-group members do not receive the respect they deserve from others.* A central tenet of ethical leadership is the duty to treat each member with respect. As Beauchamp and Bowie (1988) pointed out, people need to be treated as autonomous individuals with their own goals, and not as the means to another person's goals. Being ethical means treating other people's decisions and values with respect: Failing to do so would signify that they are being treated as means to another's ends.

Respecting Out-Group Members

A leader has an ethical responsibility to respond to out-group members. These individuals are not in the out-group without reason. They may have valid grounds for feeling alienated, unaccepted, or discriminated against, or for choosing simply to be uninvolved. No matter what the reasons are, out-group members are people who deserve to be heard by the leader and the other group members.

In summary, the impact of out-groups is substantial. When out-groups exist, they have a negative impact on community, group synergy, and the out-group members themselves. The challenge for every leader is to respond to out-group members in a way that enhances the group and its goals.

OUT-GROUP MEMBERS IN PRACTICE

While many ideas about effective leadership are abstract, these strategies for how a leader should respond to out-group members are tangible. They are concrete steps that a leader can take to handle out-group members more effectively. In reading these strategies, ask yourself how you could adopt them to improve your own leadership.

Strategy 1: Listen to Out-Group Members

More than anything else, out-group members want to be heard. Whether they perceive themselves to be powerless, alienated, or discriminated against, out-group members have a need for others to listen to them. Clearly, the fact that some people sense that they are not being heard is at the very center of why out-groups exist. Out-group members have ideas, attitudes, and feelings that they want to express; when they believe they have not been able to or will not be able to express them, they pull away and disassociate from the group.

Listening is one of the most important ways that a leader can respond to out-group members. While it requires paying attention to what people say, it also requires being attentive to what people mean. Listening is both a simple and a complex process that demands concentration, open-mindedness, and tolerance. Listening requires that a leader set aside his or her own biases in order to allow out-group members to express their viewpoints freely. When out-group members think that the leader has heard them, they feel confirmed and more connected to the larger group. Clearly, listening should be a top priority of a leader.

Strategy 2: Show Empathy to Out-Group Members

Empathy

Similar to listening, a leader also needs to show empathy to out-group members. **Empathy** is a special kind of listening that is more demanding than just listening. It requires a leader to try standing in the shoes of out-group members, and to see the world as the out-group member does. Empathy is a process in which the leader suspends his or her own feelings in an effort to understand the feelings of the out-group member.

While showing empathy comes more naturally to some than to others, it is a skill anyone can learn to improve. Techniques for showing empathy include restatement, paraphrasing, reflection, and giving support (see Table 10.1). Through the use of these techniques, a leader can assist out-group members to be understood.

Strategy 3: Recognize the Unique Contributions of Out-Group Members

Recognizing Contributions

Expectancy theory (Vroom, 1964) tells us that the first step in motivating others is to let workers know they are competent to do their jobs. Motivation builds when people know they are able to do the work. This is particularly true for out-group members. Out-group members become more motivated when a leader acknowledges their contributions to the larger group. All of us want to know that our contributions are legitimate and that others take us seriously. Out-group members want to believe that their ideas matter and that they are important to the group.

TABLE 10.1 How to Demonstrate Empathy

A leader can demonstrate empathy through four communication techniques:
1. Restatement
By restating what another person has verbalized without adding any of your own personal thoughts and beliefs, you directly acknowledge and validate another person's point of view. For example, say, "I hear you saying . . ." or "It sounds as if you feel . . ."
2. Paraphrasing
This communication technique involves summarizing in your own words what another person has verbalized. It helps to communicate to the other person that you understand what he or she is saying. For example, say, "In other words, you're saying that . . ." or "Stated another way, you're suggesting that . . ."
3. Reflection
By serving as a mirror or sounding board for another person's expressed or unexpressed emotions and attitudes, you focus on *how* something has been expressed, or the emotional dimension behind the words. This technique helps others gain an understanding of their emotions and assists them in identifying and describing those emotions. For example, say, "So you are pretty confused and angry by it all . . ." or "Am I correct in saying that you are frightened and intimidated by the process?"
4. Support
This communication technique expresses understanding, reassurance, and positive regard to let the other person know that he or she is not "in the boat alone." For example, say, "With your attitude, I know you'll do well . . ." or "I'm impressed with the progress you are making."

In many situations, it is common for out-group members to believe others do not recognize their strengths. To address these concerns, it is important for a leader to identify out-group members' unique abilities and assets, and to integrate these into the group process. For example, if an out-group member suggests a radical but ultimately successful approach to accomplish a difficult task, the leader should express appreciation to the out-group member and let her or him know that the idea was creative and worthwhile. A leader needs to let out-group members know that what they do matters—that it is significant to the larger group.

Another example of a college class in which students had to do a service-learning project helps illustrate the importance of recognizing the unique contributions of out-group members. For their project, one team in this small group communication class chose to build a wheelchair ramp for an elderly woman in the community. In the initial stages of the project, morale in the group was down because one group member (Alissa) chose not to participate. Alissa said she was quite uncomfortable using hand tools, and she chose not to do manual labor. The other team members, who had done a lot of planning on the project, wanted to proceed without her help. As a result, Alissa felt rejected and soon became isolated from the group. Feeling disappointed with her group, Alissa began to criticize the purpose of the project and the personalities of the other team members.

At that point, one of the leaders of the group decided to start being more attentive to Alissa and what she was saying. After carefully listening to many of her concerns, the leader figured out that although Alissa could not work with her hands, she had two amazing talents: She was good with music, and she made wonderful lunches.

Once the leader found this out, things started to change in the group. Alissa started to participate. Her input into the construction of the ramp consisted of playing each group member's and the elderly woman's favorite music for 30 minutes while the other group members worked on the ramp. In addition, Alissa provided wonderful sandwiches and drinks that accommodated each of the group members' unique dietary interests. By the last day, Alissa felt so included by the group, and was so often praised for providing great food, that she decided to help with the manual labor: She began raking up trash around the ramp site with a smile on her face.

Although Alissa's talents had nothing to do directly with constructing a ramp, she made a real contribution to building a successful team. Everybody was included and useful in a community-building project that could have turned sour if one out-group member's talents had not been identified and utilized.

Strategy 4: Help Out-Group Members Feel Included

William Schutz (1966) pointed out that, in small group situations, one of our strongest interpersonal needs is to know whether we belong to the group. Are we "in" or "out"? The very nature of out-groups implies that their members are on the sidelines and peripheral to the action. Out-group members do not feel as if they belong, are included, or are "in." Schutz suggested that people have a need to be connected to others. They want to be in a group, but not so much a part of the group that they lose their own identity. They want to belong, but do not want to belong so much that they lose their sense of self.

Although it is not always easy, a leader can help out-group members be more included. A leader can watch the communication cues given by out-group members and try to respond in appropriate ways. For example, if a person sits at the edge of the group, the leader can put the chairs in a circle and invite the person to sit in the circle. If a person does not follow the group norms (e.g., does not go outdoors with everyone else during breaks), the leader can personally invite the out-group member to join the others outside. Similarly, if a group member is very quiet and has not contributed, a leader can ask for that group member's opinion. Although there are many different ways to help out-group members to be included, the bottom line is that a leader needs to be sensitive to out-group members' needs and try to respond to them in ways that help the out-group members know that they are part of the larger group.

Strategy 5: Create a Special Relationship With Out-Group Members

The most well-known study on out-groups was conducted by a group of researchers who developed a theory called *leader–member exchange (LMX) theory* (Dansereau, Graen, & Haga, 1975; Graen & Uhl-Bien, 1995). The major premise of this theory, introduced in Chapter 1, is that a leader should create a special relationship with each follower. An effective leader has a high-quality relationship with all group members; this results in out-group members becoming a part of the larger group.

Lead-Member Exchange Theory

Special relationships are built on good communication, respect, and trust. They are often initiated when a leader recognizes out-group members who are willing to step out of scripted roles and take on different responsibilities. In addition, special relationships can develop when a leader challenges out-group members to be engaged and to try new things. If an out-group member accepts these challenges and responsibilities, it is the first step in forging an improved relationship between the leader and the out-group member. The result is that the out-group member feels validated and more connected to everyone else in the group.

An example of how special relationships benefit out-group members can be seen in the following example. Margo Miller was the school nurse at Central High School. She was also the unofficial school counselor, social worker, conflict mediator, and all-around friend to students. Margo noticed that there were a number of very overweight students who were not in any of the groups at school. To address this situation, she began to invite some of these students and others to exercise with her at the track after school. For some of them, it was the first time they had ever taken part in an extracurricular school program. The students and Margo called themselves the Breakfast Club because, like the characters in the movie by the same name, they were a motley crew. At the end of the semester, the group sponsored a school-wide 5K run/walk that was well attended. One overweight girl who finished the 5K said that Margo and the Breakfast Club were the best thing that had ever happened to her. Clearly, it was the special relationships that Margo created with her students that allowed out-group students to become involved and feel good about their involvement in the high school community.

**Building a
Collaborative Team**

Strategy 6: Give Out-Group Members a Voice and Empower Them to Act

Giving out-group members a voice lets them be on equal footing with other members of the group. It means the leader and the other group members give credence to the out-group members' ideas and actions. When out-group members have a voice, they know their interests are being recognized and that they can have an impact on the leader and the group. It is quite remarkable process when a leader is confident enough in his or her own leadership to let out-group members express themselves and have a voice in the affairs of the group.

Empowering others to act means a leader allows out-group members to be more involved, independent, and responsible for their actions. It includes letting them participate in the workings of the group (e.g., planning, decision making). True empowerment requires that a leader relinquish some control, giving out-group members more control. This is why empowerment is such a challenging process for a leader. Finally, empowering others is one of the larger challenges of leadership, but it is also one of the challenges that offers the most benefits for members of the out-group.

LEADERSHIP SNAPSHOT

Abraham Lincoln, 16th President of the United States

http://commons.wikimedia.org/wiki/ File:Abraham_Lincoln_head_on_ shoulders_photo_portrait.png.

Abraham Lincoln, a backwoods circuit lawyer from Springfield, Illinois, was an unlikely choice to become the 16th president of the United States. His mother died when he was 9, and he was distant from his father. As a youngster, he had little formal education but was an avid reader. Although he had a melancholy temperament, he was known for his storytelling ability and inspiriting sense of humor. After graduating from law school, he served one term in the U.S. House of Representatives and then proceeded to lose two subsequent contests for the U.S. Senate.

In 1860, he won the Republican nomination for president after ousting three formidable candidates: William Seward, a New York senator; Salmon Chase, an Ohio governor; and Edward Bates, a Missouri statesman. No one expected that a soft-spoken, unknown lawyer from rural Illinois could win the nomination, but at the convention, after three rounds of voting, Lincoln emerged as the Republican

nominee. Lincoln won the presidential election, and before he took office, six southern states seceded from the Union to form the Confederate States of America.

Lincoln began his presidency in a nation torn apart by the issue of slavery and whether slavery should be expanded, maintained, or abolished. In this context, Lincoln made a bold leadership decision: He selected for his cabinet the four archrivals who had opposed him in the presidential primary, as well as three Democrats. All of them were better known and more educated than Lincoln (Goodwin, 2005).

Lincoln's cabinet was a group of disparate politicians with strong egos who challenged the president's decisions repeatedly. Each of them had very different philosophies about the nation and slavery in particular. Some argued strongly for restricting the spread of slavery. Others argued for its abolition. Initially, the cabinet members did not view the president positively. For example, Attorney General Bates viewed Lincoln as well-meaning but an incompetent administrator. Edwin Stanton, the secretary of war, initially treated him with contempt but eventually learned to respect his competencies as commander in chief (Goodwin, 2005).

Lincoln had a remarkable ability to work with those with whom he disagreed and bring together those with disparaging opinions (Goodwin, 2005). For example, at the onset of the Civil War, Secretary of State Seward

(Continued)

(Continued)

directly challenged in writing Lincoln's response to the battle at Fort Sumter, claiming the administration was without a policy and should abandon its approach. In response, Lincoln wrote a letter to Seward explaining his own position, without insulting Seward. Instead of sending the letter, Lincoln delivered it to Seward personally. Such behavior was Lincoln's "hallmark in dealing with recalcitrant but important subordinates, generals or senators: a firm assertion of his own policy and responsibility for it, done in such as way as to avoid a personal rebuff that might create an enemy" (McPherson, 2005). Over time, Seward actually grew close to the president and became one of Lincoln's strongest supporters.

In a larger sense, Lincoln's leadership was also about bringing together a nation that was deeply divided. In 1858, well before he was elected president, Lincoln delivered his famous "House Divided" speech at the Illinois State Capitol in accepting his nomination for U.S. Senate. Based on a New Testament Bible passage (Mark 3:25), he stated, "A house divided against itself cannot stand. I believe this government cannot endure permanently half slave and half free. I do not expect the Union to be dissolved—I do not expect the house to fall—but I do expect it will cease to be divided. It will become all one thing, or all the other." In some ways, this speech foreshadowed Lincoln's style of leading and his role in addressing the debilitating and devastating impact of slavery on the country.

SUMMARY

In today's society, out-group members are a common occurrence whenever people come together to solve a problem or accomplish a task. In general, the term *out-group* refers to those people in a group who do not sense that they are a part of the larger group. Out-group members are usually people who feel disconnected, unaccepted, discriminated against, or powerless.

Out-groups form for many reasons. Some form because people are in opposition to the larger group. Others form because individuals in a group cannot identify with the larger group or cannot embrace the larger group's reality. Sometimes they form because people feel excluded or because out-group members lack communication and social skills.

Regardless of why they form, the negative impact of out-group members can be substantial. We need to be concerned about out-groups because they run counter to building community and have a negative impact on group synergy. Furthermore, out-group members do not receive the respect they deserve from those in the "in-group."

There are several specific strategies that a leader can use to respond effectively to out-group members. A leader needs to listen to out-group members, show them empathy, recognize their unique contributions, help them become included, create a special relationship with them, give them a voice, and empower them to act. A leader who uses these strategies will be more successful in his or her encounters with out-groups, and will be a more effective group leader.

GLOSSARY TERMS

empathy   224

listening   224

out-group members   219

social identity theory   219

⑤SAGE edge™

Sharpen your skills with SAGE edge at **edge.sagepub.com/northouseintro4e**

SAGE edge for students provides a personalized approach to help you accomplish your coursework goals in an easy-to-use learning environment.

10.1 CASE STUDY

Next Step

Next Step is a student organization run by graduate students in the School of Communication at a large West Coast university. The mission of Next Step is to provide students with opportunities that will help them prepare for the workforce or for more schooling. Some of the annual events that the group sponsors are résumé development workshops, a professional development day in which people from the community discuss their career paths, and workshops on interviewing skills.

Next Step has two annual bake sales to raise funds to pay for expenses such as renting meeting space, compensating speakers, and providing refreshments at group workshops. After a lukewarm fall semester bake sale, some Next Step members suggest finding a new fund-raising method, arguing that bake sales cost members money and require a lot of work for little profit.

Next Step's president, James, decides to put new fund-raising initiatives on the agenda for discussion at the group's next meeting. At that meeting, Brenna, a marketing and graphic design major, proposes that the group sell T-shirts as the winter semester's fund-raiser. Brenna believes that the college population likes to buy T-shirts and is confident that she can create a design that will appeal to students. Mallory, also a marketing major, volunteers to help promote the T-shirts. Group member Mark offers to use his employee discount at the screen shop where he works to have the shirts printed affordably.

Other Next Step members voice approval for the T-shirt fund-raiser, and the discussion moves to talking about designs for the shirts. James assigns Brenna and Mallory to survey students on their interest in buying the shirts and at what price. Brenna will also develop mock-ups of the shirt's design and bring them to the next meeting while Mark is assigned to get pricing options.

James leaves the meeting feeling positive about the direction the new fund-raiser is going, but as he loads his book back into his car, he overhears a conversation nearby. Next Step's treasurer, Nichole, calls the plan to sell T-shirts "stupid." She states she personally would never order a shirt from a student group and that Next Step is going to lose money printing the shirts. Ursula, Next Step's secretary, agrees with Nichole, calling other Next Group members "a bunch of Kool-Aid–drinking nerds" and remarking that nobody is going to buy those shirts. James is shocked. Not only does he not remember Nichole or Ursula voicing any objections to the plan at the meeting; he doesn't remember them saying anything during the meeting at all. James is concerned that two Next Step officers would talk so negatively about the group and wonders if it is fueled by the shift to selling T-shirts or something else. He makes a mental note to build an anonymous vote into the next meeting to make sure that members who don't like the idea have an opportunity to oppose it without being put in a public position.

Meanwhile, Brenna, Mallory, and Mark succeed in canvassing students, finding a reasonable price for T-shirts, and developing attractive mock-ups for Next Step members to consider. James feels confident that the positive outcome of the T-shirt committee's efforts will help Nichole and Ursula change their minds about the T-shirt sale.

However, the next day, James is working in a cubicle at the student center when Nichole enters. Before he gets a chance to leave his booth to say hi to her, Next Step's student liaison Todd comes up to Nichole and says, "Can you believe how much work those brownnosers are putting into selling T-shirts? Honestly, it's so dumb—at least no one expects us to pitch in though!" As student liaison, Todd has a pivotal role in the group and is responsible for promoting the group's efforts at other student meetings and for recruiting new members. His comments further alarm James.

James decides to act, and approaches Nichole and Todd, who were unaware that he was nearby. James makes small talk, and then reminds them about the Next Step meeting coming up in two days. Nichole rolls her eyes and says she knows about the meeting. James

asks her if everything is OK. Nichole responds, "Everything is fine. I just think that it's silly to get so involved in this T-shirt sale. We all have a lot going on for school, and this group is really just something to put on my résumé. I don't understand why we can't just stick with the easy, mindless bake sale." Todd nods in agreement and says, "Yeah, James, you can't tell me that you became president of a student group because you believe so much in its mission. We both know it's just because you want to look good when you apply for jobs this summer." Although taken aback by their attitudes, James responds that he believes in Next Step's mission and will make sure any and all concerns' regarding the fund-raiser are raised at the next meeting.

As he prepares for the upcoming meeting, James concludes that there seems to be a division, at least among the board's officers, between those who are excited about the group's mission and efforts and those who are not supportive. He wonders if other Next Step members share the attitudes expressed by Nichole, Ursula, and Todd or if they are in a minority. If they aren't, thinks James, and the division goes deeper, what does that mean for Next Step?

QUESTIONS

1. This chapter discusses several reasons that out-groups form. What is the best explanation for why Ursula, Nichole, and Todd appear to be out-group members? What impact are they having on Next Step? Do they have legitimate concerns? Discuss.

2. How could the initial meeting about fund-raising strategies have been conducted so that all members were included in the decision?

3. Of the six strategies for how leaders should respond to out-group members, do you think that certain strategies might be more appropriate or effective in this situation given the verbalized feelings about Next Step from the out-group members?

4. How could other members of the group besides James help to build the group identity and sense of cohesion in Next Step?

5. In this situation, do you think it is worth the time and effort to try to include Ursula, Nichole, and Todd? Defend your answer.

10.2 BUILDING COMMUNITY QUESTIONNAIRE

Purpose

1.   To identify your attitudes toward out-group members

2.   To explore how you, as a leader, respond to members of the out-group

Directions

1.   Place yourself in the role of a leader when responding to this questionnaire.

2.   For each of the statements below, circle the number that indicates the degree to which you agree or disagree.

Statements	Strongly disagree	Disagree	Neutral	Agree	Strongly agree
1. If some group members do not fit in with the rest of the group, I usually try to include them.	1	2	3	4	5
2. I become irritated when some group members act stubborn (or obstinate) with the majority of the group.	1	2	3	4	5
3. Building a sense of group unity with people who think differently than I is essential to what I do as a leader.	1	2	3	4	5
4. I am bothered when some individuals in the group bring up unusual ideas that hinder or block the progress of the rest of the group.	1	2	3	4	5
5. If some group members cannot agree with the majority of the group, I usually give them special attention.	1	2	3	4	5
6. Sometimes I ignore individuals who show little interest in group meetings.	1	2	3	4	5
7. When making a group decision, I always try to include the interests of members who have different points of view.	1	2	3	4	5
8. Trying to reach consensus (complete agreement) with out-group members is often a waste of time.	1	2	3	4	5
9. I place a high priority on encouraging everyone in the group to listen to the minority point of view.	1	2	3	4	5
10. When differences exist between group members, I usually call for a vote to keep the group moving forward.	1	2	3	4	5
11. Listening to individuals with extreme (or radical) ideas is valuable to my leadership.	1	2	3	4	5
12. When a group member feels left out, it is usually his or her own fault.	1	2	3	4	5
13. I give special attention to out-group members (i.e., individuals who feel left out of the group).	1	2	3	4	5
14. I find certain group members frustrating when they bring up issues that conflict with what the rest of the group wants to do.	1	2	3	4	5

Visit **edge.sagepub.com/northouseintro4e** for a downloadable version of this questionnaire.

10.2 BUILDING COMMUNITY QUESTIONNAIRE

(Continued)

Scoring

1. Sum the even-numbered items, but reverse the score value of your responses (i.e., change 1 to 5, 2 to 4, 4 to 2, and 5 to 1, with 3 remaining unchanged).

2. Sum the responses of the odd-numbered items and the converted values of the even-numbered items. This total is your leadership out-group score.

Total Score

Out-group score: _____

Scoring Interpretation

This questionnaire is designed to measure your response to out-group members.

- A high score on the questionnaire indicates that you try to help out-group members feel included and become a part of the whole group. You are likely to listen to people with different points of view and to know that hearing a minority position is often valuable in effective group work.
- An average score on the questionnaire indicates that you are moderately interested in including out-group members in the group. Although interested in including them, you do not make out-group members' concerns a priority in your leadership. You may think of out-group members as having brought their out-group behavior on themselves. If they seek you out, you probably will work with them when you can.
- A low score on the questionnaire indicates you most likely have little interest in helping out-group members become a part of the larger group. You may become irritated and bothered when out-group members' behaviors hinder the majority or progress of the larger group. Because you see helping the out-group members as an ineffective use of your time, you are likely to ignore them and make decisions to move the group forward without their input.

  If your score is 57–70, you are in the very high range.

  If your score is 50–56, you are in the high range.

  If your score is 45–49, you are in the average range.

  If your score is 38–44, you are in the low range.

  If your score is 10–37, you are in the very low range.

Improve Your Leadership Skills

If you have the interactive eBook version of this text, log in to to access the interactive leadership assessment. After completing this chapter's questionnaire, you will receive individualized feedback and practical suggestions for further strengthening your leadership based on your responses in this questionnaire.

10.3 OBSERVATIONAL EXERCISE

Out-Groups

Purpose

1. To learn to recognize out-groups and how they form
2. To understand the role of out-groups in the leadership process

Directions

1. Your task in this exercise is to identify, observe, and analyze an actual *out-group*. This can be an out-group at your place of employment, in an informal group, in a class group, in a community group, or on a sports team.

2. For each of the questions below, write down what you observed in your experiences with out-groups.

    Name of group: _____

    Identify and describe a group in which you observed an out-group.

    Observations of out-group members' actions:

    Observations of the leader's actions:

Questions

1. What is the identity of out-group members? How do they see themselves?

2. How were out-group members treated by the other members in the group?

3. What is the most challenging aspect of trying to deal with members of this out-group?

4. What does the leader need to do to integrate the out-group members into the larger group?

10.4 Reflection and Action Worksheet

Out-Groups

Reflection

1. Based on the score you received on the Building Community Questionnaire, how would you describe your attitude toward out-group members? Discuss.

2. As we discussed in this chapter, out-groups run counter to building community in groups. How important do you think it is for a leader to build community? Discuss.

3. One way to engage out-group members is to *empower* them. How do you see your own competencies in the area of empowerment? What keeps you from empowering others? Discuss.

Action

1. Using items from the Building Community Questionnaire as your criteria, list three specific actions you could take that would show sensitivity to and tolerance of out-group members.

2. In the last section of this chapter, six strategies for responding to out-group members were discussed. Rank these strategies from strongest to weakest with regard to how you use them in your own leadership. Describe specifically what you could do to become more effective in all six strategies.

3. Imagine for a moment that you are doing a class project with six other students. The group has decided by taking a vote to do a fund-raising campaign for the local Big Brothers Big Sisters program. Two people in the group have said they are not enthused about the project and would rather do something for an organization like Habitat for Humanity. While the group is moving forward with the agreed-upon project, the two people who did not like the idea have started missing meetings, and when they do attend, they are very negative. As a leader, list five specific actions you could take to assist and engage this out-group.

 Visit **edge.sagepub.com/northouseintro4e** for a downloadable version of this worksheet.

REFERENCES

Abrams, D., Frings, D., & Randsley de Moura, G. (2005). Group identity and self-definition. In S. A. Wheelan (Ed.), *Handbook of group research and practice* (pp. 329–350). London, United Kingdom: Sage.

Beauchamp, T. L., & Bowie, N. E. (1988). *Ethical theory and business* (3rd ed.). Englewood Cliffs, NJ: Prentice Hall.

Dansereau, F., Graen, G. G., & Haga, W. (1975). A vertical dyad linkage approach to leadership in formal organizations. *Organizational Behavior and Human Performance, 13*(1), 46–78.

Goodwin, D. K. (2005). *Team of rivals: The political genius of Abraham Lincoln.* New York, NY: Simon & Schuster.

Graen, G. B., & Uhl-Bien, M. (1995). Relationship-based approach to leadership: Development of leader–member exchange (LMX) theory of leadership over 25 years: Applying a multi-level, multi-domain perspective. *Leadership Quarterly, 6*(2), 219–247.

Hogg, M. A., & Abrams, D. (1988). *Social identifications: A social psychology of intergroup relations and group processes.* London, UK: Routledge.

McPherson, J. M. (2005, November 6). "Team of rivals": Friends of Abe. *The New York Times.* Retrieved from http://www.nytimes.com/2005/11/06/books/review/06mcpherson.html?pagewanted=all&_r=0

Schutz, W. (1966). *The interpersonal underworld.* Palo Alto, CA: Science & Behavior Books.

Tajfel, H., & Turner, J. C. (1979). An integrative theory of intergroup conflict. In S. Worchel & W. G. Austin (Eds.), *The social psychology of intergroup relations* (pp. 33–47). Monterey, CA: Brooks-Cole.

Tajfel, H., & Turner, J. C. (1986). The social identity theory of inter-group behavior. In S. Worchel & L. W. Austin (Eds.), *Psychology of intergroup relations* (pp. 7–24). Chicago, IL: Nelson-Hall.

Vroom, V. H. (1964). *Work and motivation.* New York, NY: Wiley.

Managing Conflict

INTRODUCTION

Conflict is inevitable in groups and organizations, and it presents both a challenge and a true opportunity for every leader. In the well-known book *Getting to Yes*, Fisher and Ury (1981) contend that handling conflict is a daily occurrence for all of us. People differ, and because they do, they need to negotiate with others about their differences (pp. xi–xii). *Getting to Yes* asserts that mutual agreement is possible in any conflict situation—if people are willing to negotiate in authentic ways.

When we think of conflict in simple terms, we think of a struggle between people, groups, organizations, cultures, or nations. Conflict involves opposing forces, pulling in different directions. Many people believe that conflict is disruptive, causes stress, and should be avoided.

As we stated in Chapter 6, while conflict can be uncomfortable, it is not unhealthy, nor is it necessarily bad. Conflict will always be present in leadership situations, and surprisingly, it often produces positive change. The important question we address in this chapter is not "How can we *avoid* conflict and *eliminate* change?" but rather "How can we *manage* conflict and

ASK THE
AUTHOR

**Is Conflict Really
Inevitable?**

produce *positive* change?" When leaders handle conflict effectively, problem solving increases, interpersonal relationships become stronger, and stress surrounding the conflict decreases.

Communication plays a central role in handling conflict. Conflict is an interactive process between two or more parties that requires effective human interaction. By communicating effectively, leaders and followers can successfully resolve conflicts to bring positive results.

This chapter will emphasize ways to handle conflict. First, we will define conflict and describe the role communication plays in conflict. Next, we will discuss different kinds of conflict, followed by an exploration of Fisher and Ury's (1981) ideas about effective negotiation as well as other communication strategies that help resolve conflict. Last, we will examine styles of approaching conflict and the pros and cons of these styles.

ASK THE AUTHOR

What Are Some Strategies for Handling Conflict?

CONFLICT EXPLAINED

Conflict has been studied from multiple perspectives, including *intra*personal, *inter*personal, and societal. Intrapersonal conflict refers to the discord that occurs *within* an individual. It is a topic often studied by psychologists and personality theorists who are interested in the dynamics of personality and factors that predispose people to inner conflicts. Interpersonal conflict refers to the disputes that arise *between individuals.* This is the type of conflict we focus on when we discuss conflict in organizations. Societal conflict refers to clashes *between societies and nations.* Studies in this field focus on the causes of international conflicts, war, and peace. The continuing crisis between the Israelis and the Palestinians is a good example of social conflict. This chapter focuses on conflict as an interpersonal process that plays a critical role in effective leadership.

The following definition, based on the work of Wilmot and Hocker (2011, p. 11), best describes conflict. **Conflict** is a felt struggle between two or more interdependent individuals over perceived incompatible differences in beliefs, values, and goals, or over differences in desires for esteem, control, and connectedness. This definition emphasizes several unique aspects of conflict (Wilmot & Hocker, 2011).

First, conflict is a *struggle*; it is the result of opposing forces coming together. For example, there is conflict when a leader and a senior-level employee oppose each other on whether or not all employees must work on weekends. Similarly, conflict occurs when a school principal and a parent disagree on the type of sex education program that should be adopted in a school system. In short, conflict involves a clash between opposing parties.

Second, there needs to be an element of *interdependence* between parties for conflict to take place. If leaders could function entirely independently of each other and their followers, there would be no reason for conflict. Everyone could do their own work, and there would be no areas of contention. However, leaders do not work in isolation. Leaders need followers, and followers need leaders. This interdependence sets up an environment in which conflict is more likely.

When two parties are interdependent, they are forced to deal with questions such as "How much influence do I want in this relationship?" and "How much influence am I willing to accept from the other party?" Because of our interdependence, questions such as these cannot be avoided. In fact, Wilmot and Hocker (2011) contend that these questions permeate most conflicts.

Third, conflict always contains an *affective* element, the "felt" part of the definition. Conflict is an emotional process that involves the arousal of feelings in both parties of the conflict (Brown & Keller, 1979). When our beliefs or values on a highly charged issue (e.g., the right to strike) are challenged, we become upset and feel it is important to defend our position. When our feelings clash with others' feelings, we are in conflict.

The primary emotions connected with conflict are not always anger or hostility. Rather, an array of emotions can accompany conflict. Hocker and Wilmot (1995) found that many people report feeling lonely, sad, or disconnected during conflict. For some, interpersonal conflict creates feelings of abandonment—that their human bond to others has been broken. Feelings such as these often produce the discomfort that surrounds conflict.

Fourth, conflict involves *differences* between individuals that are perceived to be incompatible. Conflict can result from differences in individuals' beliefs, values, and goals, or from differences in individuals' desires for control, status, and connectedness. The opportunities for conflict are endless because each of us is unique with particular sets of interests and ideas. These differences are a constant breeding ground for conflict.

In summary, these four elements—struggle, interdependence, feelings, and differences—are critical ingredients of interpersonal conflict. To further understand the intricacies of managing conflict, we'll look at the role of communication in conflict and examine two major kinds of conflict.

Communication and Conflict

When conflict exists in leadership situations, it is recognized and expressed through communication. Communication is the means that people use to express their disagreements or differences. Communication also provides the

Using Conversation

avenue by which conflicts can be successfully resolved, or worsened, producing negative results.

To understand conflict, we need to understand communication. When human communication takes place, it occurs on two levels. One level can be characterized as the *content dimension* and the other as the *relationship dimension* (Watzlawick, Beavin, & Jackson, 1967). The **content dimension** of communication involves the objective, observable aspects such as money, weather, and land; the **relationship dimension** refers to the participants' perceptions of their connection to one another. In human communication, these two dimensions are always bound together.

To illustrate the two dimensions, consider the following hypothetical statement made by a supervisor to an employee: "Please stop texting at work." The *content* dimension of this message refers to rules and what the supervisor wants the employee to do. The *relationship* dimension of this message refers to how the supervisor and the employee are affiliated—to the supervisor's authority in relation to the employee, the supervisor's attitude toward the employee, the employee's attitude toward the supervisor, and their feelings about one another. It is the relationship dimension that implicitly suggests how the content dimension should be interpreted, since the content alone can be interpreted in different ways. The exact meaning of the message to the supervisor and employee is interpreted as a result of their interaction. If a positive relationship exists between the supervisor and the employee, then the content "please stop texting at work" will probably be interpreted by the employee as a friendly request by a supervisor who is honestly concerned about the employee's job performance. However, if the relationship between the supervisor and the employee is superficial or strained, the employee may interpret the content of the message as a rigid directive, delivered by a supervisor who enjoys giving orders. This example illustrates how the meanings of messages are not in words alone but in individuals' interpretations of the messages in light of their relationships.

The content and relationship dimensions provide a lens for looking at conflict. As illustrated in Figure 11.1, there are two major kinds of conflict: conflict over content issues and conflict over relationship issues. Both kinds of conflict are prevalent in groups and organizational settings.

Conflict on the Content Level

Content conflicts involve struggles between leaders and others who differ on issues such as policies and procedures. Debating with someone about the advantages or disadvantages of a particular rule is a familiar occurrence in most organizations. Sometimes these debates can be very heated (e.g., an

FIGURE 11.1   Different Kinds of Content and Relational Conflicts

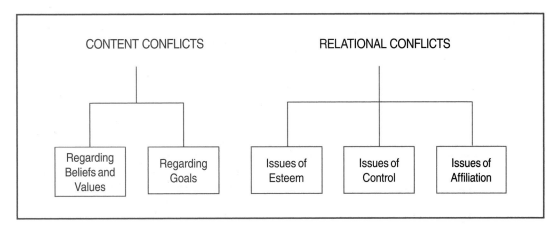

argument between two employees about surfing the Internet while working). These disagreements are considered conflicts on the content level when they center on differences in (1) beliefs and values or (2) goals and ways to reach those goals.

Conflict Regarding Beliefs and Values

Each of us has a unique system of beliefs and values that constitutes a basic philosophy of life. We have had different family situations as well as educational and work experiences. When we communicate with others, we become aware that others' viewpoints are often very different from our own. If we perceive what another person is communicating as incompatible with our own viewpoint, a conflict in beliefs or values is likely to occur.

Conflicts arising from differences in beliefs can be illustrated in several ways. For example, members of PETA (People for the Ethical Treatment of Animals) are in conflict with researchers in the pharmaceutical industry who believe strongly in using animals to test new drugs. Another example of a conflict of beliefs can occur when teachers or nurses believe they have the right to strike because of unfair working conditions, while others feel that these kinds of employees should not be allowed to withhold services for any reason. In each of these examples, conflict occurs because one individual feels that his or her *beliefs* are incompatible with the position taken by another individual on the issue.

Conflicts can also occur between people because they have different *values*. When one person's values come into conflict with another's, it can create a difficult and challenging situation. To illustrate, consider the following

LEADERSHIP SNAPSHOT

Humaira Bachal, Pakistani Educator

©Photo courtesy of Humaira Bachal.

Humaira Bachal is a 30-year-old woman who has a dangerous passion: She wants to educate children, especially girls, in her home country of Pakistan where only 57% of the children ever enter primary school.

It's hard not to worry about Bachal in the wake of the 2012 shooting of Malala Yousafzai, a teenage Pakistani girl attacked by the Taliban for speaking out in support of girls' education. But she's not afraid.

When Bachal was in ninth grade, she looked around her village of Moach Goth and saw children playing in the streets instead of being in school or studying, and at all of 14, she thought that was wrong. There were no private or government schools in her neighborhood, and Bachal had received education only because her mother had sewn clothing or sold bundles of wood for 2 cents a piece to send her children to schools elsewhere.

Bachal knew what it meant to have to fight to be educated. Her father did not want her to go to school, saying that she "was only going to get married and have children" (Rahi, 2010).

But her mother had other ideas. She wasn't educated, but believed her children should be. She labored to pay for her daughter's education herself and had to sneak her off to school, hiding Bachal's whereabouts from her father. When he found out Bachal was going to take her ninth-grade entrance exams, he became furious and beat her mother, breaking her arm. Despite this, her mother gathered her daughter's school bag and sent her on her way to the exam, which she passed.

"My mother's support at that critical moment was essential in making me who I am today," Bachal says (Faruqi & Obaid-Chinoy, 2013).

That same year while she was still being educated, Bachal started recruiting students in her neighborhood to come to a small, private school she had opened. She even went door-to-door to convince parents to send their children to the school. More than once she had a door slammed in her face and her life threatened.

"Education is a basic need and fundamental right for every human being," she says. "I want to change the way my community looks at education and I will continue to do this until my last breath" (Temple-Raston, 2013).

Pakistan has a dismal education rate: It spends half as much as neighboring India on education, and if you are a young girl in rural Pakistan, you are unlikely to ever see the inside of a classroom. There are more than 32 million girls under the age of 14 in Pakistan; fewer than 13 million of them go to school (Faruqi & Obaid-Chinoy, 2013).

In 2003, Bachal and five friends created their school, the Dream Foundation Trust Model Street School, in a two-room building with mud floors. In just over a decade, Dream Foundation has grown into a formal school with 22 teachers and 1,200 students. Children pay a rupee a day to attend classes. There are four shifts at the school, including computer classes and one for "labour boys" who work all day and attend classes in the evening. The Dream Foundation Trust also offers adult literacy classes for men and women.

But Bachal and the school are specifically interested in educating girls. Bachal will often visit fathers at their workplaces to convince them to send their daughters to school. She asks why, when the girls become teenagers, they stop coming to school. The fathers talk about honor and culture and how the girls are looked at by men as they go to school, and the men say things about them. Bachal can relate; at one point the men in her village called her immoral for becoming educated, and her brothers and father wanted to relocate to put an end to their shame (Faruqi & Obaid-Chinoy, 2013).

Bachal reaches out to mothers to make them allies in her crusade. She asks them if they want their daughters to be treated as unjustly as they have been and urges the women to help their daughters have better lives by insisting that they get an education.

Bachal's mother has no regrets about the sacrifices she made to ensure her daughters were educated, saying, "Education is essential for women. They (her daughters) have reached this potential because of their education. Otherwise they would have been slaving away for their husbands somewhere" (Rahi, 2010).

And despite the attack against Malala Yousafzai, Bachal says she isn't worried for her own safety.

"Just the opposite," she says. "It is not just one Malala or one Bachal who has raised a voice to change this situation. There are a lot of other girls who are trying to change things. Even if they kill 100 Humairas, they won't be able to stop us" (Temple-Raston, 2013).

example of an issue between Emily, a first-generation college student, and her mother. At the beginning of her senior year, Emily asks her mother if she can have a car to get around campus and to get back and forth to work. In order to pay for the car, Emily says she will take fewer credits, work more often at her part-time job, and postpone her graduation date to the following year. Emily is confident that she will graduate and thinks it is "no big deal" to extend her studies for a fifth year. However, Emily's mother does not feel the same. She doesn't want Emily to have a car until after she graduates. She thinks the car will be a major distraction and get in the way of Emily's studies. Emily is the first person in her family to get a college degree, and it is extremely important to her mother that Emily graduates on time. Deep down, her mother is afraid that the longer Emily goes to school, the more student loan debt Emily will have to pay back when she finishes.

The value conflict between Emily and her mother involves Emily's desire to have a car. In this case, both individuals are highly interdependent of one another: To carry out her decision to get a car, Emily needs her mother's agreement; to have her daughter graduate in four years, Emily's mother needs cooperation from Emily. Both individuals perceive the other's values as incompatible with their own, and this makes conflict inevitable. Clearly, the conflict between Emily and her mother requires interpersonal communication about their different values and how these differences affect their relationship.

Conflict Regarding Goals

A second common type of content-related conflict occurs in situations where individuals have different *goals* (see Figure 11.1). Researchers have identified two types of conflict that occur regarding group goals: (1) procedural conflict and (2) substantive conflict (Knutson, Lashbrook, & Heemer, 1976).

Procedural conflict refers to differences between individuals with regard to the approach they wish to take in attempting to reach a goal. In essence, it is conflict over the best means to an agreed-upon goal; it is not about what goal to achieve. Procedural conflicts can be observed in many situations such as determining how to best conduct job interviews, choose a method for identifying new sales territories, or spend advertising dollars. In each instance, conflict can occur when individuals do not agree on how to achieve a goal.

Substantive conflict occurs when individuals differ with regard to the substance of the goal itself, or what the goal should be. For example, two board members of a nonprofit human service agency may have very different views regarding the strategies and scope of a fund-raising campaign. Similarly, two owners of a small business may strongly disagree about whether or not to offer their part-time employees health care benefits. On the international level, in Afghanistan, the Taliban and those who are not members of the Taliban have different perspectives on whether or not girls should be educated. These illustrations by no means exhaust all the possible examples of substantive conflict; however, they point out that conflict can occur as a result of two or more parties disagreeing on what the goal or goals of a group or an organization should be.

Conflict on the Relational Level

Have you ever heard someone say, "I don't seem to get along with her [or him]; we have a personality clash"? The phrase *personality clash* is another way of describing a conflict on the relational level. Sometimes we do not get along with another person, not because of *what* we are talking about (conflict over content issues) but because of *how* we are talking about it. **Relational conflict** refers to the differences we feel between ourselves and others concerning how we relate to each other. For example, at a staff meeting, a manager interrupts employees and talks to them in a critical tone. The employees begin texting on their phones, ignoring the manager. A conflict erupts because both the manager and the employees feel unheard and disrespected. It is typically caused by neither one person nor the other, but arises in their relationship. Relational conflict is usually related to incompatible differences between individuals over issues of (1) esteem, (2) control, and (3) affiliation (see Figure 11.1).

Relational Conflict and Issues of Esteem

The need for esteem and recognition has been identified by Maslow (1970) as one of the major needs in the hierarchy of human needs. Each of us has needs for esteem—we want to feel significant, useful, and worthwhile. We desire to have an effect on our surroundings and to be perceived by others as worthy of their respect. We attempt to satisfy our esteem needs through what we do and how we act, particularly in how we behave in our relationships with our coworkers.

The Need for Esteem

When our needs for esteem are not being fulfilled in our relationships, we experience relational conflict because others do not see us in the way we wish to be seen. For example, an administrative assistant can have repeated conflicts with an administrator if the assistant perceives that the administrator fails to recognize his or her unique contributions to the overall goals of the organization. Similarly, older employees may be upset if newer coworkers do not give them respect for the wisdom that comes with their years of experience. So, too, younger employees may want recognition for their innovative approaches to problems but fail to get it from coworkers with more longevity who do not think things should change.

At the same time that we want our own esteem needs satisfied, others want their esteem needs satisfied as well. If the supply of respect we can give each other seems limited (or scarce), then our needs for esteem will clash. We will see the other person's needs for esteem as competing with our own or taking that limited resource away from us. To illustrate, consider a staff meeting in which two employees are actively contributing insightful ideas and suggestions. If one of the employees is given recognition for her input but the other is not, conflict may result. As this conflict escalates, the effectiveness of their working relationship and the quality of their communication may diminish. When the amount of available esteem (validation from others) seems scarce, a clash develops.

All of us are human and want to be recognized for the contributions we make to our work and our community. When we believe we're not being recognized or receiving our "fair share," we feel slighted and conflicted on the relational level with others.

Relational Conflict and Issues of Control

Struggles over issues of control are very common in interpersonal conflict. Each one of us desires to have an impact on others and the situations that surround us. Having control, in effect, increases our feelings of potency about our actions and minimizes our feelings of helplessness. Control allows us to feel competent about ourselves. However, when we see others as hindering us or limiting our control, interpersonal conflict often ensues.

Conflict Over Control

Interpersonal conflict occurs when a person's needs for control are incompatible with another's needs for control. In a given situation, each of us seeks different levels of control. Some people like to have a great deal, while others are satisfied (and sometimes even more content) with only a little. In addition, our needs for control may vary from one time to another. For example, there are times when a person's need to control others or events is very high; at other times, this same person may prefer that others take charge. Relational conflict over control issues develops when there is a clash between the needs for control that one person has at a given time (high or low) and the needs for control that others have at that same time (high or low). If, for example, a friend's need to make decisions about weekend plans is compatible with yours, no conflict will take place; however, if both of you want to control the weekend planning and your individual interests are different, then you will soon find yourselves in conflict. As struggles for control ensue, the communication among the participants may become negative and challenging as each person tries to gain control over the other or undermine the other's control.

A graphic example of a conflict over relational control is provided in the struggle between Lauren Smith, a college sophomore, and her parents, regarding what she will do on spring break. Lauren wants to go to Cancún, Mexico, with some friends to relax from the pressures of school. Her parents do not want her to go. Lauren thinks she deserves to go because she is doing well in her classes. Her parents think spring break in Cancún is just a "big party" and nothing good will come of it. As another option, her parents offer to pay Lauren's expenses to go on an alternative spring break to clean up an oil spill in the Gulf of Mexico. Lauren is adamant that she "is going" to Cancún. Her parents, who pay her tuition, threaten that if she goes to Cancún, they will no longer pay for college.

Clearly, in the above example, both parties want to have control over the outcome. Lauren wants to be in charge of her own life and make the decisions about what she does or does not do. At the same time, her parents want to direct her into doing what they think is best for her. Lauren and her parents are interdependent and need each other, but they are conflicted because they each feel that the other is interfering with their needs for control of what Lauren does on spring break.

Conflicts over control are common in leadership situations. Like the parents in the above example, the role of leader brings with it a certain inherent level of control and responsibility. When leaders clash with one another over control or when control issues exist between leaders and followers, interpersonal conflicts occur. Later in this chapter, we present some conflict management strategies that are particularly helpful in coping with relational conflicts that arise from issues of control.

Leaders' Essential Role in Conflict Management

Relational Conflict and Issues of Affiliation

In addition to wanting relational control, each of us has a need to feel included in our relationships, to be liked, and to receive affection (Schutz, 1966). If our needs for closeness are not satisfied in our relationships, we feel frustrated and experience feelings of conflict. Of course, some people like to be very involved and very close in their relationships, while others prefer less involvement and more distance. In any case, when others behave in ways that are incompatible with our own desires for warmth and affection, feelings of conflict emerge.

Relational conflict over affiliation issues is illustrated in the following example of a football coach, Terry Jones, and one of his players, Danny Larson. Danny, a starting quarterback, developed a strong relationship with Coach Jones during his junior year in high school. Throughout the year, Danny and Coach Jones had many highly productive conversations inside and outside of school about how to improve the football program. In the summer, the coach employed Danny in his painting business, and they worked side by side on a first-name basis. Both Danny and Terry liked working together and grew to know each other quite well. However, when football practice started in the fall, difficulties emerged between the two. During the first weeks of practice, Danny acted like Coach Jones was his best buddy. He called him Terry rather than Coach Jones, and he resisted the player–coach role. As Coach Jones attempted to withdraw from his summer relationship with Danny and take on his legitimate responsibilities as a coach, Danny experienced a sense of loss of closeness and warmth. In this situation, Danny felt rejection or a loss of affiliation, and this created a relational conflict.

Relational conflicts—whether they are over esteem, control, or affiliation— are seldom overt. Due to the subtle nature of these conflicts, they are often not easy to recognize or address. Even when they are recognized, relational conflicts are often ignored because it is difficult for many individuals to openly communicate that they want more recognition, control, or affiliation.

According to communication theorists, relational issues are inextricably bound to content issues (Watzlawick et al., 1967). This means that relational conflicts will often surface during the discussion of content issues. For example, what may at first appear to be a conflict between two leaders regarding the *content* of a new employee fitness program may really be a struggle over which one of the leaders will ultimately receive credit for developing the program. As we mentioned, relational conflicts are complex and not easily resolved. However, when relational conflicts are expressed and confronted, it can significantly enhance the overall resolution process.

MANAGING CONFLICT IN PRACTICE

Communication is central to managing different kinds of conflict in organizations. Leaders who are able to keep channels of communication open with others will have a greater chance of understanding others' beliefs, values, and needs for esteem, control, and affiliation. With increased understanding, many of the kinds of conflict discussed in the earlier part of this chapter will seem less difficult to resolve and more open to negotiation.

In this section, we will explore three different approaches to resolving conflict: Fisher and Ury's principled negotiation; the communication strategies of differentiation, fractionation, and face saving; and the Kilmann–Thomas styles of approaching conflict. As we discussed previously, conflict can be multifaceted and complex, and while there is no magic bullet for resolving all conflicts, knowing different approaches can help a leader employ the effective strategies for solving conflict.

Fisher and Ury Approach to Conflict

A Win-Win Situation

One of the most recognized approaches of conflict negotiation in the world was developed by Roger Fisher and William Ury. Derived from studies conducted by the Harvard Negotiation Project, Fisher and Ury (1981) provide a straightforward, step-by-step method for negotiating conflicts. This method, called **principled negotiation**, emphasizes deciding issues on their merits rather than through competitive haggling or through excessive accommodation. Principled negotiation shows you how to obtain your fair share decently and without having others take advantage of you (Fisher & Ury, 1981).

As illustrated in Figure 11.2, the Fisher and Ury negotiation method comprises four principles. Each principle directly focuses on one of the four basic elements of negotiation: people, interests, options, and criteria. Effective leaders frequently understand and utilize these four principles in conflict situations.

FIGURE 11.2   Fisher and Ury's Method of Principled Negotiation

Separate the **People** From the Problem	Focus on **Interests** Not Positions	Invent **Options** for Mutual Gains	Insist on Using Objective **Criteria**

Source: Adapted from Fisher, R., & Ury, W. (1981). *Getting to yes: Negotiating agreement without giving in.* New York, NY: Penguin Books, p. 15.

Principle 1: Separate the People From the Problem

In the previous section of this chapter, we discussed how conflict has a content dimension and a relationship dimension. Similarly, Fisher and Ury (1981) contend that conflicts comprise a *problem factor* and a *people factor.* To be effective in dealing with conflicts, both of these factors need to be addressed. In particular, Fisher and Ury argue that the people factor needs to be separated out from the problem factor.

Separating people from the problem during conflict is not easy because they are entangled. For example, if a supervisor and her employee are in a heated conversation over the employee's negative performance review, it is very difficult for the supervisor and the employee to discuss the review without addressing their relationship and personal roles. Our personalities, beliefs, and values are intricately interwoven with our conflicts. However, principled negotiation says that people and the problem need to be disentangled.

By separating people from the problem, we enable ourselves to recognize others' uniqueness. Everyone has his or her own distinct thoughts and feelings in different situations. Because we all perceive the world differently, we have diverse emotional responses to conflict. By focusing directly on the *people aspect* of the problem, we become more aware of the personalities and idiosyncratic needs of those with whom we are in conflict.

Perhaps most important, separating people from the problem encourages us to be attentive to our relationships during conflict. Conflicts can strain relationships, so it is important to be cognizant of how one's behavior during conflict affects the other party. Rather than "beat up" on each other, it is useful to work together, alongside each other, and mutually confront the problem. When we separate people from the problem, we are more inclined to work with others to solve problems. Fisher and Ury (1981) suggest that people in conflict need to "see themselves as working side by side, attacking the problem, not each other" (p. 11). Separating the people from the problem allows us to nurture and strengthen our relationships rather than destroy them.

Consider the earlier example of the supervisor and employee conflict over the negative performance review. In order to separate the people from the problem, both the supervisor and the employee need to discuss the negative review by focusing on performance criteria and behavior issues rather than personal attributes. The review indicated that the employee didn't meet performance objectives—the boss could say, "You didn't get your work done," but in separating the people from the problem, the boss would instead explain how the employee was unable to meet the requirements ("The number of contacts you made was below the required number"). The employee, on the other hand, may feel the objectives were unrealistic. Rather than telling her boss it was his fault ("You set unobtainable objectives"), the employee should make her point by providing facts about how these standards are not realistic ("The economic downturn wasn't considered when these objectives were developed"). By focusing on the problem in this way, the employer and the employee are maintaining their relationship but also confronting directly the performance review issues.

Principle 2: Focus on Interests, Not Positions

The second principle, which is perhaps the most well known, emphasizes that parties in a conflict must focus on interests and not just positions. *Positions* represent our stand or perspective in a particular conflict. *Interests* represent what is behind our positions. Stated another way, positions are the opposing points of view in a conflict while interests refer to the relevant needs and values of the people involved. Fisher and Ury (1981) suggest that "your position is something you have decided upon. Your interests are what caused you to so decide" (p. 42).

Focusing on interests expands conflict negotiation by encouraging individuals to explore the unique underpinnings of the conflict. To identify interests behind a position, it is useful to look at the basic concerns that motivate people. Some of our concerns include needs for security, belonging, recognition, control, and economic well-being (Fisher & Ury, 1981). Being attentive to these basic needs and helping people satisfy them is central to conflict negotiation.

Concentrating on interests also helps opposing parties to address the "real" conflict. Addressing both interests *and* positions helps to make conflict negotiation more authentic. In his model of authentic leadership, Robert Terry (1993) advocates that leaders have a moral responsibility to ask the question "*What is really, really going on* in a conflict situation, and what are we going to do about it?" Unless leaders know what truly is going on, their actions will be inappropriate and can have serious consequences. Focusing on interests is a good way to find out what is at the heart of a conflict.

Consider the following conflict between a college professor, Dr. Smith, and his student, Erin Crow, regarding class attendance. Dr. Smith has a mandatory attendance policy, but allows for two absences during the semester. A student's grade is lowered 10% for each additional absence. Erin is a very bright student who has gotten As on all of her papers and tests. However, she has five absences and does not want to be penalized. Based on the attendance policy, Dr. Smith would lower Erin's grade 30%, from an A to a C. Erin's position in this conflict is that she shouldn't be penalized because she has done excellent work despite her absences. Dr. Smith's position is that the attendance policy is legitimate and Erin's grade should be lowered.

In this example, it is worthwhile to explore some of the interests that form the basis for each position. For example, Erin is very reticent and does not like to participate in class. She is carrying 18 credit hours and works two part-time jobs. On the other hand, Dr. Smith is a popular professor who has twice received university-wide outstanding teaching awards. He has 20 years of experience and has a strong publication record in the area of classroom learning methodology. In addition, Dr. Smith has a need to be liked by students, and does not like to be challenged.

Given their interests, it is easy to see that the conflict between Erin and Dr. Smith over class attendance is more complex than meets the eye. If this conflict were to be settled by negotiating positions alone, the resolution would be relatively straightforward, and Erin would most likely be penalized, leaving both parties unsatisfied. However, if the interests of both Erin and Dr. Smith were fully explored, the probability of a mutually agreeable outcome would be far more likely. Dr. Smith is likely to recognize that Erin has numerous obligations that impact her attendance but are important for her economic well-being and security. On the other hand, Erin may come to realize that Dr. Smith is an exemplary teacher who fosters cohesiveness among students by expecting them to show up and participate in class. His needs for control and recognition are challenged by Erin's attendance and lack of class participation.

The challenge for Erin and Dr. Smith is to focus on their interests, communicate them to each other, and remain open to unique approaches to resolving their conflict.

Principle 3: Invent Options for Mutual Gains

The third strategy in effective conflict negotiation presented by Fisher and Ury (1981) is to invent options for mutual gains. This is difficult to do because humans naturally see conflict as an either-or proposition. We either win or lose; we get what we want, or the other side gets what it wants. We feel the results will be favorable either to us or to the other side, and we do not see any other possible options.

However, this tendency to see conflict as a fixed choice proposition needs to be overcome by inventing new options to resolve the conflict to the satisfaction of both parties. The method of principled negotiation emphasizes that we need to brainstorm and search hard for creative solutions to conflict. We need to expand our options and not limit ourselves to thinking there is a single best solution.

Focusing on the interests of the parties in conflict can result in this kind of creative thinking. By exploring where our interests overlap and dovetail, we can identify solutions that will benefit both parties. This process of fulfilling interests does not need to be antagonistic. We can help each other in conflict by being sensitive to each other's interests and making it easier, rather than more difficult, for both parties to satisfy their interests. Using the earlier example of Dr. Smith and Erin, Erin could acknowledge Dr. Smith's need for a consistent attendance policy and explain that she understands that it is important to have a policy to penalize less-than-committed students. She should make the case that the quality of her papers indicates she has learned much from Dr. Smith and is as committed to the class as she can be, given her other obligations. Dr. Smith should explain that he is not comfortable ignoring her absences and that it is unfair to other students who have also been penalized for missing class. They could agree that Erin's grade will be lowered to a B, rather than a C. While neither party would be "victorious," both would feel that the best compromise was reached given each person's unique interests.

Principle 4: Insist on Using Objective Criteria

Finally, Fisher and Ury (1981) say that effective negotiation requires that objective criteria be used to settle different interests. The goal in negotiation is to reach a solution that is based on principle and not on pressure. Conflict parties need to search for objective criteria that will help them view their conflict with an unbiased lens. Objective criteria can take many forms, including

- *precedent,* which looks at how this issue has been resolved previously;
- *professional standards,* which determine if there are rules or standards for behavior based on a profession or trade involved in the conflict;
- *what a court would decide,* which looks at the legal precedent or legal ramifications of the conflict;
- *moral standards,* which consider resolving the conflict based on ethical considerations or "doing what's right";

- *tradition,* which looks at already established practices or customs in considering the conflict; and
- *scientific judgment,* which considers facts and evidence.

For example, if an employee and his boss disagree on the amount of a salary increase the employee is to receive, both the employee and the boss might consider the raises of employees with similar positions and work records. When criteria are used effectively and fairly, the outcomes and final package are usually seen as wise and fair (Fisher & Ury, 1981).

In summary, the method of principled negotiation presents four practical strategies that leaders can employ in handling conflicts: separate the people from the problem; focus on interests, not positions; invent options for mutual gains; and insist on using objective criteria. None of these strategies is a panacea for all problems or conflicts, but used together they can provide a general, well-substantiated approach to settling conflicts in ways that are likely to be advantageous to everyone involved in a conflict situation.

Communication Strategies for Conflict Resolution

Throughout this chapter, we have emphasized the complexity of conflict and the difficulties that arise in addressing it. There is no universal remedy or simple path. In fact, except for a few newsstand-type books that claim to provide quick cures to conflict, only a few sources give practical techniques for resolution. In this section, we describe several practical communication approaches that play a major role in the conflict resolution process: differentiation, fractionation, and face saving. Using these communication strategies can lessen the angst of the conflict, help conflicting parties to reach resolution sooner, and strengthen relationships.

**The Importance
of Listening**

Differentiation

Differentiation describes a process that occurs in the early phase of conflict; it helps participants define the nature of the conflict and clarify their positions with regard to each other. It is very important to conflict resolution because it establishes the nature and parameters of the conflict. Differentiation requires that individuals explain and elaborate their own position, frequently focusing on their differences rather than their similarities. It is essential to working through a conflict (Putnam, 2010). Differentiation represents a difficult time in the conflict process because it is more likely to involve an escalation of conflict rather than a cooling off. During this time, fears may arise that the conflict will not be successfully resolved. Differentiation is also difficult because it initially personalizes the conflict and brings out feelings and sentiments in people that they themselves are the cause of the conflict (Folger, Poole, & Stutman, 1993).

The value of differentiation is that it defines the conflict. It helps both parties realize how they differ on the issue being considered. Being aware of these differences is useful for conflict resolution because it focuses the conflict, gives credence to both parties' interests in the issue that is in conflict, and, in essence, depersonalizes the conflict. Consistent with Fisher and Ury's (1981) method of negotiation, differentiation is a way to separate the people from the problem.

An example of differentiation involves a group project. Members of the group have complained to the instructor that one member, Jennifer, seldom comes to meetings; when she does come, she does not contribute to the group discussions. The instructor met with Jennifer, who defended herself by stating that the group constantly set meeting times that conflict with her work schedule. She believes they do so on purpose to exclude her. The teacher arranged for the students to sit down together, and then had them explain their differing points of view to one another. The group members said that they believed that Jennifer cared less about academic achievement than they did because she did not seem willing to adjust her work schedule to meet with them. Jennifer, on the other hand, said she believed the others did not respect that she had to work to support herself while going to school, and that she was not in total control of her work schedule.

**Resolving
Intergroup Conflict**

In the above example, differentiation occurred among group members as they attempted to assess the issues. It was a difficult process because it demanded that each participant talk about his or her feelings about why the group was having conflict. Both sides ultimately understood the other's differing viewpoints. The group and Jennifer set aside a definite time each week when they would meet, and Jennifer made sure her supervisor did not schedule her to work at that time.

Fractionation

Fractionation refers to the technique of breaking down large conflicts into smaller, more manageable pieces (Fisher, 1971; Wilmot & Hocker, 2011). Like differentiation, fractionation usually occurs in the early stages of the conflict resolution process. It is an intentional process in which the participants agree to "downsize" a large conflict into smaller conflicts and then confront just one part of the larger conflict. Fractionating conflict is helpful for several reasons. First, fractionation reduces the conflict by paring it down to a smaller, less complex conflict. It is helpful for individuals to know that the conflict they are confronting is not a huge amorphous mass of difficulties, but rather consists of specific and defined difficulties. Second, it gives focus to the conflict. By narrowing down large conflicts, individuals give clarity and definition to their difficulties instead of trying to solve a whole host of problems at once. Third, downsizing a conflict helps to reduce the emotional intensity of the dispute. Smaller conflicts carry less emotional weight (Wilmot & Hocker, 2011). Last, fractionation facilitates a better working relationship between participants in the conflict. In agreeing to address a reduced version of a conflict, the participants confirm their willingness to work with one another to solve problems.

An example of fractionation at work involves David Stedman, an experienced director of a private school that was on the verge of closing due to low enrollment. School board members were upset with David's leadership and the direction of the school, and David was disappointed with the board. The school had been running on a deficit budget for the previous three years and had used up most of the endowment money it had set aside. The school's board members saw the problem one way: The school needed more students. David knew it was not that simple. There were many issues behind the low enrollment: the practices for recruitment of students, retention of students, fund-raising, marketing, and out-of-date technology at the school, as well as bad feelings between the parents and the school. In addition to these concerns, David had responsibility for day-to-day operations of the school and decisions regarding the education of students. David asked the board members to attend a weekend retreat where, together, they detailed the myriad problems facing the school and narrowed the long list down to three difficulties that they would address together. They agreed to work on an aggressive recruitment plan, fund-raising efforts, and internal marketing toward parents so they would keep their children at the school.

In the end, the retreat was beneficial to both David and the board. The big conflict of "what to do about the school" was narrowed down to three specific areas they could address. In addition, the school board developed an appreciation for the complexity and difficulties of running the school, and David softened his negative feelings about the school board and its members' input. As a result of fractionating their conflict, David Stedman and the school board developed a better working relationship and confirmed their willingness to work on problems in the future.

Face Saving

A third skill that can assist a leader in conflict resolution is face saving. **Face saving** refers to communicative attempts to establish or maintain one's self-image in response to threat (Folger et al., 1993; Goffman, 1967; Lulofs, 1994). Face-saving messages help individuals establish how they want to be seen by others. The goal of face-saving messages is to protect one's self-image.

In conflict, which is often threatening and unsettling, participants may become concerned about how others view them in regard to the positions

Face Saving

they have taken. This concern for self can be counterproductive to conflict resolution because it shifts the focus of the conflict away from substantive issues and onto personal issues. Instead of confronting the central concerns of the conflict, face-saving concerns force participants to deal with their self-images as they are related to the conflict.

Interpersonal conflicts can be made less threatening if individuals communicate in a way that preserves the self-image of the other. Conflict issues should be discussed in a manner that minimizes threat to the participants. By using face-saving messages, such as "I think you are making a good point, but I see things differently," one person acknowledges another's point of view without making the other person feel stupid or unintelligent. The threat of conflict is lessened if participants try to support each other's self-image rather than to damage it just to win an argument. It is important to be aware of how people want to be seen by others, how conflict can threaten those desires, and how our communication can minimize those threats (Lulofs, 1994).

In trying to resolve conflicts, face saving should be a concern to participants for two reasons. First, if possible, participants should try to avoid letting the discussions during conflict shift to face-threatening issues. Similar to Fisher and Ury's (1981) principle of separating the people from the problem, this can be done by staying focused on content issues and maintaining interactions that do not challenge the other person's self-image. Second, during the later stages of conflict, face-saving messages can actually be used to assist participants in giving each other validation and support for how they have come across during conflict. Face-saving messages can confirm for others that they have handled themselves appropriately during conflict and that their relationship is still healthy.

The following example illustrates how face saving can affect conflict resolution. At a large university hospital, significant disruptions occurred when 1,000 nurses went on strike after contract negotiations failed. The issues in the conflict were salary, forced overtime, and mandatory coverage of units that were short-staffed. There was much name-calling and personal attacks between nurses and administrators. Early negotiations were inhibited by efforts on both sides to establish an image with the public that what *they* were doing was appropriate, given the circumstances. As a result, these images and issues of right and wrong, rather than the substantive issues of salary and overtime, became the focus of the conflict. If the parties had avoided tearing each other down, perhaps the conflict could have been settled sooner.

Despite these difficulties, face-saving messages did have a positive effect on this conflict. During the middle of the negotiations, the hospital ran a full-page advertisement in the local newspaper describing its proposal and why it thought this proposal was misunderstood. At the end of the ad, the hospital stated, "We respect your right to strike. A strike is a peaceful and powerful means by which you communicate your concern or dissatisfaction." This statement showed that the administration was trying to save face for itself, but also it was attempting to save face for nurses by expressing that their being on strike was not amoral, and that the hospital was willing to accept the nurses' behavior and continue to have a working relationship with them. Similarly, the media messages that both parties released at the end of the strike included affirmation of the other party's self-image. The nurses, who received a substantial salary increase, did not try to claim victory or point out what the hospital lost in the negotiations. In turn, the hospital, which retained control of the use of staff for overtime, did not emphasize what it had won or communicate that it thought the nurses were unprofessional because they had gone out on strike. The point is that these gentle face-saving messages helped both sides to feel good about themselves, reestablish their image as effective health care providers, and salvage their working relationships.

All in all, there are no shortcuts to resolving conflicts. It is a complex process that requires sustained communication. By being aware of differentiation, fractionation, and face saving, leaders can enhance their abilities and skills in the conflict resolution process.

Kilmann and Thomas Styles of Approaching Conflict

There's no doubt that people have different ways of handling conflict and that these different styles affect the outcomes of conflict. A **conflict style** is defined as a patterned response or behavior that people use when approaching conflict. One of the most widely recognized models of conflict styles was developed by Kilmann and Thomas (1975, 1977), based on the work of Blake and Mouton (1964), and is the basis for our Conflict Style Questionnaire on pages 269–271.

The Kilmann–Thomas model identifies five conflict styles: (1) avoidance, (2) competition, (3) accommodation, (4) compromise, and (5) collaboration. This model (see Figure 11.3) describes conflict styles along two dimensions: assertiveness and cooperativeness. *Assertiveness* refers to attempts to satisfy one's own concerns, while *cooperativeness* represents attempts to satisfy the concerns of others. Each conflict style is characterized by how much assertiveness and how much cooperativeness an individual shows when confronting conflict.

In conflict situations, a person's individual style is usually a combination of these five different styles. Nevertheless, because of past experiences or situational factors, some people may rely more heavily on one conflict style than on others. Understanding these styles can help you select the conflict style that is most appropriate to the demands of the situation.

FIGURE 11.3   Styles of Approaching Conflict

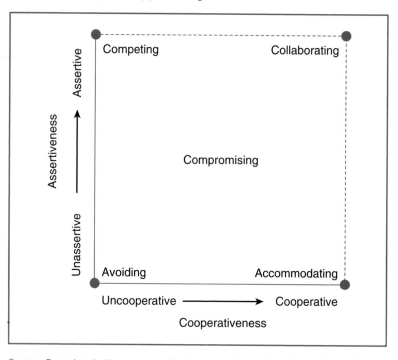

Sources: Reproduced with permission of authors and publisher from Kilmann, R. H., & Thomas, K. W. Interpersonal conflict-handling behavior as reflections of Jungian personality dimensions. *Psychological Reports*, 1975, *37*, 971–980. © *Psychological Reports*, 1975.

Avoidance

Avoidance is both an unassertive and an uncooperative conflict style. Those who favor the avoidance style tend to be passive and ignore conflict situations rather than confront them directly. They employ strategies such as denying there is a conflict, using jokes as a way to deflect conflict, or trying to change the topic. Avoiders are not assertive about pursuing their own interests, nor are they cooperative in assisting others to pursue theirs.

Advantages and Disadvantages. Avoidance as a style for managing conflict is usually counterproductive, often leading to stress and further conflict. Those who continually avoid conflict bottle up feelings of irritation, frustration, anger, or rage inside themselves, creating more anxiety. Avoidance is essentially a static approach to conflict; it does nothing to solve problems or to make changes that could prevent conflicts.

However, there are some situations in which avoidance may be useful—for example, when an issue is of trivial importance or when the potential damage from conflict would be too great. Avoidance can also provide a cooling-off period to allow participants to determine how to best resolve the conflict at a later time. For example, if Jan is so angry at her girlfriend that she throws her cell phone at the wall, she might want to go for a ride in her car or take a walk and cool down before she tries to talk to her girlfriend about the problem.

Competition

Competition is a conflict style of individuals who are highly assertive about pursuing their own goals but uncooperative in assisting others to reach theirs. These individuals attempt to resolve a struggle by controlling or persuading others in order to achieve their own ends. A competitive style is essentially a win-lose conflict strategy. For example, when Wendy seeks to convince Chris that he is a bad person because he habitually shows up late for meetings, regardless of his reasons for doing so, it is a win-lose conflict style.

Advantages and Disadvantages. In some situations, competition can produce positive outcomes. It is useful when quick, decisive action is needed. Competition can also generate creativity and enhance performance because it challenges participants to make their best efforts.

Generally, though, competitive approaches to conflict are not the most advantageous because they are more often counterproductive than productive. Resolution options are limited to one party "beating" another, resulting in a winner and a loser. Attempts to solve conflict with dominance and control will often result in creating unstable situations and hostile and destructive communication. Finally, competition is disconfirming; in competition, individuals fail to recognize the concerns and needs of others.

Accommodation

Accommodation is an unassertive but cooperative conflict style. In accommodation, an individual essentially communicates to another, "You are right, I agree; let's forget about it." An approach that is "other directed," accommodation requires individuals to attend very closely to the needs of others and ignore their own needs. Using this style, individuals confront problems by deferring to others.

Advantages and Disadvantages. Accommodation allows individuals to move away from the uncomfortable feelings that conflict inevitably produces. By yielding to others, individuals can lessen the frustration that conflict creates. This style is productive when the issue is more important to one party than the other or if harmony in the relationship is the most important goal.

The problem with accommodation is that it is, in effect, a lose-win strategy. Although accommodation may resolve conflict faster than some of the other approaches, the drawback is that the accommodator sacrifices his or her own values and possibly a higher-quality decision in order to maintain smooth relationships. It is a submissive style that allows others to take charge. Accommodators also lose because they may fail to express their own opinions and feelings and their contributions are not fully considered.

For example, Jenny's boyfriend is a sports fanatic and always wants to stay home and watch televised sports while Jenny would like to do something like go to a movie or to a club. But to make him happy, Jenny stays home and watches football.

Compromise

▶

Compromise

As Figure 11.3 indicates, **compromise** occurs halfway between competition and accommodation and involves both a degree of assertiveness and a degree of cooperativeness. Many see compromise as a "give and take" proposition. Compromisers attend to the concerns of others as well as to their own needs. On the diagonal axis of Figure 11.3, compromise occurs midway between the styles of avoidance and collaboration. This means that compromisers do not completely ignore confrontations, but neither do they struggle with problems to the fullest degree. This conflict style is often chosen because it is expedient in finding middle ground while partially satisfying the concerns of both parties.

Advantages and Disadvantages. Compromise is a positive conflict style because it requires attending to one's goals as well as others'. Compromise tends to work best when other conflict styles have failed or aren't suitable to resolving the conflict. Many times, compromise can force an equal power balance between parties.

Among the shortcomings of the compromise style is that it does not go far enough in resolving conflict and can become "an easy way out." In order to reach resolution, conflicting parties often don't fully express their own demands, personal thoughts, and feelings. Innovative solutions are sacrificed in favor of a quick resolution, and the need for harmony supersedes the need to find optimal solutions to conflict. The result is that neither side is completely satisfied. For example, Pat wants to go on a camping vacation, and Mike wants to have a "staycation," hanging around the house. In the end, they agree to spend their vacation taking day trips to the beach and the zoo.

Collaboration

Collaboration, the most preferred style of conflict, requires both assertiveness and cooperation. It is when both parties agree to a positive settlement to the conflict and attend fully to the other's concerns while not sacrificing or suppressing their own. The conflict is not resolved until each side is reasonably satisfied and can support the solution. Collaboration is the ideal conflict style because it recognizes the inevitability of human conflict. It confronts conflict, and then uses conflict to produce constructive outcomes.

Advantages and Disadvantages. The results of collaboration are positive because both sides win, communication is satisfying, relationships are strengthened, and negotiated solutions are frequently more cost-effective in the long run.

Unfortunately, collaboration is the most difficult style to achieve. It demands energy and hard work among participants as well as shared control. Resolving differences through collaboration requires individuals to take time to explore their differences, identify areas of agreement, and select solutions that are mutually satisfying. This often calls for extended conversation in which the participants explore entirely new alternatives to existing problems. For example, residents of a residential neighborhood seek to have an adult entertainment facility in their midst close or leave. The owner refuses. The residents work with city officials to find an alternative location to relocate the facility, and the city gives the facility's owner tax breaks to move.

The five styles of approaching conflict—avoidance, competition, accommodation, compromise, and collaboration—can be observed in various conflict situations. Although there are advantages and disadvantages to each style, the conflict-handling style that meets the needs of the participants while also fitting the demands of the situation will be most effective in resolving conflict.

SUMMARY

For leaders and followers alike, interpersonal conflict is inevitable. Conflict is defined as a felt struggle between two or more individuals over perceived incompatible differences in beliefs, values, and goals, or over differences in desires for esteem, control, and connectedness. If it is managed in appropriate ways, conflict need not be destructive but can be constructive and used to positive ends.

Communication plays a central role in conflict and in its resolution. Conflict occurs between leaders and others on two levels: content and relational. Conflict on the content level involves differences in beliefs, values, or goal orientation. Conflict on the relational level refers to differences between individuals with regard to their desires for esteem, control, and affiliation in their relationships. Relational conflicts are seldom overt, which makes them difficult for people to recognize and resolve.

One approach to resolving conflicts is the method of principled negotiation by Fisher and Ury (1981). This model focuses on four basic elements of negotiation—people, interests, options, and criteria—and describes four principles related to handling conflicts: Principle 1—Separate the People From the Problem; Principle 2—Focus on Interests, Not Positions; Principle 3—Invent Options for Mutual Gains; and Principle 4—Insist on Using

Objective Criteria. Collectively, these principles are extraordinarily useful in negotiating positive conflict outcomes.

Three practical communication approaches to conflict resolution are differentiation, fractionation, and face saving. Differentiation is a process that helps participants to define the nature of the conflict and to clarify their positions with one another. Fractionation refers to the technique of paring down large conflicts into smaller, more manageable conflicts. Face saving consists of messages that individuals express to each other in order to maintain each other's self-image during conflict. Together or singly, these approaches can assist leaders in making the conflict resolution process more productive.

Finally, researchers have found that people approach conflict using five styles: (1) avoidance, (2) competition, (3) accommodation, (4) compromise, and (5) collaboration. Each of these styles characterizes individuals in terms of the degree of assertiveness and cooperativeness they show when confronting conflict. The most constructive approach to conflict is collaboration, which requires that individuals recognize, confront, and resolve conflict by attending fully to others' concerns without sacrificing their own. Managing conflicts effectively leads to stronger relationships among participants and more creative solutions to problems.

GLOSSARY TERMS

$SAGE edge™

Sharpen your skills with SAGE edge at **edge.sagepub.com/northouseintro4e**

SAGE edge for students provides a personalized approach to help you accomplish your coursework goals in an easy-to-use learning environment.

11.1 CASE STUDY

Office Space

The five members of the Web programming department at a marketing company are being relocated to a new space in their building. The move came as a big surprise; the head of the company decided to cut costs by leasing less space, and with just a few days' notice, the department was relocated.

The new space is a real change from what the programmers are used to. Their old space was a big open room with one wall of floor-to-ceiling windows. Their desks all faced each other, which allowed them to easily talk and collaborate with one another. The new office space has a row of five cubicles along a wall in a long, narrow room. Four of the cubicles have windows; the fifth, which is slightly larger than the others, is tucked into a windowless corner. The cubicle walls are 6 feet tall, and when they are at their desks working, the programmers can no longer see one another.

The team leader, Martin, assigned the cubicles that each programmer has moved into. He put himself in the first cubicle with Rosa, Sanjay, and Kris in the next three cubicles with windows. Bradley was given the larger cubicle in the corner.

Bradley is the first to complain. When he sees his new space, he goes to Martin and asks for a different cubicle, one with a window. He argues that he has been employed there longer than the other programmers and should get to choose his cubicle rather than be told where

he is going to be. Because he and Martin work very closely on a number of projects, Bradley feels he should be in the cubicle next to Martin, rather than the one farthest away.

Sanjay is also upset. He is in the middle cubicle with Rosa and Kris on either side of him. Rosa and Kris used to have desks next to each other in the bigger space and would banter back and forth with one another while working. Now that they are in the row of cubicles, they still try to chat with one another, but to do so, they more or less shout to each other over Sanjay's space. When Martin offers to let him trade places with Bradley as a solution, Sanjay says he doesn't want to give up his window.

Martin leaves everyone where they are. He hasn't told them, but he purposely put Sanjay between Rosa and Kris in order to discourage their constant chatting, which he viewed as a time-wasting activity. Martin also felt like the larger cube was better for Bradley because he has more computer equipment than the other programmers.

During the next two months, the Web programming department starts to experience a lot of tension. Sanjay seems to be in a bad mood on a daily basis. When Rosa and Kris start chatting with each other over the cubicles, he asks them loudly, "Will you please just work and stop shouting to each other?" or says sarcastically, "I'm trying to work here!" As a result, either Rosa or Kris will leave her cubicle to walk down to the other's space to chat,

(Continued)

APPLICATION

(Continued)

having conversations that last longer than their old bantering back and forth used to.

Bradley stays in his corner cubicle and avoids talking to the other programmers. He believes that Martin purposely gave him what Bradley perceives is the worst cubicle but doesn't know what he did to deserve being treated this way. He is resentful of the other staff members who have windows in their cubicles and feels like Martin must think more highly of Rosa, Kris, and Sanjay than he does of Bradley. As Bradley observes Rosa and Kris spending more time talking and less time working and the crabbiness from Sanjay, he becomes very upset with Martin. It seems Martin is rewarding the programmers who behave the worst!

Bradley becomes even more reclusive at work and avoids talking to the other programmers, especially Martin. He communicates with them mainly by email messages, even though he's only a few yards away from some of them. He no longer collaborates closely with Martin; instead he tries to work on projects without involving Martin. Unfortunately, if he encounters a problem that he needs Martin's help for, Bradley will try to solve it himself. Often, Martin won't even know there is a problem that needs to be solved until Bradley realizes he can't solve it alone and the problem becomes a crisis.

The only time all five of the programmers actually see one another is in weekly staff meetings, which are held in a conference room with a large table and a dozen chairs. In their old space, they didn't have weekly meetings because they were able to talk about projects and schedules with each other whenever it was needed. In their new staff meetings, it seems like Martin is doing all the talking. Rosa and Kris sit on one side of the table and try to ignore Sanjay who sits by himself across from them. Bradley sits at the far end of the table at least two chairs away from everyone else.

After another unproductive staff meeting where no one spoke or looked at one another, Martin sits at the head of the conference table after the other programmers have left with his head in his hands. He doesn't know what has happened to the cohesive team he used to lead and why things changed. It seems absolutely ridiculous to him that this is all about space.

QUESTIONS

1. How would you describe the conflict that has arisen between the members of the Web programming department?

2. Is the conflict a relational conflict? If so, what type of relational conflict? Is there a content dimension to this conflict?

3. Using Fisher and Ury's method of principled negotiation, how would you separate the people from the problem? What do you think is really, really going on in this conflict?

4. Using the Kilmann and Thomas conflict styles, how would you characterize Sanjay's conflict style? What about Bradley's? Do Rosa and Kris have a style as well?

5. How could Martin use fractionation and face saving in attempting to resolve this conflict?

11.2 Conflict Style Questionnaire

Purpose

1. To identify your conflict style

2. To examine how your conflict style varies in different contexts or relationships

Directions

1. Think of two different situations (A and B) where you have a conflict, a disagreement, an argument, or a disappointment with someone, such as a roommate or a work associate. Write the name of the person for each situation below.

2. According to the scale below, fill in your scores for Situation A and Situation B. For each question, you will have two scores. For example, on Question 1 the scoring might look like this: 1. 2 | 4

3. Write the name of each person for the two situations here:

Person A _____   Person B _____

1 = never   2 = seldom   3 = sometimes   4 = often   5 = always

Person A	Person B	
1. ____	____	I avoid being "put on the spot"; I keep conflicts to myself.
2. ____	____	I use my influence to get my ideas accepted.
3. ____	____	I usually try to "split the difference" in order to resolve an issue.
4. ____	____	I generally try to satisfy the other's needs.
5. ____	____	I try to investigate an issue to find a solution acceptable to both of us.
6. ____	____	I usually avoid open discussion of my differences with the other.
7. ____	____	I use my authority to make a decision in my favor.
8. ____	____	I try to find a middle course to resolve an impasse.
9. ____	____	I usually accommodate the other's wishes.
10. ____	____	I try to integrate my ideas with the other's to come up with a decision jointly.
11. ____	____	I try to stay away from disagreement with the other.
12. ____	____	I use my expertise to make a decision that favors me.
13. ____	____	I propose a middle ground for breaking deadlocks.
14. ____	____	I give in to the other's wishes.
15. ____	____	I try to work with the other to find solutions that satisfy both our expectations.

(Continued)

 Visit **edge.sagepub.com/northouseintro4e** for a downloadable version of this questionnaire.

11.2 CONFLICT STYLE QUESTIONNAIRE
(Continued)

Person A	Person B
16. ____|____	I try to keep my disagreement to myself in order to avoid hard feelings.
17. ____|____	I generally pursue my side of an issue.
18. ____|____	I negotiate with the other to reach a compromise.
19. ____|____	I often go with the other's suggestions.
20. ____|____	I exchange accurate information with the other so we can solve a problem together.
21. ____|____	I try to avoid unpleasant exchanges with the other.
22. ____|____	I sometimes use my power to win.
23. ____|____	I use "give and take" so that a compromise can be made.
24. ____|____	I try to satisfy the other's expectations.
25. ____|____	I try to bring all our concerns out in the open so that the issues can be resolved.

Source: Adapted from "Confirmatory Factor Analysis of the Styles of Handling Interpersonal Conflict: First-Order Factor Model and Its Invariance Across Groups," by M. A. Rahim and N. R. Magner, 1995, *Journal of Applied Psychology, 80*(1), 122–132. In W. Wilmot and J. Hocker (2011), *Interpersonal Conflict* (pp. 146–148). Published by the American Psychological Association.

Scoring: Add up your scores on the following questions:

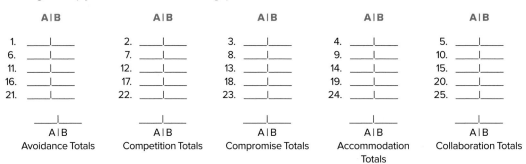

A|B	A|B	A|B	A|B	A|B
1. ___|___	2. ___|___	3. ___|___	4. ___|___	5. ___|___
6. ___|___	7. ___|___	8. ___|___	9. ___|___	10. ___|___
11. ___|___	12. ___|___	13. ___|___	14. ___|___	15. ___|___
16. ___|___	17. ___|___	18. ___|___	19. ___|___	20. ___|___
21. ___|___	22. ___|___	23. ___|___	24. ___|___	25. ___|___
___|___	___|___	___|___	___|___	___|___
A|B	A|B	A|B	A|B	A|B
Avoidance Totals	Competition Totals	Compromise Totals	Accommodation Totals	Collaboration Totals

Scoring Interpretation

This questionnaire is designed to identify your conflict style and examine how it varies in different contexts or relationships. By comparing your total scores for the different styles, you can discover which conflict style you rely most heavily upon and which style you use least. Furthermore, by comparing your scores for Person A and Person B, you can determine how your style varies or stays the same in different relationships. Your scores on this questionnaire

11.2 CONFLICT STYLE QUESTIONNAIRE

(Continued)

are indicative of how you responded to a particular conflict at a specific time and therefore might change if you selected a different conflict or a different conflict period. The Conflict Style Questionnaire is not a personality test that labels or categorizes you; rather, it attempts to give you a sense of your more dominant and less dominant conflict styles.

Scores from 21 to 25 are representative of a very strong style.

Scores from 16 to 20 are representative of a strong style.

Scores from 11 to 15 are representative of an average style.

Scores from 6 to 10 are representative of a weak style.

Scores from 0 to 5 are representative of a very weak style.

Improve Your Leadership Skills

If you have the interactive eBook version of this text, log in to to access the interactive leadership assessment. After completing this chapter's questionnaire, you will receive individualized feedback and practical suggestions for further strengthening your leadership based on your responses in this questionnaire.

APPLICATION

11.3 OBSERVATIONAL EXERCISE

Managing Conflict

Purpose

1. To become aware of the dimensions of interpersonal conflict

2. To explore how to use Fisher and Ury's (1981) method of principled negotiation to address actual conflict

Directions

1. For this exercise, you are being asked to observe an actual conflict. Attend a public meeting at which a conflict is being addressed. For example, you could attend a meeting of the campus planning board, which has on its agenda changes in student parking fees.

2. Take notes on the meeting, highlighting the positions and interests of all the people who participated in the meeting.

Questions

1. How did the participants at the meeting frame their arguments? What *positions* did individuals take at the meeting?

2. Identify and describe the interests of each of the participants at the meeting.

3. Discuss whether the participants were able to be objective in their approaches to the problem. Describe how the people involved were able to separate themselves from the problem.

4. In what ways did the participants seek to find mutually beneficial solutions to their conflict?

 Visit **edge.sagepub.com/northouseintro4e** for a downloadable version of this exercise.

11.4 REFLECTION AND ACTION WORKSHEET

Managing Conflict

Reflection

1. How do you react to conflict? Based on the Conflict Style Questionnaire, how would you describe your conflict style? How has your past history influenced your conflict style?

2. This chapter describes three kinds of relational conflict (i.e., esteem, control, affiliation). Of the three kinds, which is most common in the conflicts you have with others? Discuss.

Action

1. Briefly describe an actual conflict you had with a family member, roommate, or coworker in the recent past. Identify the positions and interests of both you and the other person in the conflict. (Note: Individuals' positions may be easier to identify than their interests. Be creative in detailing your interests and the other person's.)

2. Describe how you could *fractionate the conflict.*

3. Using Fisher and Ury's (1981) methods, describe how you could separate the person from the problem and how you could work together to address the conflict. During your discussions, how could you help the other party in the conflict save face? How could the other party help you save face?

 Visit **edge.sagepub.com/northouseintro4e** for a downloadable version of this worksheet.

REFERENCES

Blake, R. R., & Mouton, L. S. (1964). *The managerial grid.* Houston, TX: Gulf.

Brown, C. T., & Keller, P. W. (1979). *Monologue to dialogue: An exploration of interpersonal communication.* Englewood Cliffs, NJ: Prentice-Hall.

Faruqi, A. (Producer), & Obaid-Chinoy, S. (Director). (2013). *Humaira: The dreamcatcher* [Motion picture]. Pakistan: SOC films.

Fisher, R. (1971). Fractionating conflict. In C. G. Smith (Ed.), *Conflict resolution: Contributions of the behavioral sciences* (pp. 157–159). South Bend, IN: University of Notre Dame Press.

Fisher, R., & Ury, W. (1981). *Getting to yes: Negotiating agreement without giving in.* New York, NY: Penguin Books.

Folger, J. P., Poole, M. S., & Stutman, R. K. (1993). *Working through conflict: Strategies for relationships, groups, and organizations* (2nd ed.). Glenview, IL: Scott, Foresman.

Goffman, E. (1967). *Interaction ritual: Essays on face-to-face behavior.* New York, NY: Anchor Books.

Hocker, J. L., & Wilmot, W. W. (1995). *Interpersonal conflict* (4th ed.). Dubuque, IA: W. C. Brown.

Kilmann, R. H., & Thomas, K. W. (1975). Interpersonal conflict-handling behavior as reflections of Jungian personality dimensions. *Psychological Reports, 37*(3), 971–980.

Kilmann, R. H., & Thomas, K. W. (1977). Developing a forced-choice measure of conflict handling behavior: The "mode" instrument. *Educational and Psychology Measurement, 37*(2), 309–325.

Knutson, T., Lashbrook, V., & Heemer, A. (1976). *The dimensions of small group conflict: A factor analytic study.* Paper presented to the annual meeting of the International Communication Association, Portland, OR.

Lulofs, R. S. (1994). *Conflict: From theory to action.* Scottsdale, AZ: Gorsuch Scarisbrick.

Maslow, A. (1970). *Motivation and personality* (2nd ed.). New York, NY: Harper & Row.

Putnam, L. L. (2010). Communication as changing the negotiation game. *Journal of Applied Communication Research, 38*(4), 325–335.

Rahi, S. (Producer). (2010, December 10). *Humaira Bachal documentary* [Motion picture]. Dawn News. Retrieved June 10, 2013, from www.youtube.com/watch?v=3Hs2hxrY_HI

Schutz, W. C. (1966). *The interpersonal underworld.* Palo Alto, CA: Science and Behavior Books.

Temple-Raston, D. (2013, January 3). After fighting to go to school, a Pakistani woman builds her own. *Weekend Edition Sunday* [Radio news program]. Retrieved from http://www.npr.org/2013/01/06/168565152/after-fighting-to-go-to-school-a-pakistani-woman-builds-her-own

Terry, R. W. (1993). *Authentic leadership: Courage in action.* San Francisco, CA: Jossey-Bass.

Watzlawick, P., Beavin, J., & Jackson, D. D. (1967). *Pragmatics of human communication.* New York, NY: Norton.

Wilmot, W. W., & Hocker, J. (2011). *Interpersonal conflict* (8th ed.). New York, NY: McGraw-Hill.

Addressing Ethics in Leadership

INTRODUCTION

L eadership has a moral dimension because leaders influence the lives of others. Because of this influential dimension, leadership carries with it an enormous ethical responsibility. Hand in hand with the authority to make decisions is the obligation a leader has to use his or her authority for the common good. Because the leader usually has more power and control than followers have, leaders have to be particularly sensitive to how their leadership affects the well-being of others.

In recent years, there have been an overwhelming number of scandals in the public and private sectors. Accounting and financial scandals have occurred at some of the largest companies in the world, including Adelphia, Enron, Tyco International, and WorldCom. In addition, there have been stories of sexual abuse in the Catholic Church, sexual assaults within the U.S. military, and a multitude of sexual scandals in the lives of public figures including governors, U.S. senators, and mayors, to name but a few. As a result of such

ASK THE
AUTHOR

What is Ethical Leadership and Why is it Relevant?

high-profile scandals, people are becoming suspicious of public figures and what they do. The public strongly seeks moral leadership.

As mentioned in Chapter 1, "Understanding Leadership," the overriding purpose of this book is to discover "what it takes to be a leader." Closely related to this question, and perhaps even more important, is "what it takes to be an *ethical* leader." That query is the focus of this chapter. This means our emphasis will be on describing how people act when they show ethical leadership. While it is always intriguing to know whether one is or is not perceived by others to be ethical, our emphasis will not be directed toward whether you are or are not ethical, but rather we will focus on the properties and characteristics of ethical leadership. The assumption we are making is that if you understand the nature of ethical leadership, you will be better equipped to engage in ethical leadership.

Before we discuss the factors that account for ethical leadership, you may want to go to the end of the chapter and take the Ethical Leadership Style Questionnaire (12.2). It will help you understand your own ethical leadership style and at the same time introduce you to the ideas we will be discussing in this chapter.

LEADERSHIP ETHICS EXPLAINED

Defining Ethical Leadership

To begin, it is important to first define ethical leadership. In the simplest terms, **ethical leadership** is the influence of a moral person who moves others to do the right thing in the right way for the right reasons (Ciulla, 2003). Put another way, ethical leadership is a process by which a good person rightly influences others to accomplish a common good: to make the world better, fairer, and more humane.

Ethics is concerned with the kind of values and morals an individual or society finds desirable or appropriate. In leadership, ethics has to do with what leaders do and the nature of leaders' behavior, including their motives. Because leaders often have control, power, and influence over others, their leadership affects other individuals and organizations. Because of this, it is the leader's ethics—through his or her behavior, decisions, and interactions—that establish the ethical climate for an organization.

LEADERSHIP ETHICS IN PRACTICE

Leadership ethics is a complex phenomenon with multiple parts that overlap and are interconnected. When trying to practice ethical leadership, there are

FIGURE 12.1   Factors Related to Ethical Leadership

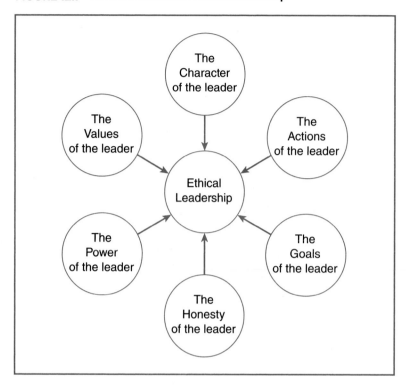

six factors (Figure 12.1) that should be of special importance to leaders. Each of these factors plays a role in who leaders are and what they do when they are engaged in ethical leadership.

1. The *charac*ter of the leader

2. The *actions* of the leader

3. The *goals* of the leader

4. The *honesty* of the leader

5. The *power* of the leader

6. The *values* of the leader

1. The Character of the Leader

The **character** of the leader is a fundamental aspect of ethical leadership. When it is said that a leader has strong character, that leader is seen as a good and honorable human being. The leader's character refers to the qualities, disposition, and core values of the leader. More than 2,000 years ago, Aristotle

The Philosopher Leader

argued that a moral person demonstrates the virtues of courage, generosity, self-control, honesty, sociability, modesty, fairness, and justice (Velasquez, 1992). Today, all these qualities still contribute to a strong character.

Character is something that is developed. In recent years, the nation's schools have seen a growing interest in character education. Misbehavior of public figures has led to mistrust of public figures, which has led to the public demanding that educators do a better job of training children to be good citizens. As a result, most schools today teach character education as part of their normal curriculum. A model for many of these programs was developed by the Josephson Institute (2008) in California, which frames instruction around six dimensions of character: *trustworthiness, respect, responsibility, fairness, caring,* and *citizenship* (see Table 12.1). Based on these and similar character dimensions, schools are emphasizing the importance of character and how core values influence an individual's ethical decision making.

Although character is clearly at the core of *who you are* as a person, it is also something you can learn to strengthen and develop. A leader can learn good values. When practiced over time, from youth to adulthood, good values become habitual, and a part of people themselves. By telling the truth, people become truthful; by giving to the poor, people become charitable; and by being fair to others, people become just. Your virtues, and hence your character, are derived from your actions.

An example of a leader with strong character is Nobel Peace Prize winner Nelson Mandela (see page 27). Mandela was a deeply moral man with a strong conscience. When fighting to abolish apartheid in South Africa, he was unyielding in his pursuit of justice and equality for all. When he was in prison and was offered the chance to leave early in exchange for denouncing his viewpoint, he chose to remain incarcerated rather than compromise his position. In addition to being deeply concerned for others, Mandela was a courageous, patient, humble, and compassionate man. He was an ethical leader who ardently believed in the common good.

Mandela clearly illustrates that character is an essential component of moral leadership. Character enables a leader to maintain his or her core ethical values even in times of immense adversity. Character forms the centerpiece of a person's values, and is fundamental to ethical leadership.

2. The Actions of the Leader

In addition to being about a leader's character, ethical leadership is about the **actions** of a leader. Actions refer to the ways a leader goes about accomplishing goals. Ethical leaders use moral means to achieve their goals. The way a

TABLE 12.1 The Six Pillars of Character

Trustworthiness	
Trustworthiness is the most complicated of the six core ethical values and concerns a variety of qualities like honesty, integrity, reliability, and loyalty.	• Be honest • Be reliable: do what you say you'll do • Have the courage to do the right thing • Don't deceive, cheat, or steal • Build a good reputation
Respect	
While we have no ethical duty to hold all people in high esteem, we should treat everyone with respect.	• Be tolerant of differences • Use good manners • Be considerate of others • Work out disagreements
Responsibility	
Ethical people show responsibility by being accountable, pursuing excellence, and exercising self-restraint. They exhibit the ability to respond to expectations.	• Do your job • Persevere • Think before you act • Consider the consequences • Be accountable for your choices
Fairness	
Fairness implies adherence to a balanced standard of justice without relevance to one's own feelings or indications.	• Play by the rules • Be open-minded • Don't take advantage of others • Don't blame others
Caring	
Caring is the heart of ethics and ethical decision making. It is scarcely possible to be truly ethical and yet unconcerned with the welfare of others. This is because ethics is ultimately about good relations with other people.	• Be kind • Be compassionate • Forgive others • Help people in need
Citizenship	
The good citizen gives more than she takes, doing more than her "fair" share to make society work, now and for future generations. Citizenship includes civic virtues and duties that prescribe how we ought to behave as part of a community.	• Share with your community • Get involved • Stay informed: vote • Respect authority • Protect the environment

Source: © 2008 Josephson Institute. The definitions of the Six Pillars of Character are reprinted with permission. www.charactercounts.org

leader goes about his or her work is a critical determinant of whether he or she is an ethical leader. We may all be familiar with the Machiavellian phrase "the ends justify the means," but an ethical leader keeps in mind a different version of this and turns it into a question: "Do the ends justify the means?" In other words, the actions a leader takes to accomplish a goal need to be ethical. They cannot be justified by the necessity or importance of the leader's goals. Ethical leadership involves using morally appropriate actions to achieve goals.

To illustrate the importance of ethical actions, consider what happened at the Abu Ghraib prison in Iraq in 2004. Because of the atrocities on 9/11, national security and intelligence gathering became a high priority. Rules and standards of interrogation were expanded, and harsh interrogation methods were approved. The government's goal was to obtain information for purposes of national security.

Problems at the prison became evident when the media reported that prisoners were being sexually abused, humiliated, and tortured by prison personnel and civilian contract employees. Gruesome photographs of demeaning actions to prisoners appeared in the media and on the Internet. To obtain intelligence information, some U.S. Army soldiers used means that violated military regulations and internationally held rules on the humane treatment of prisoners of war established by the Geneva Convention in 1948.

In the case of the Abu Ghraib prison, the goal of maintaining national security and intelligence gathering was legitimate and worthwhile. However, the means that were used by some at the prison were considered by many to be unjustified and even ruled to be criminal. Many believe that the goals did not justify the means.

In everyday situations, a leader can act in many different ways to accomplish goals; each of these actions has ethical implications. For example, when a leader rewards some employees and not others, it raises questions of fairness. If a leader fails to take into consideration an employee's major health problems and instead demands that a job be completed on short notice, it raises questions about the leader's compassion for others. Even a simple task such as scheduling people's workload or continually giving more favorable assignments to one person over another reflects the ethics of the leader. In reality, almost everything a leader does has ethical overtones.

Given the importance of a leader's actions, what ethical principles should guide how a leader acts toward others? Ethical principles for leaders have been described by many scholars (Beauchamp & Bowie, 1988; Ciulla, 2003; Johnson, 2005; Kanungo, 2001; Kanungo & Mendonca, 1996). These writings highlight the importance of many ethical standards. In addition, there are three principles that have particular relevance to our discussion of the *actions* of ethical leaders: (1) showing respect, (2) serving others, and (3) showing justice.

1. ***Showing respect.*** To show respect means to treat others as unique human beings and never as means to an end. It requires treating others' decisions and values with respect. It also requires valuing others' ideas and affirming these individuals as unique human beings. When a leader shows respect to followers, followers become more confident and believe their contributions have value.

2. ***Serving others.*** Clearly, serving others is an example of altruism, an approach that suggests that actions are ethical if their primary purpose is to promote the best interest of others. From this perspective, a leader may be called on to act in the interest of others, even when it may run contrary to his or her self-interests (Bowie, 1991). In the workplace, serving others can be observed in activities such as mentoring, empowering others, team building, and citizenship behaviors (Kanungo & Mendonca, 1996). In practicing the principle of service, an ethical leader must be willing to be follower centered. That is, the leader tries to place others' interests foremost in his or her work, and act in ways that will benefit others.

3. ***Showing justice.*** Ethical leaders make it a top priority to treat all of their followers in an equal manner. Justice demands that a leader place the issue of fairness at the center of decision making. As a rule, no one should receive special treatment or special consideration except when a particular situation demands it. When individuals are treated differently, the grounds for different treatment must be clear, reasonable, and based on sound moral values.

In addition, justice is concerned with the Golden Rule: Treat others as you would like to be treated. If you expect fair treatment from others, then you should treat others fairly. Issues of fairness become problematic because there is always a limit on goods and resources. As a result, there is often competition for scarce resources. Because of the real or perceived scarcity of resources, conflicts often occur between individuals about fair methods of distribution. It is important for a leader to establish clearly the rules for distributing rewards. The nature of these rules says a lot about the ethical underpinnings of the leader and the organization.

The challenge of treating everyone fairly is illustrated in what happened to Richard Lee when he coached his son's Little League baseball team. His son, Eric, was an outstanding pitcher with a lot of natural ability. During one of the games, Eric became frustrated with his performance and began acting very immaturely, throwing his bat and kicking helmets. When Richard saw Eric's inappropriate behavior, he immediately took his son out of the game and sat him on the bench. The player who replaced Eric in the lineup was not as good a pitcher, and the team lost the game.

Ethical Principles

LEADERSHIP SNAPSHOT

Warren Buffett and Bill and Melinda Gates, Founders, The Giving Pledge

© Getty image 71299964 by Spencer Platt.

It started with three billionaires promising to give away half their fortune during their lifetimes and now encompasses more than 150 other super-rich families from around the world promising to do the same thing (Giving Pledge, 2016).

The Giving Pledge was spearheaded in 2010 by Bill and Melinda Gates and Warren Buffett, Nos. 1 and 2 respectively on the *Forbes* list of the world's richest people, to encourage a new era in philanthropy. Instead of waiting until they die to give away their money, billionaires are encouraged by the Giving Pledge to make donations earlier in their lives while they can still choose how to spend it.

"I don't know anyone who can't live on $500 million," Buffet has said (Frank, 2011).

The pledge is simple: The signers have to be billionaires, and they have to promise to give away at least half of their fortunes during their lifetimes. There are no constraints on where the money goes; causes supported by the pledge thus far have ranged from helping farmers in Appalachia to developing a major drug used to treat breast cancer to funding Jewish schools.

The pledge is less about the financial promise than it is about a public statement meant to inspire others, say the organizers. The pledge has also created a de facto "club" of sorts, where the signers get together on a regular basis to compare notes and share ideas.

"The goal is to raise the visibility of philanthropy and the great things it can do," says Bill Gates, the founder of Microsoft. Through these gatherings, billionaires swap experiences and frustrations and debate strategies for how to give away their wealth. "People are collaborating more than they would have otherwise," Gates says (Fowler, 2012).

The pledge is just that: a nonbinding promise to give away at least half of one's fortune while alive or in a will. It doesn't impose any penalties for failing to give it away. The Giving Pledge is coordinated by the Bill & Melinda Gates Foundation, but the foundation doesn't keep track of signatories' donations.

Gates, however, doesn't think the pledge will have a problem with signatories keeping their promises. "They are making a commitment in the court of public opinion," he says (Fowler, 2012).

For some critics, the pledge has raised questions about the power of the super-wealthy using these donations to shape issues of public concern like education and health care. Some have said that the pledge is a reminder of the economic disparities between the haves and have-nots and that if you have money you can control things, including charities.

"There is already a wide financial disparity between large and small nonprofits and between those institutions that serve disadvantaged populations and those that cater to more established constituencies," writes Pablo Eisenberg of the Georgetown McCourt School of Public Policy's Center for Public & Nonprofit Leadership. "The pledges will invariably increase that gap, broadening

the inequities in our nonprofit and charitable system" (Eisenberg, 2011).

But one young billionaire, 28-year-old Facebook founder Mark Zuckerberg, signed the pledge and immediately made good on it by donating $100 million to Newark, New Jersey's public schools.

"There's so much that needs to be done, it would be better to start now," he says (Guth & Fowler, 2010).

Fellow billionaire and Giving Pledge signer Nicolas Berggruen agrees. "Wealth is an advantage, but it also is frankly a responsibility" (Guth & Fowler, 2010).

After the game, Richard received a lot of criticism. In addition to Eric being mad at him, the parents of the other players were very angry. Some of the parents came to Richard and told him that he should not have pulled his son out of the game because it caused the team to lose.

In this example, the other players' parents failed to recognize what Richard was doing as a coach. Richard made a strong effort to be fair to all the players by treating his son the way he would treat any player who acted out. He set a standard of good sportsmanship; when his own son violated the rules, he was disciplined. Richard's actions were ethical, but coaching the team as he did was not easy. He did the right thing, but there were repercussions.

This example underscores the importance of the *actions* of a leader. A leader's actions play a significant role in determining whether that leader is ethical or unethical.

3. The Goals of the Leader

The **goals** that a leader establishes are the third factor related to ethical leadership. How a leader uses goals to influence others says a lot about the leader's ethics. For example, Adolf Hitler was able to convince millions of people that the eradication of the Jews was justified. It was an evil goal, and he was an immoral leader. The al-Qaeda terrorists' attack on targets in the

Goals and Unethical Leadership

United States was motivated by a goal to seek retribution for the United States' stance on Middle East affairs. On the positive side, Mother Teresa's goal to help the poor and disenfranchised was moral. Similarly, Habitat for Humanity's goal to build houses for the disadvantaged is moral. All of these examples highlight the significant role that goals play in determining whether leadership is ethical. The goals a leader selects are a reflection of the leader's ethics.

Identifying and pursuing just and worthy goals are the most important steps an ethical leader will undertake. In choosing goals, an ethical leader must assess the relative value and worth of his or her goals. In the process, it is important for the leader to take into account the interests of others in the group or organization and, in some cases, the interests of the community and larger culture in which he or she works. An ethical leader tries to establish goals on which all parties can mutually agree. An ethical leader with ethical goals will not impose his or her will on others.

Jacob Heckert, president of a regional health insurance company, is an example of a leader who used his leadership for worthwhile goals. Jacob believed in community service and advocated, but did not demand, that his employees engage in community service as well. Because he had several friends with diabetes and two of his employees had died of end-stage renal disease, Jacob was particularly interested in supporting the National Kidney Foundation. To promote his cause, he urged his entire company of 4,000 employees to join him in raising money for the National Kidney Foundation's 5K. Each employee who signed up was responsible for raising $100. Everyone who participated received a free water bottle and T-shirt.

On the day of the rally, Jacob was surprised when more than 1,800 employees from his company showed up to participate. The rally was a great success, raising more than $180,000 for the National Kidney Foundation. The employees felt good about being able to contribute to a worthy cause, and they enjoyed the community spirit that surrounded the event. Jacob was extremely pleased that his goals had been realized.

4. The Honesty of the Leader

Another major factor that contributes to ethical leadership is **honesty**. More than any other quality, people want their leaders to be honest. In fact, it could be said that being honest is synonymous with being ethical.

When we were children, we were frequently told by grown-ups to "never tell a lie." To be good meant telling the truth. For leaders, the lesson is the same. To be an ethical leader, a leader needs to be honest.

Dishonesty is a form of lying, a way of misrepresenting reality. Dishonesty may bring with it many negative outcomes, the foremost of which is that it creates distrust. When a leader is not honest, others come to see that leader as undependable and unreliable. They lose faith in what the leader says and stands for, and their respect for this individual is diminished. As a result, the leader's impact is compromised because others no longer trust and believe what he or she says.

Dishonesty also has a negative effect on a leader's interpersonal relationships. It puts a strain on how the leader and followers are connected to each other. When a leader lies to others, the leader in essence is saying that manipulation of others is acceptable. For example, when a boss does not come forth with a raise he promised, an employee will begin to distrust the boss. The long-term effect of this type of behavior, if ongoing, is a weakened relationship. Dishonesty, even when used with good intentions, contributes to the break-down of relationships.

Emerging From Scandal

But being honest is not just about the leader telling the truth. It also has to do with being open with others and representing reality as fully and completely as possible. This is not an easy task because there are times when telling the complete truth can be destructive or counterproductive. The challenge for a leader is to strike a balance between being open and candid, and at the same time monitoring what is appropriate to disclose in a particular situation.

An example of this delicate balance can be seen in a story about Dan Johnson. Dan was hired to work as an executive with a large manufacturing company. The new job required Dan and his family to leave the small Michigan community they lived in, giving up jobs and friends, to move to Chicago. The family put its house on the market and began looking for a new home and jobs in Chicago. A few days after Dan started, his boss, Justin Godfrey, took him aside and told him that he should not sell his Michigan house at that time. Justin suggested that Dan postpone his move by using his wife's job as an excuse when people inquired why the family had not moved to Chicago. Justin could not tell him any more, but Dan knew something major was about to happen. It did. The company announced a merger a few months later, and Dan's job in Chicago was eliminated. Justin was required to keep the merger news quiet, but if he had not confided the little information that he did, members of Dan's family would have uprooted their lives only to have them uprooted again. They would have experienced not only financial losses but emotional ones as well.

This example illustrates that it is important for a leader to be authentic. At the same time, it is essential that leaders be sensitive to the attitudes and feelings of others. Honest leadership involves a wide set of behaviors, which includes being truthful in appropriate ways.

5. The Power of the Leader

Another factor that plays a role in ethical leadership is **power**. Power is the capacity to influence or affect others. A leader has power because he or she has the ability to affect others' beliefs, attitudes, and courses of action. Religious leaders, managers, coaches, and teachers are all people who have the potential to influence others. When they use their potential, they are using their power as a resource to effect change in others.

The most widely cited research on power is French and Raven's (1959) work on the bases of social power. French and Raven identified five common and important bases of power: referent power, expert power, legitimate power, reward power, and coercive power (see Table 12.2). Each of these types of power increases a leader's capacity to have an impact on others, and each has the potential to be abused.

Power and Ethics

Since power can be used in positive ways to benefit others or in destructive ways to hurt others, a leader needs to be aware of and sensitive to how he or she uses power. How a leader uses power says a great deal about that leader's ethics. Power is not inherently bad, but it can be used in negative ways.

As discussed in Chapter 1, "Understanding Leadership," there is dark side of leadership where a leader uses his or her influence or power for personal ends. Unfortunately, there are many examples in the world of such leaders. One example was Saddam Hussein, the president of Iraq from 1979 to 2003. Recognized widely as a brutal dictator, Hussein was a Sunni Muslim (a minority in Iraq), a sect of Islam that has a centuries-old conflict with the country's majority Shi'a Muslims and ethnic Kurds. When Hussein assumed power, he used his security forces to systematically murder anyone who opposed him. Many of these were genocidal massacres of innocent Iraqi citizens who were

TABLE 12.2   Five Bases of Power

1. Referent power	Based on followers' identification and liking for the leader	Example: A college professor who is highly admired by students
2. Expert power	Based on the followers' perceptions of the leader's competence	Example: A person with strong knowledge about a software program
3. Legitimate power	Associated with having status or formal job authority	Example: A judge who presides over a court case
4. Reward power	Derived from having the capacity to provide benefits to others	Example: A supervisor who can give bonuses to employees
5. Coercive power	Derived from being able to penalize or punish others	Example: A teacher who can lower a student's grade for missing class

Source: Based on French and Raven (1959).

Shi'a Muslims and ethnic Kurds. The number of Iraqis murdered by Hussein's forces is unknown, but it is believed to be more than 250,000. Another example of a leader using power in unethical and destructive ways is Jim Jones, an American who set up a religious cult in the country of Guyana, and who led more than 900 of his followers to commit suicide by drinking cyanide-laced punch. While these are extreme examples, power can also be abused in everyday leadership. For example, a supervisor who forces an employee to work every weekend by threatening to fire the worker if she or he does not comply is being unethical in the use of power. Another example is a high school cross-country track coach who is highly admired by his runners, but who requires them to take costly health food supplements even though the supplements are not proven effective by standard medical guidelines. There are many ways that power can be abused by a leader. From the smallest to the largest forms of influence, a leader needs to try to be fair and caring in his or her leadership.

The key to not misusing power is to be constantly vigilant and aware of the way one's leadership affects others. An ethical leader does not wield power or dominate, but instead takes into account the will of the followers, as well as the leader's own will. An ethical leader uses power to work with followers to accomplish their mutual goals.

6. The Values of the Leader

A final factor that contributes to understanding ethical leadership is **values**. Values are the ideas, beliefs, and modes of action that people find worthwhile or desirable. Some examples of values are peace, justice, integrity, fairness, and community. A leader's ethical values are demonstrated in everyday leadership.

Values and Leadership

Scholar James MacGregor Burns suggested that there are three kinds of leadership values: ethical values, such as kindness and altruism; modal values, such as responsibility and accountability; and end values, such as justice and community (Ciulla, 2003). **Ethical values** are similar to the notion of character discussed earlier in this chapter. **Modal values** are concerned with the means or actions a leader takes. **End values** describe the outcomes or goals a leader seeks to achieve. End values are present when a person addresses broad issues such as liberty and justice. These three kinds of values are interrelated in ethical leadership.

In leadership situations, both the leader and the follower have values, and these values are seldom the same. A leader brings his or her own unique values to leadership situations, and followers do the same. The challenge for the ethical leader is to be faithful to his or her own leadership values while being sensitive to the followers' values.

For example, a leader in an organization may value community and encourage his or her employees to work together and seek consensus in planning. However, the leader's followers may value individuality and self-expression. This creates a problem because these values are seemingly in conflict. In this situation, an ethical leader needs to find a way to advance his or her own interests in creating community without destroying the followers' interests in individuality. There is a tension between these different values; an ethical leader needs to negotiate through these differences to find the best outcome for everyone involved. While the list of possible conflicts of values is infinite, finding common ground between a leader and followers is usually possible, and is essential to ethical leadership.

In the social services sector, where there are often too few resources and too many people in need, leaders constantly struggle with decisions that test their values. Because resources are scarce, a leader has to decide where to allocate the resources; these decisions communicate a lot about the leader's values. For example, in mentoring programs such as Big Brothers Big Sisters, the list of children in need is often much longer than the list of available mentors. How do administrators decide which child is going to be assigned a mentor? They decide based on their values and the values of the people with whom they work. If they believe that children from single-parent households should have higher priority, then those children will be put at the top of the list. As this example illustrates, making ethical decisions is challenging for a leader, especially in situations where resources are scarce.

CULTURE AND LEADERSHIP ETHICS

Culture and Ethics

The world today is globally connected in ways it never has been before. Through your lifetime, you will undoubtedly be exposed to and work with individuals from cultures very different than your own. As a leader, it is important to recognize that not every culture shares the same ethical ideals as yours. Different cultures have different rules of conduct, and as a result, leadership behaviors that one culture deems ethical may not be viewed the same way by another culture.

For example, Resick, Hanges, Dickson, and Mitchelson (2006) found that Nordic European cultures such as Denmark and Sweden place more importance on a leader's character and integrity—defined as a leader behaving in a manner that is just, honest, sincere, and trustworthy—than Middle Eastern cultures such as those in Egypt, Turkey, and Qatar.

Another example is the use of bribery in business practices. Bribery (offering money or gifts in exchange for favorable treatment or influence) to obtain business is forbidden for U.S. companies, no matter where on the globe they are doing business, and offenders can face jail terms and large fines. However, in some countries, bribery is a norm, and business can't be transacted without it. In China, for example, it is expected in business relationships that there will be the giving of carefully chosen gifts to convey respect and that the business relationship is valued by the giver. It is considered a matter of business etiquette (Pitta, Fung, & Isberg, 1999). And, until 1999, bribes were tax deductible and seen as a necessary part of conducting business in Germany.

SUMMARY

There is a strong demand for ethical leaders in our society today. This chapter answers the question "What does it take to be an ethical leader?" Ethical leadership is defined as a process in which a good person acts in the right ways to accomplish worthy goals. There are six factors related to ethical leadership.

First, *character* is fundamental to ethical leadership. A leader's character refers to who the leader is as a person and his or her core values. The *Six Pillars of Character* are trustworthiness, respect, responsibility, fairness, caring, and citizenship.

Second, ethical leadership is explained by the *actions* of the leader—the means a leader uses to accomplish goals. An ethical leader engages in showing respect, serving others, and showing justice.

Third, ethical leadership is about the *goals* of the leader. The goals a leader selects reflect his or her values. Selecting goals that are meaningful and worthwhile is one of the most important decisions an ethical leader needs to make.

Fourth, ethical leadership is concerned with the *honesty* of the leader. Without honesty, a leader cannot be ethical. In telling the truth, a leader needs to strike a balance between openness and sensitivity to others.

Fifth, *power* plays a role in ethical leadership. A leader has an ethical obligation to use power for the influence of the common good of others. The interests of followers need to be taken into account, and the leader needs to work *with* followers to accomplish mutual ends.

Finally, ethical leadership is concerned with the *values* of the leader. An ethical leader has strong values and promotes positive values within his or her organization. Because leaders and followers often have conflicting values, a leader needs to be able to express his or her values and integrate these values with others' values.

In summary, ethical leadership has many dimensions. To be an ethical leader, you need to pay attention to who you are, what you do, what goals you seek, your honesty, the way you use power, and your values.

GLOSSARY TERMS

actions　276

character　275

end values　285

ethical leadership　274

ethical values　285

goals　282

honesty　282

modal values　285

power　284

values　285

⑤SAGE edge™

Sharpen your skills with SAGE edge at **edge.sagepub.com/northouseintro4e**

SAGE edge for students provides a personalized approach to help you accomplish your coursework goals in an easy-to-use learning environment.

12.1 CASE STUDY

The Write Choice

Each semester, community college professor Julia Ramirez requires her students to do a 10-hour community service project at a nonprofit agency of their choice and write a paper about the experience. In the paper, they are to discuss their volunteer experience and incorporate concepts presented in class into this reflection. This is the sixth semester that Professor Ramirez has used this assignment, and she has always received positive feedback about the benefits of the assignment from her students and the nonprofits.

The community college that Professor Ramirez works at is making an effort to be "green" and, in order to cut down on paper usage, requests that faculty and staff utilize online tools for giving and receiving assignments and providing feedback to students. Professor Ramirez takes advantage of these green initiatives, requiring her community learning papers to all be turned in electronically at noon on the last Friday before exams. She likes having the papers turned in electronically because it has significantly cut down on late papers and it is now very easy to check student work for plagiarism.

That day has arrived, and Professor Ramirez downloads her student papers from the class webpage and begins to grade them. The papers are informal in nature, written in first-person narrative as if the students were talking directly to Professor Ramirez. After grading a number of papers, Professor

Ramirez comes to the paper written by student Kelly Declan. Kelly's paper reads less like a personal narrative and more like a brochure for the organization where she volunteered. At first, Professor Ramirez is impressed with the amount of detail that Kelly retained from volunteering, but after reading part of the paper, she becomes suspicious. To be safe, Professor Ramirez decides to copy a passage from Kelly's paper into her Internet search engine to see if it matches any other published sources. It does; in fact, it is a direct match for an online brochure of a similar organization in a neighboring state. Professor Ramirez tests a few more sections from Kelly's paper and finds that 90% of it was plagiarized from this one source on the Internet.

Plagiarism is taken very seriously at the college. Students accused of plagiarism are reported to the student review board, and if the board confirms that a student's work is not his or her own, the student is dismissed from the college. Students who have been dismissed for plagiarism are able to reapply to the college after waiting one semester, and if they are readmitted, they are placed on academic probation for a year.

Despite the college's policy, Professor Ramirez is conflicted about how to deal with this situation. She knows that Kelly had a very difficult semester. Her mother is ill with cancer, and during the semester, Kelly drove twice a week to her hometown two hours away to

(Continued)

(Continued)

take her mother to doctor's appointments and chemotherapy. Knowing this, Professor Ramirez accommodated Kelly's schedule during the semester so that she did not have to drop the course. This is also Kelly's last semester before graduation, and she will be the first person in her family to graduate from college. Kelly also has a job lined up after graduation, for which Professor Ramirez wrote her a letter of recommendation, and if she does not graduate, she will most likely lose the job. Losing the job will be certain if Kelly is ejected from the college.

Professor Ramirez decides not to report the incident of plagiarism to the review board right away. She chooses instead to approach Kelly one-on-one and will proceed based on what Kelly has to say. During their meeting, it is apparent to Professor Ramirez that Kelly did complete the required service hours but was overwhelmed when it came to writing the paper.

Kelly had let the assignment go until the very end and then when she had to write it, she could only come up with one page rather than the three pages required. She added the plagiarized information to make the paper reach the required length. Kelly is genuinely remorseful and admits she is terrified of the consequences.

In the end, Professor Ramirez gave Kelly a zero for the assignment, but she still passed the class with a grade of a B. She did not feel that having Kelly kicked out of school would benefit the college or Kelly. Despite going against college policy, Professor Ramirez believes her behavior is consistent with her personal values of acknowledging that people make mistakes and deserve second chances. She personally felt that this behavior was out of character for Kelly and, had Kelly not been under tremendous personal and academic stress, she wouldn't have acted in this way.

QUESTIONS

1. Even though Professor Ramirez deviated from the college's policy regarding plagiarism, do you feel that she acted ethically?

2. If you were a student in this class and learned Professor Ramirez made an exception for this student, would you think she acted ethically? Explain.

3. In Table 12.1, the Six Pillars of Character are detailed. Which of these six pillars did Professor Ramirez display in consideration for her student, and how?

4. Professor Ramirez's actions ultimately brought into question whether or not the ends justify the means. Do you feel that her leniency in this case made her a stronger or more ethical leader? Explain.

12.2 SAMPLE ITEMS FROM THE ETHICAL LEADERSHIP STYLE QUESTIONNAIRE

Purpose

1. To develop an understanding of your ethical leadership style
2. To understand how your preferred ethical leadership style relates to other ethical leadership styles

Directions

1. Please read the following 10 hypothetical situations in which a leader is confronted with an ethical dilemma.
2. Place yourself in the role of the leader or manager in the situation.
3. For each situation, indicate with an "X" your *most preferred response*. Your most preferred response is the response that best describes why you would do what you would do in that particular situation. Choose only one response. There are no right or wrong answers.

Response alternatives explained:

- *I would do what is right:* this option means you follow a set of moral rules and do what is expected of you when facing an ethical dilemma. You focus on fulfilling your moral obligations and doing your duty.
- *I would do what benefits the most people:* this option means you try to do what is best for the most people overall when facing an ethical dilemma. You focus on what will result in happiness for the largest number of individuals.
- *I would do what a good person would do:* this option means that you pull from who you are (your character) when facing an ethical dilemma. You act out of integrity and you are faithful to your own principles.
- *I would do what shows that I care about my close relationships:* this option means that you give attention to your relationships when facing an ethical dilemma. You may give special consideration to those with whom you share a personal bond or commitment.
- *I would do what benefits me the most:* this option means that you do what is best for accomplishing your personal goals and objectives when facing an ethical dilemma. You are not afraid to assert your own interests when resolving problems.
- *I would do what is fair:* this option means that you focus on treating others fairly when facing an ethical dilemma. You try to make sure the benefits and burdens of decisions are shared equitably between everyone concerned.

Situations

1. You are the leader of a manufacturing team and learn that your employees are falsifying product quality results to sell more products. If you report the matter, most of them will lose their jobs, you may lose yours, and your company will take a significant hit to its reputation. What would you do in this situation?

   ☐ A. I would do what is right.
   ☐ B. I would do what benefits the most people.
   ☐ C. I would do what a good person would do.
   ☐ D. I would do what shows that I care about my relationships.

(Continued)

 Visit **edge.sagepub.com/northouseintro4e** for a downloadable version of this questionnaire.

12.2 SAMPLE ITEMS FROM THE ETHICAL LEADERSHIP STYLE QUESTIONNAIRE

(Continued)

    ☐ E. I would do what benefits me the most.
    ☐ F. I would do what is fair.

2. You have an employee who has been having performance problems, which is making it hard for your group to meet its work quota. This person was recommended to you as a solid performer. You now believe the person's former manager had problems with the employee and just wanted to get rid of the person. If you give the underperforming employee a good recommendation, leaving out the performance problems, you will have an opportunity to pass the employee off to another group. What would you do in this situation?

    ☐ A. I would do what is right.
    ☐ B. I would do what benefits the most people.
    ☐ C. I would do what a good person would do.
    ☐ D. I would do what shows that I care about my relationships.
    ☐ E. I would do what benefits me the most.
    ☐ F. I would do what is fair.

3. Your team is hard-pressed to complete a critical project. You hear about a job opening that would be much better for one of your key employees' career. If this individual leaves the team, it would put the project in danger. What would you do in this situation?

    ☐ A. I would do what is right.
    ☐ B. I would do what benefits the most people.
    ☐ C. I would do what a good person would do.
    ☐ D. I would do what shows that I care about my relationships.
    ☐ E. I would do what benefits me the most.
    ☐ F. I would do what is fair.

4. An employee of yours has a child with a serious illness and is having trouble fulfilling obligations at work. You learn from your administrative assistant that this employee claimed 40 hours on a timesheet for a week when the employee actually only worked 30 hours. What would you do in this situation?

    ☐ A. I would do what is right.
    ☐ B. I would do what benefits the most people.
    ☐ C. I would do what a good person would do.
    ☐ D. I would do what shows that I care about my relationships.
    ☐ E. I would do what benefits me the most.
    ☐ F. I would do what is fair.

5. You are a manager, and some of your employees can finish their quotas in much less than the allotted time to do so. If upper management becomes aware of this, they will want you to increase the quotas. Some of your employees are unable to meet their current quotas. What would you do in this situation?

    ☐ A. I would do what is right.
    ☐ B. I would do what benefits the most people.
    ☐ C. I would do what a good person would do.
    ☐ D. I would do what shows that I care about my relationships.
    ☐ E. I would do what benefits me the most.
    ☐ F. I would do what is fair.

12.2 SAMPLE ITEMS FROM THE ETHICAL LEADERSHIP STYLE QUESTIONNAIRE

(Continued)

6. You are an organization's chief financial officer, and you are aware that the chief executive officer and other members of the senior leadership team want to provide exaggerated financial information to keep the company's stock price high. The entire senior management team holds significant stock positions. What would you do in this situation?

   ☐ A. I would do what is right.
   ☐ B. I would do what benefits the most people.
   ☐ C. I would do what a good person would do.
   ☐ D. I would do what shows that I care about my relationships.
   ☐ E. I would do what benefits me the most.
   ☐ F. I would do what is fair.

7. Two new employees have joined your accounting team right out of school. They are regularly found surfing the Internet or texting on their phones. Your accounting work regularly requires overtime at the end of the month to get the financial reports completed. These employees refuse to do any overtime, which shifts work to other team members. The other team members are getting resentful and upset. What would you do in this situation?

   ☐ A. I would do what is right.
   ☐ B. I would do what benefits the most people.
   ☐ C. I would do what a good person would do.
   ☐ D. I would do what shows that I care about my relationships.
   ☐ E. I would do what benefits me the most.
   ☐ F. I would do what is fair.

8. You are the director of a neighborhood food cooperative. A member—a single parent with four children—is caught shoplifting $30 in groceries from the co-op. You suspect this person has been stealing for years. You consider pressing charges. What would you do in this situation?

   ☐ A. I would do what is right.
   ☐ B. I would do what benefits the most people.
   ☐ C. I would do what a good person would do.
   ☐ D. I would do what shows that I care about my relationships.
   ☐ E. I would do what benefits me the most.
   ☐ F. I would do what is fair.

9. You have been accused of discriminating against a particular gender in your hiring practices. A new position opens up, and you could hire a candidate of the gender you've been accused of discriminating against over a candidate of another gender, even though the latter candidate has slightly better qualifications. Hiring the former candidate would let you address this accusation and improve your reputation in the company. What would you do in this situation?

   ☐ A. I would do what is right.
   ☐ B. I would do what benefits the most people.
   ☐ C. I would do what a good person would do.
   ☐ D. I would do what shows that I care about my relationships.
   ☐ E. I would do what benefits me the most.
   ☐ F. I would do what is fair.

(Continued)

APPLICATION

APPLICATION

12.2 SAMPLE ITEMS FROM THE ETHICAL LEADERSHIP STYLE QUESTIONNAIRE

(Continued)

10. You are a professor. One of your best students buys an essay online and turns it in for a grade. Later in the term, the student begins to feel guilty and confesses to you that the paper was purchased. It is the norm at the university to fail a student guilty of plagiarism. You must decide if you will flunk the student. What would you do in this situation?

☐ A. I would do what is right.
☐ B. I would do what benefits the most people.
☐ C. I would do what a good person would do.
☐ D. I would do what shows that I care about my relationships.
☐ E. I would do what benefits me the most.
☐ F. I would do what is fair.

Scoring

To score the questionnaire, sum the number of times you selected items A, B, C, D, E, or F. The sum of A responses represents your preference for *Duty Ethics,* the sum of B responses represents your preference for *Utilitarian Ethics*, the sum of C responses represents your preference for *Virtue Ethics*, the sum of D responses represents your preference for *Caring Ethics*, the sum of E responses represents your preference for *Egoism Ethics*, and the sum of F responses represents your preference for *Justice Ethics*. Place these sums in the Total Scores section that follows.

Total Scores

A. Duty Ethics: _____

B. Utilitarian Ethics: _____

C. Virtue Ethics: _____

D. Caring Ethics: _____

E. Egoism Ethics: _____

F. Justice Ethics: _____

Scoring Interpretation

The scores you received on this questionnaire provide information about your ethical leadership style; they represent your preferred way of addressing ethical dilemmas. Given a situation with an ethical dilemma, this questionnaire points to what ethical perspective is behind the choices you would make to resolve the dilemma. As you look at your total scores, your highest score represents your primary or dominant ethical leadership style, your second-highest score is the next most important, and so on. If you scored 0 for a category, it means that you put lower priority on that particular ethical approach to guide your decision making when facing ethical dilemmas.

- *If you scored higher on Duty Ethics*, it means you follow a set of moral rules and do what is expected of you when facing an ethical dilemma. You focus on fulfilling your moral obligations and doing your duty.

12.2 SAMPLE ITEMS FROM THE ETHICAL LEADERSHIP STYLE QUESTIONNAIRE

(Continued)

- *If you scored higher on Utilitarian Ethics*, it means that you try to do what is best for the most people overall when facing an ethical dilemma. You focus on what will result in happiness for the largest number of individuals.
- *If you scored higher on Virtue Ethics*, it means that you pull from who you are (your character) when facing an ethical dilemma. You act out of integrity and you are faithful to your own principles.
- *If you scored higher on Caring Ethics*, it means that you give attention to your relationships when facing an ethical dilemma. You may give special consideration to those with whom you share a personal bond or commitment.
- *If you scored higher on Egoism Ethics*, it means that you do what is best for accomplishing your personal goals and objectives when facing an ethical dilemma. You are not afraid to assert your own interests when resolving problems.
- *If you scored higher on Justice Ethics*, it means that you focus on treating others fairly when facing an ethical dilemma. You try to make sure the benefits and burdens of decisions are shared equitably between everyone concerned.

By comparing your scores regarding each of these ethical perspectives, you can get a sense of what is important to you when addressing an ethical concern. Obviously, if you scored low on in any of these categories, it suggests that you give less priority to that ethical perspective. All of the ethical perspectives have merit, so there is no "best" perspective to maintain.

This questionnaire is intended as a self-assessment exercise. Although each ethical approach is presented as a discrete category, it is possible that one category may overlap with another category. It is also possible that you may have an ethical leadership style that is not fully captured in this questionnaire. Since this questionnaire is an abridged version of an expanded questionnaire, you may wish to take the entire questionnaire to gain a more accurate reflection of your ethical approach. It can be taken at www.leaderdecisionmakingsurvey.com.

APPLICATION

APPLICATION

12.3 OBSERVATIONAL EXERCISE

Ethical Leadership

Purpose

1. To become aware of the dimensions of ethical leadership
2. To assess how actual leaders exhibit ethical leadership

Directions

1. For this exercise, you must observe a public presentation of a leader in your community. This can be a pastor, a college president, a mayor, a city commissioner, the head of a social service agency, or some other community leader.

2. Record what you observe about the leader's ethics in the categories that follow. Try to be thorough in your descriptions of the leader's presentation.

Leader's name: _____ Leader's title: _____

Occasion: _____

1. The **character** of the leader: What was the leader like? What kind of person was the leader? What were the leader's strengths and weaknesses?

2. The **actions** of the leader: How does this leader go about accomplishing goals? Where does the leader stand on (1) showing respect, (2) serving others, and (3) showing justice?

3. The **goals** of the leader: What were the leader's main goals? Were the leader's goals clear to you and others in the audience? How would you assess the value and worth of those goals?

4. The **honesty** of the leader: What did you observe about this leader's honesty? Was the leader open and forthright? How authentic did you find this leader to be?

5. The **power** of the leader: Based on French and Raven's (1959) types of power, what kind of power did this leader exhibit? What did you observe about how this leader would use his or her power with others?

6. The **values** of the leader: Based on the presentation, what do you think this leader values? What is important to this leader? What values did this leader promote in his or her presentation?

 Visit **edge.sagepub.com/northouseintro4e** for a downloadable version of this exercise.

12.3 OBSERVATIONAL EXERCISE

(Continued)

Questions

1. What is your overall assessment of this leader's ethics?

2. What specific examples in the leader's presentation were particularly revealing of the leader's ethics?

3. Which factors of ethical leadership (character, actions, goals, honesty, power, and values) were most apparent in the leader's presentation? Discuss.

4. On a scale from 1 to 10, how would you describe this speaker's ethical leadership? Defend your answer.

APPLICATION

12.4 REFLECTION AND ACTION WORKSHEET

Ethical Leadership

Reflection

1. This chapter suggests that leadership has a *moral dimension* and that leaders have a responsibility to use their authority for the common good. Do you agree? Discuss.

2. When you consider the *character of a leader* and *what a leader does* (the leader's actions), which of these two factors is more important with regard to ethical leadership? Can a person with bad character be an ethical leader? Discuss your answers.

3. In this chapter, the circumstances at Abu Ghraib prison are used as an example of unethical leadership. Do you agree with this assessment? How do you view what happened at Abu Ghraib? What factors explain the leadership ethics in this situation?

4. This chapter includes a story about Richard Lee, the father who coached his son's Little League baseball team. What was your reaction to the story? Do you think Richard was an ethical leader? How would you have responded in this situation?

Action

1. Based on your responses to the Ethical Leadership Styles Questionnaire, what are your core values? Do you think other people know your core values? Are you comfortable talking about these values with others? In your planning for the future (e.g., next five years), how will your values influence what you do? Discuss.

2. *Character* is a fundamental aspect of ethical leadership. What are your character strengths and weaknesses? List three specific actions you could take to strengthen your character.

3. In the Observational Exercise (12.3), you observed and analyzed the ethical leadership of a specific leader. If you were to apply the same analysis to your own leadership, how would you describe yourself? What factors best explain the ethics of your own leadership? If you were to try to become a more ethical leader, what specific changes should you make in your leadership? Discuss.

 Visit **edge.sagepub.com/northouseintro4e** for a downloadable version of this worksheet.

REFERENCES

Beauchamp, T. L., & Bowie, N. E. (1988). *Ethical theory and business* (3rd ed.). Englewood Cliffs, NJ: Prentice Hall.

Bowie, N. E. (1991). Challenging the egoistic paradigm. *Business Ethics Quarterly, 1*(1), 1–21.

Ciulla, J. B. (2003). *The ethics of leadership*. Belmont, CA: Wadsworth/Thomson Learning.

Eisenberg, P. (2011, January 11). Unintended consequences of Giving Pledge's good intentions. *Chronicle of Philanthropy*. Retrieved from http://onphilanthropy.com/2011/pablo-eisenberg-unintended-consequences-of-giving-pledges-good-intentions/

Fowler, G. (2012, September 19). More billionaires sign on to giving money away. *The Wall Street Journal*. Retrieved from http://online.wsj.com/article/SB10000872396390443995604578003043533208534.html

Frank, R. (2011, October 27). The biggest gift in the world. *WSJ Magazine*. Retrieved from http://online.wsj.com/article/SB1000142405297020464450457665351080182 6824.html

French, J. R., Jr., & Raven, B. (1959). The bases of social power. In D. Cartwright (Ed.), *Studies in social power* (pp. 150–167). Ann Arbor, MI: Institute for Social Research.

Giving Pledge. (2016). *Current pledgers*. Retrieved from http://givingpledge.org/index.html

Guth, R. A., & Fowler, G. A. (2010, December 9). 16 tycoons agree to give away fortunes. *The Wall Street Journal*. Retrieved from http://online.wsj.com/article/SB100014240527487034935045760079825009394 82.html

Johnson, C. R. (2005). *Meeting the ethical challenges of leadership* (2nd ed.). Thousand Oaks, CA: Sage.

Josephson Institute. (2008). *The Six Pillars of Character*. Los Angeles, CA: Author.

Kanungo, R. N. (2001). Ethical values of transactional and transformational leaders. *Canadian Journal of Administrative Sciences, 18*(4), 257–265.

Kanungo, R. N., & Mendonca, M. (1996). *Ethical dimensions of leadership*. Thousand Oaks, CA: Sage.

Pitta, D. A., Fung, H.-G., & Isberg, S. (1999). Ethical issues across cultures: managing the differing perspectives of China and the USA. *Journal of Consumer Marketing, 16*(3), 240–256.

Resick, C. J., Hanges, P. J., Dickson, M. W., & Mitchelson, J. A. (2006). A cross-cultural examination of the endorsement of ethical leadership. *Journal of Business Ethics, 63*(4), 345–359.

Velasquez, M. G. (1992). *Business ethics: Concepts and cases* (3rd ed.). Englewood Cliffs, NJ: Prentice Hall.

CHAPTER 13

Overcoming Obstacles

INTRODUCTION

"Life is difficult." That is the first sentence in Scott Peck's famous book *The Road Less Traveled* (1978). Although hard for some to accept, Peck told us that life is not going to be easy. Obstacles and struggles are an integral part of life. In the work setting, the same is true. Because obstacles always will be present, one of the most important things a leader can do is to help others overcome these obstacles.

ASK THE
AUTHOR

Should Leaders Help Their Followers Around Obstacles?

OBSTACLES EXPLAINED

What is an obstacle? It is a hindrance, problem, or hurdle that gets in the way of followers and makes it difficult for followers to reach their goal. Obstacles get in the way of what followers intend to do. Obstacles come in many forms. It could be a physical thing (e.g., bad work space), a psychological issue (e.g., closed-mindedness), or a task-related issue (e.g., a complex work process). In essence, anything that has a negative impact on follower performance could be called an obstacle. There are many examples of obstacles. For a busy person who wants to learn to play the guitar, an obstacle could be finding enough time to practice. For a new employee in a large hospital, an obstacle could be learning where the different departments in the building are located. Or, for a fifth-year senior who isn't going to graduate, an obstacle could be a lack of motivation.

Obstacles are important for leaders to recognize because they provide clear cues for what leaders can do to help followers. Addressing obstacles can be very direct and practical. While some leadership theories are rather esoteric and prescribe certain leadership strategies (e.g., be authentic), addressing obstacles is a very concrete approach to leadership. For example, if a leader asks followers "How can I help you?" or "What problems are you having?" their answers will point directly to how the leader can adapt his or her behavior to help the followers with their work. Maybe followers want more direction or need to be challenged more; either way, if the leader asks them about their concerns, the obstacles can be remedied. Learning about and dealing with obstacles is a very effective way to improve your leadership.

OVERCOMING OBSTACLES IN PRACTICE

Engaging With Obstacles

Whether it is by listening to their complaints, encouraging them, or providing counsel, there are many ways a leader can be helpful to his or her followers. The first challenge in helping people with obstacles is to figure out what the problems are; the second challenge is determining what should be done to solve them. If a leader does this, followers will be more motivated, productive, and satisfied with their work.

Research conducted by House (1971, 1996) on **path–goal leadership** directly addresses how a leader can assist others in overcoming obstacles that hinder productivity. Path–goal leadership suggests that a leader should choose a style that best fits the needs of individual group members and the work they are doing. The leader should help these individuals define their goals and the paths they wish to take to reach those goals. When obstacles arise, the leader needs to help individuals confront them. This may mean helping them to navigate around the obstacles, or it may mean helping them remove the obstacles. The leader's job is to help group members reach their goals by directing, guiding, and coaching them along the way.

Based on ideas set forth in path–goal leadership theory, this chapter addresses the **obstacles** that followers may face and how a leader can help followers overcome them. Although people encounter many obstacles in their lives, this chapter highlights *seven* major obstacles derived from path–goal

FIGURE 13.1 Obstacles Hindering Goal Achievement

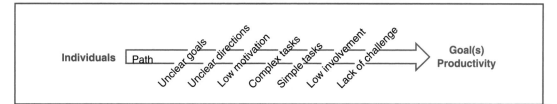

theory (see Figure 13.1). In the following section, each of the obstacles will be described, and the various ways leaders can respond to these obstacles will be explored.

Obstacle 1: Unclear Goals

We have all known people who selected their career goals early in life. You may remember a grade school friend who said she was going to be a doctor and then subsequently went to college and medical school and became a neurosurgeon. You may remember a high school friend who said he was going to be in the movies and subsequently made it big in Hollywood. These people stand out because they were especially goal oriented—they knew what they wanted to do, *and* they did it. The problem is that these people are the *exception* and not the *rule*. For most people, finding their life goal is a real challenge.

The same is true in leadership situations. It is not uncommon for individuals to be unclear or confused about their goals. Whether it is the salesperson who is required to meet a new sales quota, a hospital volunteer who is supposed to help patients, or a high school student who must write a term paper, people are often unclear about the goal or how to reach it.

Sometimes the goal is not known, sometimes it is obscure, and sometimes it is hidden among a tangle of competing goals. When goals are not clearly articulated and understood, individuals are less likely to be successful in achieving them. Furthermore, they will be less excited about their work and less gratified about their accomplishments.

It cannot be stressed enough that *the leader needs to make goals clear and understandable.* Just as leaders need to provide a map in articulating their vision (see Chapter 7, "Creating a Vision"), they must help others see the goal, the end toward which everything else is being directed. All members of a group deserve a clear picture of where their efforts are being directed. When the goal is vague, the leader needs to clarify it. Similarly, if the goal is embedded in a complex set of related goals, the leader needs to identify a specific goal for group members and explain how it fits with all the other goals.

Clarifying Goals

The following list provides a few examples of leaders expressing clear goals. The examples may not be glamorous, but they exemplify good leadership.

Football coach to team: "The goal for the defensive team this season is to try to sack the opposing quarterback at least two times in every game."

High school physical education teacher to students: "At the beginning of every class you are required to jog one lap around the track."

Orchestra conductor to orchestra: "Our upcoming rehearsals are going to be difficult because the pieces we are playing are really challenging. If we practice together every week for five hours, this concert could be our best all year."

Staff supervisor at a geriatric facility to volunteer staff: "By helping the staff to fold the laundry of the patients living here, you will help to reduce the spiraling costs of our facility."

College speech teacher to students: "In this speech assignment, you must make sure to do three things: (1) tell the audience what you are going to tell them, (2) tell them, and (3) tell them what you have told them."

In each of these examples, the leaders are helping individuals identify and clarify the goals of their work. The individuals doing the work will be more effective and more satisfied as a result of knowing their goals.

Obstacle 2: Unclear Directions

The Need for Clear Directions

Anyone who has ever bought something that needed to be assembled (e.g., a computer table or futon frame) knows how frustrating it is when the directions are missing from the box, impossible to follow, or written in a foreign language. No matter how much you want to put the product together, you cannot do it. This is what happens in work situations when leaders are not clear with their directions. Bad directions lead to ineffective performance.

A leader needs to *define the path* to the goal by giving clear directions. Directions that are vague, confusing, rambling, imprecise, or incomplete are not helpful to anyone. In fact, unclear directions can have a debilitating effect on individuals. People lose their capacity to move forward when they do not have clear directions on how to proceed. Some individuals are lost without directions. They may have a picture of where they are headed, but they do not know *how* to get there.

Giving clear directions takes thought and skill. For example, students in a classroom want clear directions for their assignments. If the assignment is a term paper, an effective teacher describes in detail the required components. The teacher might require a two-paragraph introduction, a thesis sentence, a conceptual framework, a review of the literature, a discussion section, a conclusion, and a bibliography. When clear directions are given, students have a sense of personal control because they know what is required of them. When people know *what* they are supposed to do and *when* they are supposed to do it, they can accomplish their work more easily.

While giving clear directions is important, it is also important to be aware that individuals vary in their need for direction. Some people want very elaborate, specific instructions, while others want general directions that allow them to proceed on their own. It is the leader's job to adapt directions to the needs of each individual.

Much like drivers who are relieved to have the navigation system tell them what interstate exit to take, followers want direction from a calm leader who tells them what they need to do and when they need to do it. When they make a mistake or lose their way, they want the leader to redirect them. Most important, group members want directions that are not evaluative or critical. If they make mistakes, they want to be corrected in a kind manner. A good leader will give directions that are helpful but not judgmental. People appreciate straightforward directions, and like to hear the leader say they "have arrived" when they get their work done.

Obstacle 3: Low Motivation

What should a leader do when individuals are not motivated? How does a leader encourage followers to work when they do not want to work? How can a leader make people excited about work? Answers to questions such as these have been of interest to leaders for a long time. In fact, hundreds of articles and books have been written in an effort to explain the underpinnings of human motivation (see Herzberg's motivation-hygiene theory, 1968; Maslow's hierarchy of needs theory, 1954; and Skinner's work on behaviorism, 1953). All these writings point to the complexity and challenges leaders face in trying to motivate others.

Path–goal leadership incorporates **expectancy theory** as a way to motivate others (House, 1996; Vroom, 1964). Expectancy theory suggests that people will be more highly motivated when the effort they put into a task leads to an expected outcome that they value. This occurs for individuals when they feel competent, they get what they expect, and they value what they do. If a leader can help individuals in these three areas, then motivation will be high.

Overcoming Low Motivation

Help Others Feel Competent

All of us have a need to feel **competent**. We want to present ourselves in a way that suggests to others (and ourselves) that we know what we are doing. Whether it is learning how to play the guitar, how to swing a golf club, or how to play blackjack, we all want to give a good performance. Letting individuals know that they are competent is the first step in helping them become more highly motivated. For example, after completing a complex assignment, an employee would be gratified to hear the manager say, "You did that assignment exactly the way it needed to be done."

Help Others Get What They Expect

People are also more highly motivated when their expectations are met. Knowing that effort will lead to an expected outcome is very important. Achieving an expected result makes the effort worthwhile, but it is disheartening and unmotivating when work does not lead to an expected outcome. In a sense, when individuals do not achieve the results they expect, they distrust the way the system works.

A leader should make sure the outcome that individuals expect from their effort is achievable and will likely occur. A leader must be aware of what outcome individuals expect, and confirm if those outcomes are realistic.

For example, if a salesperson is given a new quota to meet, he or she may expect a pay increase or financial reward for achieving that goal. It is up to the leader to clarify for the salesperson whether or not that reward is possible.

Another example that illustrates this point involves a university instructor who taught a course in public relations. The instructor assigned each group in the class a client for which the student was to develop a campaign, and gave the students a basic outline from which to work. One group struggled with the assignment; the instructor met often with these students outside class to help them develop their plan. At the end of the semester, the group submitted a very basic plan that met the minimum requirements for the assignment and received a C grade. Members of the group were very upset with their grade and argued that they deserved a higher score because they had done a lot of work, completed every task the instructor had given them in their meetings, and met the requirements for the assignment outlined in the syllabus. The instructor pointed out that higher grades were given to those who went beyond the minimum requirements. It was clear to the teacher that her expectations and those of her students were not the same. As a result, when she taught the class again, the teacher specified that the requirements outlined in the syllabus were only a starting point: Higher grades were for those who met and exceeded these requirements in developing their campaign plans. This example illustrates the importance of a leader and the group members having a mutual understanding of the expected outcomes.

LEADERSHIP SNAPSHOT

Bill Courtney, Head Coach, Manassas High School Football

© Matt Carr/Contributor/Getty Images Entertainment/Getty Images

Football coaches have challenges as part of the job: finding and grooming talented players, tough opposing defenses, injured team members. But in 2002, when Bill Courtney volunteered to coach Manassas High School's struggling football team in North Memphis, Tennessee, an inner-city community, he faced some huge obstacles.

Manassas had had a record of 5–95 for the past 10 years, a roster of only 17 players, a lack of equipment, and a reputation for the being the district's "doormat team." It was rumored that larger schools would pay to have Manassas be their homecoming game's opponent so they would be guaranteed a win.

But Courtney found the personal obstacles faced by his players just as daunting. The players all lived in poverty, most didn't have a father at home, and some lived with a single grandparent or other relative. All of them had close family members who had gone to jail, but few had any who had been to college.

"When you're in generational abject poverty and just hopelessness and loss and you're surrounded by it, and that's all you see coming up, then that's all that you expect life is," said Courtney. "If that's what your reality is and that's all you see and you've never traveled more than 10 miles from the neighborhood you were born in, then why would anyone expect [you] to have a road map to success?" (Ward-Henninger, 2013).

For Courtney, it became more than just teaching the basics of block, hit, and tackle. A man who knows what it is to grow up without a father, he found the job morphed into becoming a coach of his players' character, resolve, and integrity. As he quoted often to his players, "The measure of a man's character is determined not by how he handles his wins, but by how he handles his failures."

One of Courtney's players, Chavis Daniels, joined the team after spending 15 months in a juvenile detention facility and had serious anger issues. At one point, he was suspended for several games during the team's season for fighting with an assistant coach. The fact Daniels wasn't just kicked off the team speaks to Courtney's commitment to the individuals and to the impact it ultimately has on those young men. Despite the suspension, Daniels wanted to remain on the team because "without football I've got nothing" (Lindsay & Martin, 2012).

(Continued)

(Continued)

But coaching doesn't come without sacrifices for Courtney. The owner of a successful lumber company and the father of four children of his own, he admits that neither of these gets the attention it deserves during football season.

In 2009, the team did the unthinkable: They went 9–1. While the players were winning on the field, the coach was fighting other battles off the field. Linebacker O. C. Brown, at 6-foot-2 and 315 pounds, had a real shot at playing college football, but academically couldn't qualify. The coaching staff tried to arrange for tutors, only to be told no one would come to Brown's North Memphis neighborhood to tutor him. The coaches hit upon a unique solution: Brown would live during the week with one of the assistant coaches at his suburban home and receive tutoring there. They succeeded: Brown achieved the required score on his college entrance exam and was signed to play at the University of Southern Mississippi.

Another student, Montrail Brown, was an academic standout, but an undersized football player. He, too, dreamt of college. After suffering a midseason knee injury that took him off the field, he stopped coming to school. Courtney reached out to him, reminding him that football doesn't build character; it reveals character, and character is about how you handle your failures. Williams continued his physical therapy and was ultimately able to play in the playoff game. One of the team's assistant coaches, Jeff Germany, successfully found a donor willing to pay 100% of Montrail's college expenses.

"There's a story under every helmet," Courtney says. All of his players are "equally important to me" and "willing to lay it on the line for [me]."

"The only way you do that is to build a relationship with your players and find out who they are: what their fears are, what excites them and what hurts them and how you can yell at one kid to motivate him but you have to pat another on the fanny right next to him because they're motivated by different stimulus. I believe you surround yourself with good talent and you let players win games after you've won your players" (Ward-Henninger, 2013).

Not only does a leader need to be sensitive to what others expect from his or her work and make sure these expectations are realistic, but he or she must also ensure that these expected outcomes are realized. For example, if a student is promised additional points for doing an extra-credit assignment, the teacher must make sure the student receives them. Similarly, if a worker expects a raise in pay if he or she meets the new sales quota, the leader needs to make sure the employee receives the pay increase.

Help Others Value What They Do

The third aspect of motivating others has to do with outcomes. When people place a high value on what they are doing, they are more motivated. Without a *valued* outcome, people are not motivated to put effort toward a goal.

An example about playing a musical instrument may illustrate this. When Judy, a high school student, takes up a musical instrument (the trumpet), her first concern is about competence. She wonders, "Can I play this thing?" After taking lessons for a period, Judy's thoughts turn to whether or not she can do a solo recital. With long and hard practice, she is successful in the recital. Finally, she asks herself, "What is all of this worth?" This final phase is about the value of the outcome. If Judy really wants to become a good trumpet player, she will continue to be motivated to practice and play. If she does not find real value in playing, her motivation will subside, and she may quit playing altogether.

As a leader, the challenge is to help others see the value in their work performance. Whether this is done through monetary rewards, positive personal feedback, or giving special achievement awards, the key is to help others feel good about those things toward which they are directing their energies.

In summary, the leader's challenge to motivate others is threefold: to help others feel *competent*, to help others get what they *expect*, and to help others see the overall *value* of their work. When all three of these conditions are met, individuals will be more highly motivated about their work.

**Leadership and
Problem Solving**

Obstacle 4: Complex Tasks

Sometimes the obstacle facing people is the task itself. When a task is unstructured, ambiguous, or complex, it creates an obstacle for individuals. People are often frustrated and threatened when confronting complex tasks. Some individuals may even be overwhelmed.

When a task is *complex*, the leader needs to use a **directive leadership** style— to "take charge" and clarify the path to the goal. Directive leaders give others instruction, including what is expected of them, how it is to be done, and a timeline for when it should be completed. Being directive means setting clear standards of performance and making rules and regulations clear for others. When a leader simplifies complex tasks, it helps followers to feel more competent about their work.

Being Directive

The following example illustrates how a supervisor effectively used *directive leadership* to help one employee become more productive in her work. Jill Jones was one of four administrative staff working for a team of 45 people in product development at a large corporation. Her job was to do payroll, scheduling, requisitions, and a number of other secretarial tasks as needed. Jill had multiple tasks to coordinate but often seemed overwhelmed about which task to do first. Jill's supervisor recognized that she was having difficulty with her job and decided that Jill needed some guidance in managing her work demands. To reduce Jill's stress, the supervisor reassigned one of Jill's overdue work assignments to another employee. Next, the supervisor met with Jill and asked her to list all of her work responsibilities and the day of the month that each had to be completed. The supervisor had Jill fill out a calendar detailing the days of the week when each specific task needed to be completed (e.g., Monday 9 A.M. to noon—payroll; Tuesday, 3–5 P.M.—requisitions). Jill felt relieved after she worked through this process with her supervisor, and the whole process was win-win. Jill felt better about her work, and her boss was getting more work done. The manager had removed obstacles that were keeping Jill from adequately carrying out her job assignments.

To summarize, Jill was facing a *complex group of tasks*, and her supervisor responded appropriately with *directive leadership*. By reducing the complexity of the task, the supervisor effectively assisted Jill in feeling competent and successful about her work.

Obstacle 5: Simple Tasks

Sometimes the obstacle to people's success is not complexity but simplicity. Like complex tasks, simple and repetitive tasks can have a negative impact on motivation. There is little excitement in doing the same job over and over again. With no variety or nuance, simple tasks become dull and uninteresting.

Being Supportive

For work like this, it is important for a leader to use a **supportive leadership** style. The supportive style provides what is missing—the human connection—by encouraging others when they are engaged in tasks that are boring and unchallenging. Supportive leadership offers a sense of human touch for those engaged in mundane mechanical activity.

If you have ever observed people in a weight room at a fitness center, you have seen how support works to counter the unpleasantness of mundane work. People who lift weights are usually engaged in a very simple activity. Doing repetitions is not complex. However, weight rooms are often marked by camaraderie and supportiveness between the people lifting. People spot for each other and often engage in friendly banter and conversation. Their social interaction works to make their repetitive tasks more tolerable and interesting.

To identify situations that involve mundane tasks, you need not look very far. Consider the following situations: working on an assembly line in an automobile plant, swimming laps as part of training for a swim team, washing dishes at a restaurant, or studying vocabulary cards for a foreign-language quiz. Many jobs and many aspects of nearly every job have a simplicity to them that can be negative.

The solution to this problem is for a leader to be supportive and nurturing. A good leader senses when jobs are mundane and tries to give people the missing ingredient—social support. Although social support can take a variety of forms (e.g., being friendly, talking about the other's family, or giving compliments), the bottom line is that social support shows care for the well-being and personal needs of the follower. When the task is not challenging, an effective leader will provide stimulation in the form of social support.

Obstacle 6: Low Involvement

Having a voice in what happens is very important to people. When people are not involved in a group or an organization, their productivity goes down, and the group or organization suffers. People want to have an identity that is unique from others', but they also want to be included and to fit in with others. By expressing their own thoughts and opinions on different issues, individuals are able to sense that they are contributing to a group. When individuals sense they are not heard, their participation decreases, they contribute less, and often they disengage from the group.

Leaders should use a **participative leadership** style to address the issue of low involvement. Participative leaders invite others to share in the ways and means of getting things done. They work to establish a climate that is open to new and diverse opinions. This leader consults with others, obtains their ideas and opinions, and integrates their suggestions into the decisions regarding how the group or organization will proceed.

A brief example may help to illustrate the importance of involvement. Oakwood Bistro is a small, upscale restaurant in a college town. It employs about 20 people as bartenders, cooks, and waitstaff. The bistro has two managers, whom we will call Managers A and B. Manager A is very authoritarian and strict. She stresses rules and procedures. She interacts very little with the staff and seldom asks anyone for opinions or feedback. Although Manager A is very competent and runs a tight ship, very few employees like working shifts when she is in charge.

The opposite is true when Manager B is in charge. Manager B is a democratic leader who is friendly with everyone. He is as interested in what the staff and customers are saying as he is in the rules and procedures of the place. He has nicknames for everyone who works at the bistro. In addition, he holds weekly "gripe" sessions during which staff members can express their opinions and make suggestions for how to improve things. Needless to say, individuals like to work for Manager B, and he is effective in his role.

Clearly, Manager B in the above example is a participative leader who allows people to be involved in the workings of the restaurant. The staff appreciates this involvement. In groups or organizations where everyone is involved, there are synergistic effects that create remarkable outcomes. Commitment to the group goes up, and group cohesiveness grows exponentially.

Low Involvement

Obstacle 7: Lack of a Challenge

**The Need
for a Challenge**

Some people do not work well because they are not *challenged* by what they are doing. Without a challenge, these people find work uninteresting and not worthwhile. As a result, these people work less hard, or they quit and move on to something that they find more engaging.

A leader should adopt an **achievement-oriented leadership** style in dealing with individuals who are not challenged. Achievement-oriented leadership is characterized by a leader who challenges individuals to perform at the highest level possible. This leader establishes a high standard of excellence and seeks continuous improvement. In addition to expecting a lot from followers, an achievement-oriented leader shows a high degree of confidence that people can reach those challenging goals.

An achievement-oriented leader continually challenges others to excel and pushes people to higher levels of success. He or she sets standards of excellence and challenges others to meet those standards. In the classroom, these leaders are the teachers who use an A+ grade as a way of coaxing students to do superior work. On the football field, they are the coaches who promote effort by placing stars on players' helmets for outstanding performance. At work, they are the managers who give end-of-the-year bonuses for individuals who go the extra mile or do more than they are expected to do. An achievement-oriented leader is always looking for ways to challenge people to perform at the highest level possible.

It is important to point out that, while achievement-oriented leadership is good for some people, it is not for everyone. Although some people thrive on competition and like being pushed to do their best, there are those who are internally motivated and do not need a nudge from the achievement-oriented leader. It is the leader's responsibility to assess followers' needs to determine when achievement-oriented leadership is indicated and for whom.

SUMMARY

Challenges and difficulties will always be present for people in the workplace. A leader plays a critical role in helping people overcome these obstacles. Most important, effective leaders help individuals define their goals and the paths they wish to take to meet those goals. Based on expectancy theory, leaders can help others be motivated by helping them to feel competent, to receive what they expect from their work, and to see the overall value of their work.

If the obstacle a person faces is a *complex task*, the leader should provide *directive leadership*. If the obstacle is a task that is too *simple or mundane*, however, the leader needs to give *supportive leadership*. Sometimes leaders have followers who are *uninvolved* in the group or organization; for these individuals, the leader should adopt a *participative leadership* style. At other times, for followers who are not *challenged*, the leader should incorporate an *achievement-oriented leadership* style.

Obstacles will always exist and present a challenge in all endeavors. The sign of a good leader is one who is willing to help individuals overcome these obstacles so that they can more effectively move toward and accomplish their goals.

GLOSSARY TERMS

achievement-oriented leadership 312

competent 306

directive leadership 309

expectancy theory 305

obstacles 302

participative leadership 311

path–goal leadership 302

supportive leadership 310

$SAGE edge™

Sharpen your skills with SAGE edge at **edge.sagepub.com/northouseintro4e**

SAGE edge for students provides a personalized approach to help you accomplish your coursework goals in an easy-to-use learning environment.

13.1 CASE STUDY

Book Quiz Blues?

As a community service project, Trey Morgan volunteered to coach a Book Quiz team of fourth graders at a local elementary school. As a college student majoring in education, Trey was excited for the opportunity to work one-on-one with children to prepare them for the competition. He felt it would give him a good indication of how much he would like teaching and whether he would be a good teacher.

The Book Quiz is a competition where teams of students read 10 books and compete with other teams, answering questions about the books. The teams have 10 weeks to prepare by reading the books and doing practice quizzes.

Trey's team members were selected by their teacher, who mandated that all students in her class be on a team. Trey spent an hour each week with his team. He made a chart, and as the students finished reading the books, he would put a star next to their name. He also established that the first student to finish all the books would get a prize.

After three weeks, one of the team members, Claire, had finished five of the books already and was moving way ahead of the other team members. Shelby had admitted to starting to read four of the books, but "they were boring" so she stopped reading them. Marco, who announced at the first meeting that he would win the prize for reading all 10 books first, had read three of them, but his progress had slowed considerably. Every time a new star was added to Claire's name on the chart,

Marco became visibly discouraged and frustrated. Garrett, on the other hand, wasn't progressing at all. He was still reading the same 80-page book he started the first week. Trey observed that during their meetings Garrett would get up frequently and move around the room. He also liked to spin in circles, often hitting the other kids accidentally with his swinging arms. When Trey tried to encourage Garrett to go for the prize, he shrugged and said, "I can't win that. I don't read fast like Claire and Marco."

At the six-week point, Trey panicked. His Book Quiz guidebook said that each team member should have read at least five of the books by now. Claire had only read one additional book in the past three weeks because she had joined the track team and had little time after track practice and homework for reading. Marco had read four books, but didn't seem interested in any of the remaining books. Garrett finally finished the one he started, and Shelby had started them all but not completed one. Trey hadn't even begun to quiz the students on the books because there was no point if they hadn't read them. He did have Marco and Claire work together on the four books they had both read, writing questions and quizzing each other.

With four weeks left, Trey has to figure out a way to get his team motivated and focused. He has given up any hopes of winning, but does want his team to at least make a good showing.

As he tries to give them a pep talk, encouraging them to focus so they "won't look like idiots in the competition," Garrett interrupts.

"Who cares if we look like idiots?" he asks. "I didn't ask to be on this team. I got put on this team. It's a stupid competition."

Marco gets mad. "Garrett, we are going to lose because you and Shelby won't read. I don't like losing, and when we do, it will be your fault."

Shelby and Claire both start to cry, with Claire saying she feels awful because she can't read as much anymore and she is letting everyone down. "I have too much to do," she wails.

Garrett gets up and spins in circles.

Marco looks at Trey. "Aren't you going to do something?" he demands angrily.

Trey thinks to himself that if he does anything it will be to change his major to business.

QUESTIONS

1. Obviously, things are not working out well for Trey and his team. If you were Trey, how would you have proceeded from the beginning to help the team avoid or overcome its obstacles?

2. Based on the seven obstacles discussed in this chapter, identify which obstacles each of the team members (Claire, Shelby, Marco, and Garrett) is facing.

3. Some of Trey's team members seem to lack motivation. Based on *expectancy theory*, how could Trey help his team members *feel competent*, *get what they expect*, and *value what they do*?

4. Based on how his team is feeling and doing, identify three specific things Trey could do to help his students.

13.2 PATH–GOAL STYLES QUESTIONNAIRE

Purpose

1. To identify your path–goal styles of leadership
2. To examine how your use of each style relates to other styles of leadership

Directions

1. For each of the statements below, circle the number that indicates the frequency with which you engage in the expressed behavior.
2. Give your immediate impressions. There are no right or wrong answers.

When I am the leader . . .	Never	Seldom	Sometimes	Often	Always
1. I give clear explanations of what is expected of others.	1	2	3	4	5
2. I show interest in followers' personal concerns.	1	2	3	4	5
3. I invite followers to participate in decision making.	1	2	3	4	5
4. I challenge followers to continuously improve their work performance.	1	2	3	4	5
5. I give followers explicit instructions for how to do their work.	1	2	3	4	5
6. I show concern for the personal well-being of my followers.	1	2	3	4	5
7. I solicit followers' suggestions before making a decision.	1	2	3	4	5
8. I encourage followers to consistently raise their own standards of performance.	1	2	3	4	5
9. I give clear directions to others for how to proceed on a project.	1	2	3	4	5
10. I listen to others and give them encouragement.	1	2	3	4	5
11. I am receptive to ideas and advice from others.	1	2	3	4	5
12. I expect followers to excel in all aspects of their work.	1	2	3	4	5

Scoring

1. Sum the responses on items 1, 5, and 9 (directive leadership).
2. Sum the responses on items 2, 6, and 10 (supportive leadership).
3. Sum the responses on items 3, 7, and 11 (participative leadership).
4. Sum the responses on items 4, 8, and 12 (achievement-oriented leadership).

 Visit **www.sagepub.com/northouseintro4e** for a downloadable version of this questionnaire.

13.2 Path–Goal Styles Questionnaire

(Continued)

Total Scores

Directive leadership: _____

Supportive leadership: _____

Participative leadership: _____

Achievement-oriented leadership: _____

Scoring Interpretation

This questionnaire is designed to measure four types of path–goal leadership: directive, supportive, participative, and achievement-oriented. By comparing your scores on each of the four styles, you can determine which style is your strongest and which is your weakest. For example, if your scores were directive leadership = 21, supportive leadership = 10, participative leadership = 19, and achievement-oriented leadership = 7, your strengths would be directive and participative leadership, and your weaknesses would be supportive and achievement-oriented leadership. While this questionnaire measures your dominant styles, it also indicates the styles you may want to strengthen or improve.

If your score is 13–15, you are in the high range.

If your score is 6–12, you are in the moderate range.

If your score is 3–5, you are in the low range.

Improve Your Leadership Skills

If you have the interactive eBook version of this text, log in to access the interactive leadership assessment. After completing this chapter's questionnaire, you will receive individualized feedback and practical sugsgestions for further strengthening your leadership based on your responses in this questionnaire.

APPLICATION

13.3 Observational Exercise

Obstacles

Purpose

1. To develop an understanding of the practical value of path–goal leadership as a strategy for helping followers reach their goals

2. To identify *Obstacles* that limit group effectiveness

3. To investigate how a *leader's style* helps followers overcome *obstacles* to goal achievement

Directions

1. Observe a meeting, practice, or session of one the following groups (or a similar group): a sports team practice, a class project group meeting, a weekly staff meeting at work, a fraternity or sorority council meeting, or a planning meeting for a nonprofit organization.

2. Record what you observe at the meeting. Be specific in your descriptions.

   General observations of the meeting:

   Observations of the leader's behavior:

   Observations of group members' behaviors:

Questions

1. What are the *goals* of the individuals or group you observed? Are the goals clear?

2. What are the major obstacles confronting the individuals in the group?

3. What style of leadership did the leader exhibit? Was it appropriate for the group?

4. If you were leading the group, how would you lead to help group members?

 Visit **www.sagepub.com/northouseintro4e** for a downloadable version of this exercise.

13.4 REFLECTION AND ACTION WORKSHEET

Obstacles

Reflection

1. When it comes to helping people who are having problems, how do you view your own abilities? Are you comfortable with setting goals and giving directions to others?

2. One of the central responsibilities of a leader is to help his or her followers become motivated. This means helping them feel *competent*, helping them meet their *expectations*, and helping them *value* what they do. How would you apply these three principles in a leadership situation?

3. As you reflect on the *obstacles* discussed in the chapter, which obstacles would you be most and least effective at addressing? Why?

Action

1. To be an effective leader requires that you *clarify the goal* and *define the path* to the goal. What specific things could you do in an upcoming leadership situation to clarify the goal and define the path for others?

2. As you look at your results on the Path–Goal Styles Questionnaire, what scores would you like to change? Which styles would you like to strengthen? How can you make sure you exhibit the most effective style the next time you are leading a group?

3. People vary regarding their need to be helped. Some want a lot of assistance, and others like to be independent. Are you prepared to adapt your leadership to be helpful to those who need it? Discuss.

 Visit **www.sagepub.com/northouseintro4e** for a downloadable version of this worksheet.

APPLICATION

References

Hart, B. (2005, June 10). GPS voice fine for some of life's roads but not for others. *Deseret News* (Salt Lake City, UT). Retrieved from http://www.deseretnews.com/article/600140296/GPS-voice-fine-for-some-of-lifes-roads-but-not-for-others.html?pg=all

Herzberg, F. (1968). *Work and the nature of man.* New York, NY: World.

House, R. J. (1971). A path-goal theory of leader effectiveness. *Administrative Science Quarterly, 16*(3), 321–328.

House, R. J. (1996). Path-goal theory of leadership: Lessons, legacy, and a reformulated theory. *Leadership Quarterly, 7*(3), 323–352.

Lindsay, D. [Producer], & Martin, T. J. [Director]. (2012). *Undefeated* [Motion picture]. United States: Spitfire Studios.

Maslow, A. H. (1954). *Motivation and personality.* New York, NY: Harper & Row.

Peck, M. S. (1978). *The road less traveled.* New York, NY: Simon & Schuster.

Skinner, B. F. (1953). *Science and human behavior.* New York, NY: Free Press.

Vroom, V. H. (1964). *Work and motivation.* New York, NY: Wiley.

Ward-Henninger, C. (2013, February 19). Coach Bill Courtney and Manassas make "Undefeated" a true underdog story. *MaxPreps.com.* Retrieved from http://www.maxpreps.com/news/pPAP2YAMCEmkJtpd2TK7Bg/coach-bill-courtney-and-manassas-make-undefeated-a-true-underdog-story.htm

Glossary

ability a natural or acquired capacity to perform a particular activity

accommodation an unassertive but cooperative conflict style that requires individuals to attend very closely to the needs of others and ignore their own needs

achievement-oriented a leader who challenges individuals to perform at the highest level possible, establishes a high standard of excellence, and seeks continuous improvement

actions the ways one goes about accomplishing goals

administrative skills competencies a leader needs to run an organization in order to carry out the organization's purposes and goals

authentic leadership an emerging leadership approach that looks at the authenticity of leaders and their leadership

authoritarian leadership style a style of leadership in which leaders perceive subordinates as needing direction and need to control subordinates and what they do

avoidance a conflict style that is both unassertive and uncooperative, and characterized by individuals being passive and ignoring conflict situations rather than confronting them directly

behavior approach an approach to leadership research that focuses on behavior and examines what leaders do and how they act

challenge to stimulate people to commit themselves to change

change a move toward something different; a shift away from the way things currently are

character one's qualities, disposition, and core values

charisma magnetic charm and appeal; a special personality characteristic that gives people the capacity to do extraordinary things

cohesiveness a sense of "we-ness"; the cement that holds a group together, or the esprit de corps that exists within a group

collaboration a conflict style that requires both assertiveness and cooperation and occurs when both parties agree to a positive settlement to the conflict and attend fully to the other's concerns while not sacrificing or suppressing their own

competent a leader who presents himself in a way that suggests to others (and himself) that he knows what he is doing

competition a conflict style of individuals who are highly assertive about pursuing their own goals but uncooperative in assisting others to reach their goals

compromise a conflict style that involves both a degree of assertiveness and a degree of cooperativeness

conceptual skills capabilities that involve working with concepts and ideas, the thinking or cognitive aspects of leadership

concern for people refers to how a leader attends to the people in the organization who are trying to achieve its goals

concern for production refers to how a leader is concerned with achieving organizational goals

confidence feeling positive about oneself and one's ability to succeed

conflict   a felt struggle between two or more interdependent individuals over perceived incompatible differences in beliefs, values, and goals, or over differences in desires for esteem, control, and connectedness

conflict style   a patterned response or behavior that people use when approaching conflict

consideration behavior   a relationship leadership behavior in which the leader creates camaraderie, respect, trust, and regard with followers

content conflicts   involve struggles between leaders and others who differ on issues such as policies and procedures

content dimension   involves the objective, observable aspects of communication

contingency theory   a leadership theory that focuses on the match between the leader's style and specific situational variables

democratic leadership style   a style of leadership in which leaders treat subordinates as fully capable of doing work on their own and work with subordinates, trying hard to treat everyone fairly, without putting themselves above subordinates

determination   being focused and attentive to tasks; showing initiative, persistence, and drive

differentiation   an interaction process that occurs in the early phase of conflict that helps participants define the nature of the conflict and clarify their positions with regard to each other

directive leadership   a leader sets clear standards of performance and makes rules and regulations clear for others

emotional intelligence   concerned with a person's ability to understand his or her own and others' emotions, and then to apply this understanding to life's tasks; the ability to perceive and express emotions, to use emotions to facilitate thinking, to understand and reason with emotions, and to manage emotions effectively within oneself and in relationships with others

empathy   a process in which an individual suspends his or her own feelings in an effort to fully understand the feelings of another individual

employee orientation   a relationship leadership behavior in which the leader takes an interest in workers as human beings, values their uniqueness, and gives special attention to their personal needs

end values   the outcomes or goals a leader seeks to achieve

ethical leadership   a process by which a good person rightly influences others to accomplish a common good

ethical values   concerned with the character or virtuousness of the leader

expectancy theory   people will be more highly motivated when they are capable of performing their work, the effort they put into a task leads to an expected outcome, and they value the outcome

face saving   communicative attempts to establish or maintain one's self-image or another's self-image in response to threat

fractionation   the technique of breaking down large conflicts into smaller, more manageable pieces

Gallup Organization   a public opinion research organization that conducts political polling and research in other areas of the social sciences

goals   the aims or outcomes an individual seeks to achieve

"Great Man" theories   early trait theories of leadership that focused on identifying the innate qualities and characteristics possessed by great social, political, and military leaders (see also trait approach)

honesty   telling the truth and representing reality as fully and completely as possible

initiating structure   task leadership in which the leader organizes work, defines role responsibilities, and schedules work activities

integrity   adhering to a strong set of principles and taking responsibility for one's actions; being honest and trustworthy

intelligence having good language skills, perceptual skills, and reasoning ability

interpersonal skills people skills; those abilities that help a leader to work effectively with subordinates, peers, and superiors to accomplish the organization's goals

laissez-faire leadership style a style of leadership, sometimes labeled nonleadership, in which leaders ignore workers and their work motivations and engage in minimal influence

leader-member exchange (LMX) theory conceptualizes leadership as a process that is centered on the interactions between leaders and followers

leadership a process whereby an individual influences a group of individuals to achieve a common goal

leadership style the behaviors of leaders, focusing on what leaders do and how they act

learned behaviors actions or behaviors people acquire through experience; ingrained things they come to understand throughout their life

listening paying attention to what people say while being attentive to what people mean

map a laid-out path to follow to direct people toward their short- and long-term goals

mission the goal toward which a group is working, which provides organization to the rest of its activities

modal values concerned with the means or actions a leader takes

norms the rules of behavior that are established and shared by group members

obstacle a problem that hinders group productivity

out-group individuals in a group or an organization who do not identify themselves as part of the larger group, and who are disconnected and not fully engaged in working toward the goals of the group

participative leadership a leader invites others to share in the ways and means of getting things done

path-goal leadership leadership in which a leader should choose a style that best fits the needs of individual group members and the task they are doing

path-goal theory a leadership theory that examines how leaders use employee motivation to enhance performance and satisfaction

personal style unique habits regarding work and play, which have been ingrained over many years and influence one's current style

philosophy of leadership a unique set of beliefs and attitudes about the nature of people and the nature of work that have a significant impact on an individual's leadership style

picture an ideal image of where a group or an organization should be going

positive psychology the "scientific" study of what makes life most worth living

power the capacity to influence or affect others

principled negotiation an approach to conflict that decides issues on their merits rather than through competitive haggling or through excessive accommodation

problem-solving skills one's cognitive ability to take corrective action in a problem situation in order to meet desired objectives

process behaviors behaviors used by leaders to help group members feel comfortable with each other and at ease in the situations in which they find themselves

production orientation task leadership in which the leader stresses the production and technical aspects of the job

realized strengths personal attributes that represent our strongest assets

relational approach an approach to leadership research that examines the nature of relations between leaders and followers

relational conflicts refer to the differences we feel between ourselves and others concerning how we relate to each other

relationship behaviors   behaviors used by leaders that help subordinates feel comfortable with themselves, with each other, and with the situation they find themselves in

relationship dimension   refers to the participants' perceptions of their connection to one another

relationship-oriented leadership   leadership that is focused primarily on the well-being of subordinates, how they relate to each other, and the atmosphere in which they work

servant leadership   an emerging leadership approach that emphasizes the "caring principle" with leaders as "servants" who focus on their followers' needs in order to help these followers become more autonomous, knowledgeable, and like servants themselves

situational approach   an approach to leadership research based on the premise that different situations demand different kinds of leadership

skill   a competency developed to accomplish a task effectively

sociability   capable of establishing pleasant social relationships; being sensitive to others' needs and concerned for their well-being

social identity theory   explains why and how individuals identify with particular social groups and how these identifications affect their behavior

social perceptiveness   having insight into and awareness of what is important to others, how they are motivated, the problems they face, and how they react to change

spiritual leadership   an emerging leadership approach that examines how leaders use values, a sense of "calling," and membership to motivate followers

standards of excellence   the expressed and implied expectations for performance that exist within a group or an organization

status quo   the current situation; the way things are now

strategic planning   a conceptual skill, the cognitive ability to think and consider ideas to develop effective strategies for a group or an organization

strengths   attributes or qualities of an individual that account for successful performance; positive features of ourselves that make us effective and help us flourish

structure   a blueprint for the work of a particular group that gives form and meaning to the purposes of its activities

supportive   a leader who provides what is missing—the human connection—by encouraging others when they are engaged in tasks that are boring and unchallenging; offers a sense of human touch for those engaged in mundane mechanical activity

synergy   the group energy created from two or more people working together, which creates an outcome that is different from and better than the sum of the individual contributions

task behaviors   behaviors used by leaders to get the job done

task-oriented leadership   leadership that is focused predominantly on procedures, activities, and goal accomplishments

technical competence   having specialized knowledge about the work we do or ask others to do

themes of human talent   relatively stable, fixed characteristics—similar to personality traits—that are not easily changed

Theory X   a general theory created by Douglas McGregor in which leaders assume that people dislike work, that they need to be directed and controlled, and that they want security—not responsibility

Theory Y   a general theory created by Douglas McGregor in which leaders assume that people like work, that they are self-motivated, and that they accept and seek responsibility

trait   a distinguishing personal quality that is often inherited (e.g., intelligence, confidence, charisma, determination, sociability, or integrity)

trait approach   an approach to leadership research that focuses on identifying the innate qualities and characteristics possessed by individuals (see also "Great Man" theories)

transformational leadership theory   a theory that describes leadership as a process that changes people and organizations

unrealized strengths   personal attributes that are less visible

values   the ideas, beliefs, and modes of action that people find worthwhile or desirable

vision   a mental model of an ideal future state

weaknesses   limiting attributes that often drain our energy and result in poor performance

Index